THE 'B' SPECIALS

Vice-Admiral Sir Arthur Hezlet has lived in Northern Ireland, his family and ancestral home, since retiring from the Royal Navy in 1963 after a distinguished naval career. He was at one time the Director of the Royal Naval Staff College at Greenwich and later became the Flag Officer Scotland and Northern Ireland.

He began to write on his retirement, and his first two books, *Submarine and Sea Power* and *Aircraft and Sea Power* were published in 1967. They received considerable critical acclaim. During the last few years, residing in Co Londonderry, he has had first-hand experience of the Ulster crisis and has considerable local knowledge of the situation. He is a member of the Military History Society of Ireland and of the International Institute of Strategic Studies.

THE 'B' SPECIALS

A history of the
Ulster Special Constabulary

SIR ARTHUR HEZLET

UNABRIDGED

PAN BOOKS LTD : LONDON

First published 1972 by Tom Stacey Ltd
This edition published 1973 by Pan Books Ltd,
33 Tothill Street, London SW1

ISBN 0 330 23789 6

Printed in Great Britain by
Richard Clay (The Chaucer Press), Ltd, Bungay, Suffolk

'That historians should show partiality for their own country I would allow, but not that they should make statements about it that contradict the facts. There are enough errors of ignorance to which historians are liable and which a man may hardly avoid. But if we write falsely from intention – be it for country or for friends or for favour – what better are we than those who make their living by such means.'

Polybius *c* 150 BC

Contents

I	The Birth of the Specials	1
II	1921, the First Year of Operations	28
III	The 'Troubles' – 1922	53
IV	Order Restored – 1922–5	94
V	The Struggle for Existence	121
VI	The Wartime USC, 1939–45	138
VII	Post World War II, 1945–56	153
VIII	The 1956–62 Campaign	171
IX	The Last Phase, 1962–9	201
X	The Hunt Report and Disbandment	218

APPENDICES
I	Roll of Honour	251
II	Contingent at Royal Review	253
III	A Typical Sub-District	255
	Notes on Sources	257
	Bibliography	258
	Index	261

List of lIustrationS

(*between pages 78 and 79*)

B Specials in 1921 (*Illustrated London News*)
B Specials at Westminster Abbey, 1921 (*Radio Times Hulton Picture Library*)
An A Special Constabulary mobile platoon
Sir James Craig addressing Special Constables (*Illustrated London News*)
Rolls-Royce armoured cars (*Illustrated London News*)
Border farmers with the County Commandant (*Illustrated London News*)
A Specials in ambush exercise, 1922
An A Special church parade, 1922
B Specials soon after the issue of ex-British uniforms, 1922
A Lancia armoured lorry used by A Specials
Under canvas at Coagh Camp
Children and armoured car in Cavour Street (*Illustrated London News*)

(*between pages 174 and 175*)

A and B Specials on parade near Enniskillen, April 1923 (*Impartial Reporter*)
The 1935 riots in Belfast (*News Letter*)
Small arms training
Revolver practice
Fire with movement
B Specials during a rifle competition
Lord Brookborough meeting B Specials
B Specials discover an IRA dugout
Magherafelt Court House after fire, 1956 (*Radio Times Hulton Picture Library*)
Captain Terence O'Neill and Major Maclaren

B Specials being inspected by the Governor of Northern Ireland

The Inspector General of the RUC inspecting B Specials, 1963

B Specials on parade at Enniskillen in the 1960s

Foreword

When I was approached by the ex-District Commandants of the Ulster Special Constabulary to write their history, I was already engaged on another book on a very different subject. I decided to change horses in mid-stream and comply with their request because I believed that the B Specials were the victims of political circumstances following a mendacious propaganda campaign. I thought it important that the truth should be written in the hope that the record could be set straight. My position is therefore of an advocate whose purpose is to put his clients' case. This does not mean that this book is counter-propaganda; it is what I believe to be a true history in which I have been guided by the extract from Polybius quoted on page v. I made it absolutely clear to the ex-District Commandants that I would only undertake the book on the condition that everything in it was my work alone, and it would not necessarily be a reflection of their own views.

With a subject that is bound to cause controversy it is as well to declare my position. I am an Ulsterman and proud of it. Having said that, I would add that I am a United Kingdom Ulsterman who has spent his entire working life outside the Province in the service of the Crown, as did my father and grandfather. We all, however, unlike so many people of the North of Ireland, returned to live in the Province. For three generations we have not been members of a political party or of the Orange Order, Royal Black Institution, Apprentice Boys or any similar body, mainly because of the servicemen's dislike of politics. I describe my nationality as 'British first' and 'Irish second' in the same way as someone on the other side of the Irish Sea could be 'British' and 'Scottish'.

This has not been an easy book to write for two reasons. The first has been the time available. My publisher, for very good reasons, has insisted that it be completed in under six months which has left me less time for research and to allow people to criticize my drafts than I would have liked. No doubt anyone who wishes to point out any errors or omissions will not hesitate to do so and I shall be interested to receive their comments. The second difficulty is that I have been writing for two quite different sets of readers. I wanted, of course, to produce a history which ex-members of the USC would wish to possess and which would interest them. I also wanted to set down information about the Force which will be a genuine contribution to the history of the period. These two have not always been compatible and if I jump from 10 Downing Street somewhat abruptly to a cratered road crossing the border on a dark night, that is the reason.

It is customary in a foreword to acknowledge by name the help that one has received. In the unsettled position of this Province I do not intend to do this. I hope that all the people who have let me interview them, or have answered my questionnaires, and they range widely from personages who have held high office to ex B-men themselves, will accept this as my thanks. I also wish to thank the person who has read and criticized my drafts and the lady who did all the typing.

Atlantic Ocean

LONDON...

T Y R O N...

FERMANAGH

IRISH FREE STATE

	H.Q. INSPECTOR GENERAL
	H.Q. COUNTY COMMANDANTS
	H.Q. AREA COMMANDANTS
•	'B' SPECIAL SUB-DISTRICTS
□	'A' SPECIAL PLATOONS

THE
ULSTER SPECIAL
CONSTABULARY
1923

Irish

Sea

ANTRIM

DOWN

MAGH

0   5   10   15   20   25
miles

NORTHERN
IRELAND

Coleraine
Ballycastle
Ballymoney
Cushendall
The Glens
Clough
RY
Maghera
Ballymena
Larne
ANTRIM
Magherafelt
Antrim
Carrickfergus
Lough
Neagh
BELFAST
Newtownards
Irish
Lisburn
Comber
Sea
annon
Lurgan
Hillsborough
Portadown
Dromore
Ballynahinch
Armagh
Banbridge
DOWN
Downpatrick
RMAGH
Keady
Rathfriland
Bessbrook
Newry
Newcastle
Cullaville
Warrenpoint
Mourne
Mts.
LOUTH
Kilkeel

0   5   10   15   20   25
miles

CHAPTER ONE

The Birth of the Specials

By the middle of 1920, when the formation of a Special Constabulary was first considered, Ireland was rapidly degenerating into anarchy. If the reasons for its formation are to be understood, the situation at that time and the events which had led up to it must be related in a certain amount of detail. The course of the rebellion in the whole of Ireland will have to be followed as an essential background to the story.

After the Easter Rising in 1916, the country had been relatively quiet for some three years. At the end of 1918 there was a general election in the United Kingdom and the extreme Republican Sinn Fein party gained a landslide victory in the South of Ireland, winning seventy-three seats, reducing their predecessors, the more moderate Nationalists, to six seats. Although the Home Rule Bill for Ireland had become law in 1914 and was merely suspended until the end of the war, this was not enough for the Sinn Feiners who demanded nothing less than an independent Republic as proclaimed during the Easter Rising. The Sinn Fein Party, described by Winston Churchill as 'an untamed, untutored band of haters', refused to take their seats at Westminster, declared their independence and established a Republican Parliament in Dublin which elected a cabinet. The victory of Sinn Fein at the polls was to a large extent the result of the political activity of the 1916 rebels released from English prisons. They were able to claim that it was Sinn Fein which had been responsible for prevent-

ing conscription in Ireland and at the same time were able to
stir up anti-British feeling by making martyrs and national
heroes of the executed leaders of the 1916 Rising. Sinn Fein
was not at all particular in its methods and intimidation of
rival candidates and voters was rife. Throughout 1919 it did
its best to cripple the legitimate government of Ireland, which
was direct rule from Westminster through Dublin Castle.
Rival courts and local government bodies were set up and the
ordinary machinery was boycotted. The movement even
opened consulates abroad and entered into communication
with foreign powers.

Although it had much genuine support, Sinn Fein depended
a great deal upon intimidation for its success. This was applied by its military counterpart, the Irish Republican Army,
which had grown out of the Volunteers of the 1916 Rising.
The IRA had expanded greatly with the threat of conscription
but by the beginning of 1919, with the victory of Sinn Fein at
the polls, it had melted away again. The advocates of physical
force were determined to keep the IRA in being and decided
that the only way to do this was to start active operations
before it was too late. So began the campaign of outrage and
assassination of the servants of the Crown, which began with
the ambush and murder of two policemen who were escorting
a load of dynamite at Soloheadbeg in Co Tipperary in January
1919. On 23 June a District Inspector was shot dead in the
market square at Thurles in the same county and from then
on, political crime in the South of Ireland gradually increased.
Although the IRA were still weak and very short of arms and
ammunition, they had enough to cause plenty of trouble. Their
policy was to try and neutralize the Royal Irish Constabulary
who were the principal law enforcement agency in Ireland.
Sinn Fein and the Irish Republican Army were in fact separate bodies and they followed separate courses. By August
1919 the IRA became dissatisfied with the political progress
and told Sinn Fein that if this was the best they could do, they
would resort to more militant methods. The moderate Sinn
Feiners objected at first but later gave way and thereafter the

movement adopted a complementary policy to the IRA. The Dail outlawed the RIC as agents of the British and the campaign against them was intensified. During the remainder of 1919 another twelve policemen were murdered and just under a hundred fired at or assaulted. The police were therefore in great danger and had to work under very difficult conditions: they and their families were treated as outcasts and they even had difficulty in buying food and clothes which had to be supplied directly to them by the Government. This boycott against the police was enforced by intimidation: anyone helping them was liable to be shot or assaulted or have his property destroyed. The most disturbing feature of the campaign was that no one had been apprehended, let alone convicted, for any of these crimes.

The terrorists were confident that the vast majority of people were too frightened to report them to the police and would certainly not give evidence in court. Furthermore, most people could be coerced into sheltering gunmen and giving them food for fear of the reprisals which they knew they were ruthless enough to enforce.

There were two police forces in Ireland in 1920: the Royal Irish Constabulary and the Dublin Metropolitan Police. The Dublin police, 1,100 strong, were unarmed and organized much as any British urban force. The 10,000 strong Royal Irish Constabulary, on the other hand, were armed not only with pistols but with rifles, and were organized as a paramilitary force or gendarmerie quite unlike anything in Great Britain. This had been found necessary because of the peculiar conditions in Ireland where it had to deal with frequent outbreaks of disorder against the Government. The Royal Irish Constabulary was first established in 1836 and had a fine history and reputation and, in general, excellent relations with the public. It was composed entirely of Irishmen, some 60 per cent of the officers being Protestants and 40 per cent Roman Catholics, including General Sir Joseph Byrnes, the Inspector-General. These proportions were reversed in the rank and file, some 70 per cent being Roman Catholic and 30 per cent

Protestant.[1] Unfortunately by this time the Dublin Metropolitan Police had become practically useless. Unarmed and living in their homes spread all over the city, they were at the mercy of gunmen and did not dare to do anything to counter the terrorists.

In the autumn of 1919, the Government began to take sterner measures, proscribing Sinn Fein, banning the meetings of its Parliament and suppressing the leading Republican newspaper. At the same time it attempted a political solution and decided to introduce the Better Government of Ireland Bill to replace the Home Rule Act of 1914. This Bill which proposed Partition was in the end reluctantly accepted in the North but was ignored in the South. These measures had little effect and 1919 ended with an unsuccessful attempt to murder the Viceroy, Field Marshal Lord French, as he was returning to Dublin.

The year 1920 started badly. On 21 January Mr Redmond, an Assistant Commissioner of the Dublin Metropolitan Police, was shot dead in the street on his way home by two gunmen. No attempt was made by the bystanders to apprehend the murderers and they escaped. The Government thereupon offered a £10,000 reward for information leading to the arrest and conviction of any of the murderers of policemen. They then arrested and deported fifty leading Sinn Feiners for sedition under the Defence of the Realm Act and this drastic move was followed shortly afterwards by a curfew in Dublin from midnight to 5 AM.

Early in 1920 there was also a great increase in political crime and murder and the assault on the police was intensified. On 30 March, the IRA issued a proclamation referring to the RIC as spies and traitors and warned prospective recruits not to join. During the first six months of 1920 forty attacks were made on police stations, in which most of the RIC lived, and although the majority of these were repulsed, fifteen stations were totally destroyed and a quantity of arms and ammunition fell into the hands of the IRA. These attacks had already led to the evacuation of most of the small police stations which were garrisoned by only three or four constables, as they could not withstand a prolonged attack by large numbers of well-armed terrorists. In order to prevent the re-occupation of the abandoned stations, the IRA burnt no less than 351 of them and damaged 105 more. In this same period fifty-three policemen were killed and seventy were wounded. These murders were generally carried out in a cowardly manner: the police, conspicuous in their uniform, being shot down by a number of safely concealed gunmen. When resistance was put up, even by a single policeman, the IRA generally took to their heels: they preferred to catch their victims unawares or unarmed. Most of the IRA were young men directed by ruthless fanatics. Unemployment was heavy; emigration had been stopped during the war and conscription had not been brought into force. There were therefore a lot of young men with nothing to do in Ireland. The result of these attacks was that the police lost control of many districts and there were, in consequence, many other outrages, including nearly a hundred mail raids and nineteen attacks on coastguard stations. In this same period, fifteen civilians were murdered by the IRA and another forty-one wounded. The worst case was that of a Dublin Resident Magistrate who was dragged off a tramcar in broad daylight in a crowded street and shot dead. Not a person lifted a finger to help him and no one could be found to assist in tracking down the gunmen. It was becoming harder to bring the perpetrators of crimes to justice. The Sinn Fein courts threatened reprisals to anyone who even attended the Crown courts, and the IRA intimidated juries and witnesses to such an extent that no convictions could be obtained. In the Assizes held throughout Ireland in the spring, although there was an appalling list of violent crimes that had been committed, there were few cases before the courts and, to make matters even more difficult, thirty-three courthouses had been burned down during the first six months of the year.

The Sinn Fein Revolt was, therefore, firstly a civil disobedience campaign which aimed to make the ordinary administration of the country impossible, and secondly a campaign of violence and outrage directed mainly at the police and anyone who helped them, but also at people who refused to support the civil disobedience campaign. The third and last campaign, which was by no means the least significant, took the form of mendacious but nevertheless most efficient propaganda. The Irish have always been good propagandists and their efforts proved to be of extreme importance to Sinn Fein as the Government made little effort to refute or counter them in any way. Their propaganda was readily believed by the liberal press and politicians in Great Britain, who did not hesitate to use it to embarrass the Government. The Press in Ireland now mainly supported Sinn Fein, partly from necessity and partly out of genuine conviction. Undoubtedly if they opposed Sinn Fein their offices and presses were in danger of destruction and they ran the risk that no one would dare to buy their papers. Even the correspondents for British newspapers were subjected to intimidation.

By the early spring of 1920 it was obvious that more effective measures would be required to restore order in Ireland and the Government decided that, first of all, it needed new leaders. At the end of March, General Sir Nevil Macready was appointed GOC in C to command the troops. He had been the London Metropolitan Commissioner of Police since September 1918 and the original intention was that he should command both the army and the police. He managed to convince the Prime Minister that this was not practicable. The Inspector General of the RIC, General Sir Joseph Byrnes, had already been given indefinite leave of absence and shortly afterwards his deputy, Mr Moorhouse Davies, resigned. On 11 March the City Commissioner for Belfast, Mr J. Smith, was appointed Inspector General with Mr A. Walsh as his Deputy.[2] Later Major General H. M. Tudor was sent as Police Adviser to the Viceroy to command both the RIC and the Dublin Metropolitan Police. Finally at the end of April, a further change was made at the very top and Sir Hamar Greenwood replaced Mr Ian Macpherson as Chief Secretary for Ireland.

The need to increase the strength of the RIC to deal with the campaign of terror was obvious. Apart from the actual casualties, intimidation both of the policemen themselves and their families had caused many resignations from the force. At the same time recruiting was almost at a standstill and overall strength was falling dramatically. The position of the police in the south of Ireland at this time was not easy. These men were Irishmen who would have to live in the country after Home Rule was introduced, and they had to consider their position if the Government of the country was to be Sinn Fein. It says a great deal for the RIC that the morale of the force was as high as it was. As early as January it had been decided that the wastage of the RIC would have to be made good from England. Recruiting began there on 1 January 1920, and large numbers of ex-soldiers came forward. The first of these men arrived in Ireland at the end of March and began a period of six weeks' intensive training. By the end of May, 1,500 'Black and Tans', as they came to be known by the Irish, had arrived.[3]

The escalation of the trouble as well as the fall in strength of the police meant that the army had to be used more and more. The army stationed in Ireland was about 30,000 strong: it consisted of about thirty battalions of Infantry and seven regiments of cavalry with the usual complement of other arms. It was nominally organized into two Infantry Divisions, a Cavalry Brigade and the Dublin Military District. All units were under strength and their training programmes had been disrupted by demobilization after the war. Training was, in any case, for trench warfare and not for dealing with terrorists. Most of the soldiers were very young and their officers inexperienced. To date the army had been employed mainly in guarding Government buildings, in providing escorts for stores and prisoners and in trying to cope with a large number of calls for help from outlying police stations when they came under attack. Casualties up to the middle of 1920 were small compared to those suffered by the police, no more than five soldiers having been killed and two wounded.

In April the number of prisoners detained under the Defence of the Realm Act was over three hundred, half in Mountjoy prison, Dublin, and half in England. The policy of internment was, however, undermined by the Government's decision to release internees if they went on hunger strike. On 30 April the Prime Minister conferred in London with the Viceroy, the new Chief Secretary and other ministers. At this meeting Lord French said firmly that either a truce should be made with the rebels or outright measures of war should be taken against them. He estimated that only 10 per cent of the population wanted a republic but that most wanted some form of Home Rule. Mr Bonar Law put forward views provided by Sir Edward Carson who was not at the meeting. Sir Edward wanted to know why outlying police stations had been given up and pointed out that this policy surrendered whole districts to the IRA and left any loyalists there helpless. He therefore advocated an enlarged police force. The Viceroy pointed out that something of the order of three times the number of troops would be needed to protect all the outlying police stations and that a better solution would be to make the army more mobile. At another conference of ministers in London on 11 May at which General Macready was present, it was decided to send another eight battalions of troops to Ireland and to raise the number of motor vehicles available to the army from 193 to 427 in order to make it more mobile. This reinforcement made the army in Ireland larger than in the rest of Great Britain and there was talk of raising a Special Emergency Gendarmerie for Ireland. This project never reached fruition but in early June it was decided to form an Auxiliary Division of the RIC recruited, like the 'Black and Tans', in Great Britain. These Auxiliaries were to act in independent companies and to be used as mobile striking forces against the IRA. They were mostly young ex-army officers and the first of them arrived at the end of July when, like the 'Black and Tans', they began a six weeks' training course. In spite of all these measures, Sinn Fein lawlessness continued throughout the

whole of the south of Ireland. Republican Courts sat everywhere and their findings were enforced even more ruthlessly
by the Irish Republican Army. Sinn Fein had by this time
gained many unwilling adherents who joined because they
were resigned to the fact that it was the only real force to be
reckoned with in Ireland. The greater part of Ireland, except
for north-east Ulster, was now in a state in which no loyalist or
person of property was safe.

Nearly all the terrorism so far had been in the three southern provinces of Ireland and there had been very little in
Ulster, especially in the six counties which had substantial
Protestant populations. Here, although Sinn Fein had made
considerable progress among the Catholics, the IRA were very
weak and quite unable to intimidate the bulk of the population
in the way that they had in the south. The Protestant population was fanatically loyal to the Crown and the British con-
nection and had a violent hatred of Sinn Fein and all that it
stood for. They heartily agreed with Sir Edward Carson when
he said 'we in Ulster will tolerate no Sinn Fein – no Sinn Fein
organization, no Sinn Fein methods'. The northern Irish Protestants, unlike the English, were completely immune to Sinn
Fein propaganda. It was their firm conviction that you could
believe very little of what the native Irish told you. Since
1914, when they had been promised that the six northern
counties would be exempted from Home rule, the Province
had been fairly quiet. It had contributed more to the war effort
than the rest of Ireland put together. It held the south of
Ireland, with its Easter Rising, its opposition to conscription
and its relatively poor recruiting, in contempt. As the spring
and summer of 1920 wore on, however, tension increased as
minor Sinn Fein outrages spread to the North. Up to the
middle of 1920 these incidents were confined to a few raids on
private houses for arms and a bomb attack on Ballynahinch
RIC Station in Co Down. In June, however, the IRA attacked
the RIC Barracks at Crossgar in Co Down and Cookstown in
Co Tyrone and were beaten off in both places. They succeeded
in burning the courthouse in Derrylin in Co Fermanagh and

also four vacated RIC barracks elsewhere and shot a police sergeant dead in Co Armagh.

It was obvious that if nothing was done the disorders would become worse in the North. The RIC in Ulster, controlled centrally from Dublin, were inclined to adopt the same tactics as in the South. They abandoned the smaller police stations and concentrated in the larger ones and were apt to shut and bolt the door at sunset and not emerge until the morning. Terrorists could therefore move freely at night, attack the loyal population in their homes, destroy their property and even kidnap them. Thus the Protestant population of the North decided to take measures to protect themselves. In the middle of 1920, vigilante groups of various kinds began to be formed and, using their own arms, to mount guards at night and to patrol their areas against intruders. The most active organizer of an unofficial police force of this kind was Captain Sir Basil Brooke in Co Fermanagh. Captain Brooke had just left the army and returned home to farm and manage his estate at Colebrooke. Visits to Dublin during the spring of 1920 revealed to him the appalling state of affairs in the South of Ireland and brought home to him the danger should the trouble spread to the North. He did his best to get the authorities in Dublin Castle to organize an official Special Constabulary but his requests were cold shouldered. He was told that while the authorities welcomed the offer of the loyalists of the North to help maintain law and order, under no circumstances would they be allowed to carry arms. The suggestion was that they should wear arm bands and carry whistles! It seemed clear that, as little help could be expected from Dublin or the RIC, the loyalists would have to arm and protect themselves. Many of the rifles imported for the old pre-war Ulster Volunteer Force were still available as well as sporting guns. In retrospect one can see why Dublin Castle was reluctant to arm the 'Black North'. Their policy for the restoration of order in Ireland was to disarm the whole population and only leave weapons in the hands of the security forces. This would have been quite satisfactory if the army and police could have protected the people, but they could not: they had already largely lost control.

An early success for the unofficial vigilantes was at Lisbellaw in Co Fermanagh on 8–9 June 1920. A group was hastily organized by Mr George E. Liddle for the defence of the village as the RIC had been withdrawn from the local barracks and they were defenceless. Armed patrols were formed on the approach roads and arrangements were made to guard the railway station, the courthouse and the abandoned RIC barracks. Lookouts were stationed in the tower of Lisbellaw Parish Church. The stationmaster was requested to report at once should the telegraph wires to the station be cut, as this was rightly predicted to be a certain indication that the village was about to be attacked. The attack came on the very first night, which was clear and moonless and the first warning was, as expected, the cutting of the telegraph wires. An advance party of the IRA was permitted to reconnoitre the village without being molested, and later the incendiaries with their petrol tins were actually allowed to start work on the courthouse before the alarm was given by ringing the church bells. The fifty raiders were taken completely by surprise, there was heavy firing and a number of people were wounded. The IRA scattered and broke into two groups, one of which fled along the road to Enniskillen, and the other into the mountains towards Tempo. At dawn, several revolvers, bicycles and torches were taken as trophies, having been abandoned by the IRA in their retreat. In spite of several messages sent, summoning help from the RIC and the army, they did not appear until nearly lunch time the next day. The population of Lisbellaw were indignant at this failure to protect them and furious when they found that the soldiers had orders to disarm the victors. After a great deal of parleying they were persuaded not to do this but instead to pursue the IRA.

The problem of law and order in Ulster was not only one of competing with the IRA. It was complicated by the fact that rival mobs of Roman Catholics and Protestants, especially in the cities of Belfast and Londonderry, were liable to clash and very serious fighting often resulted. The history of this sort of disturbance goes back many years. In the early spring of 1920 there had been a minor riot at a football match in Belfast between Protestant and Catholic teams but this disturbance was brought under control by the police. It was the beginning, however, of a series of spasmodic outbursts lasting for nearly three years. Vigilantes were also organized in the city of Londonderry by groups of ex-soldiers to try and keep order in the streets at night. In spite of this, in June 1920, the city erupted after being kept in a state of tension for some time by IRA gunmen who had arrived from the South. On 19 June, rival loyalist and nationalist gangs clashed in the Waterside district of Londonderry. Firearms were used and the rioting spread to the whole city. By 21 June, trade and business were at a standstill and it was dangerous to venture on to the streets. Next day two civilians were killed and two wounded by the indiscriminate firing; burning of property and looting were widespread. Order was finally restored by troops and police on 26 June by isolating four districts of the city from each other and by imposing a curfew. Many loyal citizens of the North were eager to help and in the same month the Ulster ex-Servicemen's Association in Belfast sent a telegram to the King pledging their support to restore law and order and offering the services of 3,000 trained ex-Service men.

July started quietly in Ulster and the traditional Orange parades of the 'Twelfth' went off without incident in spite of Sinn Fein efforts to provoke trouble by Republican flag waving and writing of slogans on walls. But soon signs appeared that the situation was further deteriorating. Minor Sinn Fein activities continued: postmen were held up; threatening letters were sent; trams were interfered with and another abandoned RIC barracks was burnt. On 17 July, Colonel Smyth, the Divisional Commissioner of the RIC in Munster, was murdered by the IRA in the County Club at Cork. Colonel Smyth was a native of Banbridge in Co Down and his assassination caused an outburst of fury in the North. There was serious rioting at Banbridge, Dromore and Hillsborough and later on a smaller scale at Bangor and Newtownards and, in these predominantly Protestant towns, local Sinn Fein property suffered severely. Two people were killed and efforts were made to get employers to dismiss all Sinn Fein workers. By far the worst trouble, however, was in Belfast. Many Protestant shipyard workers, who had joined the army, found on their return from the war that their jobs had been taken by Catholics who had stayed at home. When these Catholics openly supported Sinn Fein, it only needed an incident such as the murder of Colonel Smyth, to bring matters to a head. On 21 July, a meeting of Belfast Unionist workmen in their dinner hour decided to expel all Catholics from the shipyards and serious attacks were made on them, several being assaulted and others thrown into the harbour. Order was restored after an hour and a half by troops and police. Wild rumours followed by attacks on workers of both sides as they went home culminated in fierce sectarian rioting throughout the city. Police and soldiers were fired on by a Sinn Fein mob and returned the fire. The rioting went on until 24 July, eighteen people being killed, some 200 injured and half a million pounds' worth of damage done.

On 23 July 1920, a conference was held in London between ministers and officers of the Irish Administration. Mr Lloyd George presided and most of the cabinet were present as well as Generals Macready and Tudor and Sir James Craig, then Parliamentary Secretary to the Admiralty. The picture presented to the cabinet was gloomy. The Civil Courts in Ireland had ceased to function and no one was paying taxes. It was feared that by September the Royal Irish Constabulary would have ceased to exist as a police force. It was probable that because of the campaign of terror against them and their families half of them would have resigned and the rest would be pinned down in their barracks, able only to sortie occasionally to make reprisals. In fact the situation was now worse than it had ever been before. Most of the meeting was concerned with the question of whether it would be better to seek an immediate truce with Sinn Fein or, by a policy of repression, to restore law and order so that the Better Government of Ireland Act could be brought into force. In general, the civil members of the Irish Administration seemed to favour a truce and felt that repression would fail and deprive the Government of the few friends it had left in Ireland. General Tudor believed that a policy of repression could succeed and defeat the terrorists but the police would have to be better supported by the Government. The recent release of hunger strikers had lowered the morale of the police badly, and the fact that still not a single murderer of a policeman had been brought to justice was even more depressing. He advocated trial of terrorists by court martial, identity cards for all, passport control for anyone entering Ireland, restriction on movement and a policy of fining areas in which outrages occurred. He also wanted all prisoners sent to Great Britain and the GPO purged of traitors. It was an inescapable fact, however, that if a policy of repression was to be followed many more police and troops would have to be found. Mr Winston Churchill, the Secretary of State for War, asked what would happen if the Protestants of the northern six counties were given arms and charged with keeping law and order in their own area so that the police and troops now stationed there could be used in the South of Ireland. Mr Wylie, one of the Dublin Castle law officers who was present, said at once that such a policy would be disastrous. He thought Sinn Fein would arm an equal number of men in the North and it would simply lead to civil war. Sir John Anderson, Under Secretary for Ireland, went further and said that he did not know whether law and order could be kept in the North in this way but it was certain that it would set the south of Ireland ablaze and might well lead to a massacre of Protestants in the South and West. General Tudor said he knew that the people of Ulster were determined that law and order should be maintained in the province and wanted to get their unofficial special constabulary recognized. He was however very much against using an irregular force for the purpose and was also opposed to a reconstitution of the pre-war Ulster Volunteer Force. Sir James Craig, on the other hand, said that Mr Winston Churchill's proposal was quite practicable providing it was made official and legal. Special Constables could be properly sworn in and take the Oath of Allegiance. With their own officers and military discipline he was confident that they could keep order in the Six Counties. He believed that they would be able to prevent mob law or the Protestants from running amok. The Prime Minister noted that this proposal could release seven battalions and several thousand police and directed that it should be further examined.

In the South of Ireland three reinforcements of troops amounting to ten battalions in all arrived during the summer, but many of these were below strength and in August operations were seriously impeded by orders to hold them ready for withdrawal again because of industrial trouble in Great Britain. The policy of reinforcing the RIC with 'Black and Tans' went ahead and by September the police were again up to strength. The Government decided not to introduce martial law as yet but to rely on a policy of greater mobility, using armoured cars and lorries, and at the same time to strengthen the law. The Restoration of Order in Ireland Act came into effect on 9 August and provided for courts martial for a wider range of offences than permitted by the Defence of the Realm Act and for military courts of enquiry to be held instead of inquests. It also made it easier for the authorities to impose curfews, restrict traffic and imprison terrorists on suspicion. In the second half of 1920, however, the 'troubles' escalated in the South of Ireland. The IRA had by now expanded considerably and had arms for about 3,000 men. In August they took an oath of allegiance to Dail Eireann. In the six months from June to December 1920 no less than 127 policemen were murdered, 192 wounded and another 113 attacked in some way. Casualties among the soldiers increased to forty-seven killed and 118 wounded, with another eighty-six attacks on them. Finally thirty civilians were murdered and sixty-nine injured, most of whom were suspected of giving information to the authorities and were shot in reprisal by the IRA. There were over 2,000 raids for arms by the IRA mostly in September, and 894 mail raids. At the same time another thirty-nine courthouses were burnt down, as well as 167 vacated police barracks and twenty-six coastguard stations and lighthouses. Attacks on occupied police barracks continued and eleven were destroyed but many other attacks were repulsed. In the late autumn, the IRA began to form flying columns and what they called 'active service units' of men who were known to have committed crimes and were 'on the run'. In November the IRA perpetrated two atrocities, the murder of fourteen Intelligence Officers in their billets in Dublin on 'Bloody Sunday' and the ambush of seventeen Auxiliaries by a large force of IRA at Macroom in Co Cork, in which a number of wounded men were butchered and mutilated. At the same time there were encouraging signs. The strength of the Royal Irish Constabulary recruited in the form of the 'Black and Tans' and the Auxiliaries had risen well above the 1919 figure and at the end of the year stood at 12,755. The number of the IRA who were arrested, tried by court martial and convicted, increased dramatically. From the introduction of the Restoration of Order in Ireland Act until the end of the year, there were 1,584 arrests, 809 court martials and 635 convictions. On 21 November some 500 members of the IRA were arrested and interned, and on 9 December martial law was declared in Counties Cork, Kerry, Tipperary and Limerick. Without doubt the security forces at this time were pressing the IRA hard. At the Guildhall Banquet on 9 November, Mr Lloyd George said, prematurely as it transpired, 'we have murder by the throat'. In December, after long debate, the Better Government of Ireland Act received the Royal assent.

Whilst this savage campaign was being waged in the South and allegations of reprisals were being made against the 'Black and Tans' and the Auxiliaries, the six northern counties were far from tranquil. August started quietly, but on the 15th a Sinn Fein flag was hoisted on the border of a Unionist locality in Belfast and the police were attacked by a Catholic mob when they tried to remove it. Another provocative act caused an affray in Banfoot in Co Armagh. Tension throughout the

province remained high because of the many Sinn Fein outrages in the South. In the Six Counties telephone wires were
cut by the IRA, English and Belfast newspapers were destroyed, Drumquin and Ballycastle RIC barracks were attacked
and the courthouse at Omagh burned. A number of mail raids
occurred and there was a great deal of intimidation by both
sides. By far the worst disturbances were triggered by another
incident which had its origin in the South. In March, Alder-
man MacCurten, the Lord Mayor of Cork and a member of
the IRA was murdered by an extremist Republican group and
a local inquest found, in a manifestly political verdict,[4] that he
had been killed by the police. There was not a shred of evidence to implicate the RIC but it was considered prudent to
move the local District Inspector to Lisburn in Co Antrim as
he was clearly a marked man. On 22 August, an IRA murder
gang followed him to Lisburn and shot him dead on his way
home from church. Serious rioting at once broke out in the
town and the local Sinn Feiners, indeed practically the whole
Catholic community, were driven from their homes and out of
the town. The few police available were quite unable to cope
and a considerable number of special constables had to be
sworn in to assist them, order being gradually restored. On 24
August, after the arrival of these Lisburn refugees, the trouble
spread to Belfast where a Sinn Fein mob attacked loyalist
workmen in the Ballymacarett area on their way back to work
after their midday meal. Next day the military were called out
and were shot at by a Sinn Fein crowd and they had to return
the fire. Wholesale sectarian rioting then engulfed the whole
city for the best part of a week, twenty-two people being killed
and over 300 injured. On 31 August, by which time a curfew
had been ordered, the riots died down of their own accord but
terror, unrest and a wholesale polarization of the communities
followed. In September 1920, as a reprisal for the eviction of
the Roman Catholics from Lisburn, Sinn Fein ordered a boycott of Belfast goods in the rest of Ireland.

On 2 September 1920 these events resulted in an important
conference of ministers in London presided over by Mr Bonar

Law, the Lord Privy Seal. Colonel Sir James Craig, still the Parliamentary and Financial Secretary to the Admiralty, was present and was clearly in a mood to press for decisive action. He declared the situation in Ulster was deteriorating rapidly and that the loyal population was losing faith in the Government's will to protect them. They were threatening recourse to arms and there was a danger of civil war. In addition to a request that there should be an Under Secretary appointed to Belfast and that the troops and police there should come under his authority instead of directly under that of Dublin, he made the first definite proposals for a Special Constabulary to be raised in Ulster. His proposals were for 2,000 full-time Special Constables to assist the RIC to re-establish police stations effectively throughout the Six Counties. This force was to be armed and organized on military lines. He further proposed that a part-time force of Special Constables should be raised from the loyal population for use when required, suggesting that a much larger number should be sworn in than normally required in order to provide for reliefs and ensure that as large a proportion of the population as possible were brought under discipline. This force would come under the RIC Divisional Commissioner in Ulster but should be commanded by local officers and should be allowed to drill and practise musketry. They would be required to do duty near their homes and should be armed when necessary. Sir James Craig also proposed that in the event of a general rising by the rebels which was beyond the security forces' capacity to control or in the event of the withdrawal of the army from the North of Ireland, the pre-war Ulster Volunteer Force should be rearmed for the defence of the country.

The meeting came to the decision that it was right to separate Ulster administratively and that it was desirable to form a force of Special Constables at once. The next day the Ulster Unionist Council issued a statement demanding full and immediate protection of those whose lives and property were imperilled by the disturbances. The Council also earnestly appealed to all loyal subjects of the King to assist the authorities in maintaining law and order. A deputation which included members of the Ulster Unionist Labour Association was sent to London and saw Mr Bonar Law and other members of the cabinet on 7 September. The following day, a council of ministers presided over by the Prime Minister agreed that the Chief Secretary for Ireland should take the necessary steps to organize a force of Special Constables[5] and appoint an Under Secretary for Belfast. No mention was made of the rearming or recalling of the Ulster Volunteer Force. The formation of a Special Constabulary was viewed with disfavour by General Macready, who feared that it might sow the seeds of civil war and necessitate the intervention of the army, so proving a drain on his resources. He still favoured a force of eight garrison battalions specially raised in Great Britain for service in Ireland which would be soldiers under military discipline. The Government, however, stuck to its decision not to raise such a force. Sir Henry Wilson, the Chief of the Imperial General Staff, was also nervous about arming Special Constables without putting them under military discipline.

In Ulster itself tension was further increased by the murder of Captain Lendrum, a Resident Magistrate in Co Clare who was an Ulsterman from Trillick in Co Tyrone. On 22 September Captain Lendrum was ambushed in his car between Ennistymon and Ennis and shot. While still alive he was buried up to his neck in the sand to wait for the tide to come in and drown him. Finally he was thrown on a manure heap. I make no apology for recalling this atrocity against one who was admitted to be a fair and just magistrate, for unless some such cases are mentioned it is difficult to understand the pressures and tensions of the time and the hatreds that exist in Ireland to this day.

From July onwards, the Unionists in Co Armagh had begun to organize themselves for their own protection and there were indications that the Ulster Volunteer Force was being reorganized in all six counties. The strength of the police and army had proved totally inadequate in both Lisburn and Belfast and this was why the Justices of the Peace in Lisburn had officially sworn in a considerable number of Special Constables. Committees were formed to organize defence in many places. In October there were vigilantes in Dromore, Banbridge and Rathfriland in Co Down and in Maghera, Castledawson and Moneymore in Co Londonderry, as well as at various places in Co Antrim. It was in Co Fermanagh, however, that most progress was made and several thousand men were now organized. Few of these Special Constables were as yet official and sworn, but many carried their own arms and assisted the RIC as much as they could. There was friction in Lisburn in November when the RIC prosecuted some of the Special Constables for riot.[6]

In October and November, there was some rioting in Belfast and another four people were killed. The army had to open fire on one occasion and the police made baton charges against both Protestant and Catholic mobs. In the rest of the Six Counties, the IRA continued its campaign and in the last three months of the year there were attacks on the RIC barracks at Tempo and Carnlough. At the former a police sergeant was shot dead before the place was relieved by the local unofficial Special Constabulary, and in the latter 150 IRA were repulsed by eight policemen after a battle lasting three hours. Two other members of the RIC were murdered and ten police patrols were fired upon in other parts of the Province. In addition there were over thirty raids by the IRA for arms; Torr Head coastguard station was attacked and there were the usual mail raids and cutting of telephone wires.

Towards the end of October, Dublin Castle announced the formation of a Special Constabulary. No new legislation was required as the Special Constables (Ireland) Acts of 1832 and 1914 were still in force. Under these Acts 'Their Excellencies the Lords Justice and General-Governors of Ireland' approved applications by local authorities to enrol Special Constables.[7] All law-abiding citizens between the ages of twenty-one and forty-five were invited to apply for enrolment to assist the authorities in the maintenance of order and the prevention of crime. In theory the Special Constables could be raised anywhere in Ireland but in practice it was only attempted in the North. There were to be three classes: the A Specials who were to be whole time, the B Specials part-time, and the C Specials listed as available for use in emergency. The A Specials were enrolled for a period of six months and were to be armed, equipped, uniformed and paid the same wages as the regular members of the RIC. The B Specials were to carry out duties in their own districts on about one night a week and were also to attend training drills. They were to be armed as necessary and were to act with the regular police. They were unpaid but were given an allowance to cover the wear and tear of their clothes. At first they had no uniform but were issued with caps and armlets. It was intended that they should be under their own officers, but on duty would act under the regular police. Class C Specials were simply listed as available for emergency service. They would be expected to do occasional drills but would only have caps and armbands. They would be unpaid and would use their own arms for which they would be given permits.

The Special Constabulary was to be under the command of Lieutenant-Colonel C. G. Wickham, the Divisional Commissioner of the RIC for Ulster in Belfast. He answered partly to General Tudor, in Dublin, and partly to Sir Ernest Clark, the new Under Secretary in Belfast, but in practice he had considerable independence. Under the Divisional Commissioner, a County Commandant was appointed for each county, appointments parallel to the County Inspectors of the RIC with whom they had to co-operate closely. Within the counties the force was divided into districts under District Commandants and the Districts into Sub-Districts under Sub-District Commandants. The first County Commandants to be appointed were:

Antrim and Belfast	Lieutenant-Colonel W. R. Goodwin, CMG, DSO
Down	Major D. Ker
Fermanagh	Captain Sir Basil Brooke, Bart
Londonderry	Lieutenant-Colonel G. Moore-Irvine
Armagh	Captain C. H. Ensor
Tyrone	Colonel J. K. McClintock

Applications for enrolment as Special Constables were considered by Selection Committees appointed in each county. The Selection Committees were formed of Justices of the Peace who were invited 'to co-opt other inhabitants of the county who should be of various classes in order that an accurate knowledge of each candidate may be available'. A perusal of the lists of these Committees shows that they included a large number of retired officers of the services. The Committees were told to select 'only men of unquestionable fidelity and efficiency'. The age limit of forty-five was to be strictly applied to Class A but the Committees were given discretion to accept older candidates for classes B and C. After acceptance by the Selection Committee the names were sent to the local District Inspector of Police for final vetting. Subsequently they were formally appointed by two Justices of the Peace and had to take an oath.[8] Class A Special Constables had to pass a medical examination and were sent to a training camp at Newtownards for a six weeks' course. The A Specials took the same oath as the RIC and were governed by the same code of discipline. This was at General Tudor's request and it caused some misgivings, as the A Specials were determined that the Government in Dublin should not go back on the assurance that they had been given on enlistment that they would only be required to serve in the six counties.

Attitudes to the formation of the Special Constabulary varied widely. The ordinary loyal Unionist of the six counties welcomed the decision to form the Specials simply because he wanted law and order and he wished to be defended against IRA murderers, arsonists and intimidators. He was determined that the country should not sink into anarchy as the three southern provinces had done. He needed a Special Constabulary because the RIC was now of very limited use and, he suspected, had Sinn Fein traitors in its ranks. The British Army was under strength and fully occupied with the 'troubles' in the South and with the communal riots in Belfast and Londonderry, leaving the rest of the six counties wide open to IRA attack. Sir James Craig and the Ulster Unionist

Party with whom we may group the Orange Order also wanted law and order preserved and were, in addition, determined that the IRA was not going to obtain a united Ireland by force against the will of the people of the six counties as a whole, and that the political solution of partition promised by the British Government should be upheld. They were confident that a Special Constabulary raised from the loyal population of the North was a suitable instrument and could prove a disciplined and effective force. This confidence was based on their experience of the excellent discipline of the pre-war Ulster Volunteer Force which had never got out of hand nor killed a soul, and the fact that the new Special Constabulary would contain a substantial proportion of demobilized soldiers from the British Army who were already trained and disciplined. In Dublin, Generals Macready and Tudor viewed the whole business with distaste. General Macready had an ambivalent attitude towards Ulster. He had been sent to the North in 1914 to command the proposed operations against the Ulster Volunteer Force and, in spite of their splendid subsequent record as the 36th (Ulster) Division in France, he still thought of them as the enemy. He was outspokenly opposed to the action of the officers at the Curragh who had resigned rather than march against Ulster. He was therefore opposed to the formation of the Specials in principle which he thought of as a resurrection of the Ulster Volunteer Force. General Tudor did not share his prejudices but he was already having difficulty with the discipline of the 'Black and Tans' and the Auxiliaries who were proving difficult to control in the face of the intense provocation of the IRA, and he believed that the control of a Special Constabulary which he thought of as untrained irregulars would be impossible. The Royal Irish Constabulary viewed the Specials with mixed feelings. Although grateful for the reinforcement and conscious that they would give confidence to the law-abiding majority, they were apprehensive of the effect not only on the Catholic population but also on the Catholic members in the police force. The Irish Administration in Dublin Castle were also opposed to the scheme, particularly the Under Secretaries, Sir John Anderson and Mr McMahon, and the assistant Attorney General, Mr Wylie. They were afraid that the arming of the Special Constabulary would simply lead to civil war in the North, an area which up to now had been quiet.

Some moderate Catholics in the North, although they had misgivings, were prepared to support the scheme if they could be given assurances that it was going to be administered properly. Sir Ernest Clark, the Under Secretary in Belfast, gave them these assurances and said that if sufficient Catholics joined, Catholic units could be formed to keep order in Catholic areas. In spite of this encouragement, nothing came of the scheme because Catholics were discouraged from joining by their Church and most of their political organizations. The Ancient order of Hibernians certainly discouraged its members from becoming Special Constables and the Nationalist Party felt that the Special Constabulary was simply a way to impose partition on the six counties by force of arms. Sinn Fein regarded the Specials as an excuse for arming the Orangemen and an act even more atrocious than the creation of the 'Black and Tans'! Their fury was natural as they saw that the Specials might well mean that they would be unable to intimidate and subdue the North by force. Their skilful propaganda set about blackening the image of the Special Constables, trying to identify them with the worst elements of the Protestant mobs in Belfast. They sought to magnify and distort every incident and to stir up hatred of the force even before it started to function. The Irish Republican Army were more direct. They announced their intention of treating any Catholics who joined as traitors and of dealing with them accordingly. Loyal Roman Catholics had to be brave men to volunteer as Special Constables and the majority preferred not to get involved. The likely consequences were shown on 4 December when four IRA men in Belfast tried to murder Special Constable McCullough, a Roman Catholic.

The Special Constabulary, therefore, raised by the British Government through the Irish Administration in Dublin

Castle, became an almost completely Protestant force, not because the Government desired this but because practically every Roman Catholic organization in Ireland discouraged their members from joining. Without a doubt this suited the Unionists and the Orange Order, and these organizations encouraged their members to join. The Specials themselves were relieved that the danger of being infiltrated by Sinn Fein traitors, as the GPO, the RIC, the Irish Railways and even the Dublin Castle administration had been, was accordingly reduced. Against Sinn Fein propaganda, however, they were virtually defenceless. For the most part dour and silent men employed by a Government which had virtually no counter-propaganda machinery, their actions were even more likely to be misrepresented than those of the British troops and police in the South. The original reason which led to their formation was the shortage of troops and regular police in Ireland, coupled with the demand of the loyal population in the North for protection. They were raised to help keep law and order in the face of an attempt by the IRA to seize power against the wishes of the majority of the people in Northern Ireland.

NOTES

1. It has been difficult to find the exact percentages. Lloyd George in a Memorandum in 1922 said the RIC was 82 per cent Catholic.

2. The reasons for these changes have never really come to light. It seems likely that there was some disagreement between General Byrnes and the authorities in Dublin Castle but of what kind and under what circumstances remains a mystery.

3. Their nickname was after a famous pack of hounds and they were given it because their early uniform was a mixture of khaki and dark green.

4. They found a verdict of murder against the RIC District Inspector Swanzy, the Viceroy and Lloyd George!

5. It is of interest that the typewritten cabinet minutes originally referred to a force of Special Constables in Ulster, but the word Ulster was crossed out and Ireland substituted in ink.

6. It was, of course, very difficult to know if a Special Constable in plain clothes was trying to restore order or taking part in a riot.

7. By the Act, a 'credible witness' had to swear an oath before Justices of the Peace to say that the ordinary police force was 'not sufficient for the preservation of the public peace', etc.

8. The actual oath which Special Constables had to take before a Justice of the Peace, was:

'I do swear that I will well and truly serve our Sovereign Lord the King in the Office of Special Constable without favour or affection, malice or ill-will, and that I will to the best of my power cause the Peace to be kept and preserved, and prevent all offences against the persons and properties of his Majesty's subjects; and that while I continue to hold the said office I will to the best of my skill and knowledge discharge all the duties thereof faithfully according to law. So help me God.'

CHAPTER TWO

1921, The First Year of Operations

Recruiting for the new Special Constabulary[1] began in Belfast on 1 November 1920, in Cos Fermanagh and Tyrone on 15 November and in the remaining counties by 27 November. At first, volunteers for Class A were easier to obtain than for Class B, 1,700 applying in Belfast alone. The first batches of A Specials soon began their six weeks' training at Newtownards Camp. Here under the command of Major J. McCallum, DSO, MC, they were instructed in police duties, in the use of arms, in drill and in discipline and they received their uniform, clothing and equipment. The training was a fairly simple task as the majority had served in the army during the war and had only just been demobilized. On 6 December, on completion of this course, the first two platoons of A Specials were inspected by Colonel Wickham. They then took up duty, the first in Belfast and the second in the border area of Co Down. Each platoon had two officers, a Head Constable, four Sergeants and sixty Special Constables. They were armed with rifles and organized in four sections each under a sergeant. The platoons were fully mobile and each had, in addition to a Ford car for the officer in charge, two armoured cars and four Crossley tenders, one of the latter for each section. Roughly half the A Specials were organized in these platoons and half were sent as reinforcements to RIC stations all over the province. The number of A Specials sworn in by the end of the year amounted to 1,500.

By the middle of November, 750 B Specials had been enrolled in Belfast and by the Middle of January, 945 B men
had been sworn in in Co Fermanagh. Only 180 were reported
on duty in Co Armagh in February but recruiting was reported brisk in Londonderry. Co Fermanagh held its lead,
however, with a strength of 500 in February and 2,200 in
March. General Ricardo, a resident in Co Tyrone, who had
commanded a brigade of the 36th (Ulster) Division during the
war, was worried at the lack of recruits for Class B in his
county and suggested that it might be better to enrol a smaller
number of Class A in their place. He believed that this would,
in any case, be more acceptable to moderate Roman Catholics
and could not be construed as a wholesale arming of the Protestant population. His advice, however, was not taken and
meetings were held all over the Province to try and get recruits. The establishment for the B Specials was laid down in
January as ten times the combined strength of the RIC and the
A Specials in a county. This target for the Province, which
amounted to some 30,000 men, was never reached. Unfortunately, recruiting was best in the solid Protestant areas where
the Specials were not so necessary, and worst in the Nationalist areas where the IRA were particularly active. On 23
November 1920, Sir Basil Brooke, who had been appointed
County Commandant for Fermanagh, issued a public order to
all who wished to join the Specials. The following is an extract, 'You have now the great test of your loyalty before you
... when called upon to fight the agents of Murder, Anarchy
and Terrorism. For it is these three that you are asked to
destroy – and to destroy with the utmost vigour.

Be, however, tolerant in your actions, for there are many of
other persuasions, who, while disapproving of these deeds of
violence, are yet unable to take an active part in suppressing
them. . . .'

The Belfast Special Constabulary was organized on different lines from the counties. The districts corresponded with
the RIC police divisions of the city and a sub-district was
attached to each police station. The City Commandant and the

Special Constabulary therefore worked in very close touch with the Commissioner of Police for the city and the RIC. They were armed with pistols and truncheons which were kept in the police stations and issued to patrols as necessary. On 4 February, the first patrols of B Specials began work in Belfast and great care was taken to use them where there were no Roman Catholics. By May there were 1,480 Specials in the City and they manned thirty-two beats while another forty-three more were planned. In the early stages many of the B Specials in country districts carried their own arms which was a somewhat hazardous business. When available they were armed with service rifles from RIC stocks which they drew from a police station before going on duty and returned immediately afterwards. By midsummer there were still only enough rifles for the men actually out on patrol and so these rifles had to be used every night by different men. The B Specials reported for duty in civilian clothes but wore their policemen's caps and they were generally issued with RIC pattern waterproof coats and armbands as well. Training in the early stages was very sketchy. Fortunately nearly half of the men were ex-soldiers who knew how to handle a rifle and they were able to instruct their civilian colleagues.

On 17 November 1920, general orders for the Special Constabulary were issued. In each county an advisory board consisting of three magistrates, the County Inspector of the RIC and the County Commandant of the Special Constabulary was established and all questions affecting discipline and general welfare could be referred to it. In disciplinary cases it had the power to recommend dismissal, or that service should be determined. Generally Special Constables would be allowed to resign rather than be dismissed but any offences against the ordinary law would be tried in the civil courts. For lesser offences, Special Constables could be fined up to £5 or could be reprimanded. In January 1921 a memorandum laid down the principles for the relations between the RIC and the Special Constabulary. The County Inspector of the RIC was to be responsible for all the barrack reinforcements of A

Special Constables as well as the permanent police, whereas the County Commandant would command the A Special Platoons, and the B and C Specials. The regular police were to deal with all people arrested and cases in which civilians were killed or injured and, of course, all civil crime. It was stressed that co-operation was very important and that information should be freely exchanged. The original orders issued by the Divisional Commissioner also laid down that the Special Constabulary were not to make raids or searches without the permission of the County Inspector of the RIC and when this was obtained, a member of the regular RIC would have to be present. All patrols were to be accompanied by an RIC Constable and the patrols themselves were to be ordered by the regular RIC. The early orders state, 'Special Constables will not under any circumstances act on their own initiative. In particular an order to fire must come from the senior member of the RIC present'. Patrolling in this way was carried out in the city of Belfast and in Co Antrim in the early days. It soon fell into disuse in country districts however, mainly because there were nothing like enough RIC constables to accompany the patrols and because of the reluctance of the RIC to leave their barracks at night. These orders were not re-issued after the first edition and A Specials were soon recognized as having the same powers as the regular RIC. The Tyrone Special Constables Handbook of 18 February 1921, says, 'In the event of a Patrol not being accompanied by an RIC representative, the Special Sergeant then must act on his own initiative'. In the Fermanagh Special Orders to Head Constables issued in February, the responsibility for the ordering of patrols is laid upon the Head Special Constable of the Sub-District and no mention is made of the RIC. Emphasis is put on secrecy, 'Sergeants must impress on their men the importance of keeping absolutely to themselves any orders or information or location of patrols, which they may receive'. Fire is to be opened 'only in extreme circumstances ... and only when it is quite certain that the person or vehicle challenged is endeavouring to evade search'. The rule that houses were not to be searched unless the RIC were present was however reaffirmed and 'The use of "Party Expressions" and words likely to give offence when passing the houses of the "other side" is strictly forbidden when on duty'. This led to the RIC complaint that the activities of the Specials were, to a large extent, unknown to them and in consequence Colonel Wickham directed that 'the Special Constabulary, when going on patrol, must inform the local District Inspector and invite him or his representative to accompany the patrol'. In practice this invitation was seldom accepted. Although no actual orders seem to exist, the separate patrolling by the Special Constabulary was clearly recognized as an essential part of their duties by the authorities during the first quarter of 1921. Although the relations between the RIC and the Special Constabulary were good in many places, they were often bad. The Specials who did nearly all their work at night had not much time for regular police who bolted themselves in their barracks during the dark hours. In some places the Specials were convinced that the RIC were infiltrated by Sinn Feiners and so they were reluctant to report intelligence to them or even to reveal where they were patrolling. Many members of the RIC were hostile to the Specials and very ready to lay charges against them for any breaches of the rules.

In January 1921 there were signs that internment under the Restoration of Order in Ireland Act had decreased IRA activities in the North. Nevertheless in this month alone there were four attacks on police, four of whom were killed and six wounded. The Special Constabulary suffered its first fatal casualty when the IRA ambushed five police who were escorting a postman at Crossmaglen in Co Armagh. The postman was killed, Special Constable Robert Compston later died of his wounds and an RIC constable was also wounded. Elsewhere a vacated barracks was burnt and there were ten IRA raids for arms mostly near the borders of Co Fermanagh. In February there were signs that IRA activity was being stirred up from outside the province. On 6 February came the sole attack on the police during the month when bombs were thrown at a patrol at Warrenpoint, and Special Constable John Cummings was killed and two others were wounded. There were a dozen raids by the IRA for arms in February, four attacks on police stations, two on coastguard stations, two attempts to enforce the boycott of Belfast goods and a number of bridges were destroyed and roads trenched to prevent mobile police patrols operating in Nationalist areas. Belfast and Londonderry were kept quiet by curfew and constant patrolling by the military and police including the Special Constabulary.

As early as December 1920, police reports had begun to show that the efforts of the Special Constabulary were having beneficial results in the Province. The situation in Newry was said to be improving due to patrolling by Specials and in Co Down 'Sinn Fein was less aggressive due to the restraining influence of the Special Constabulary'. In February a decrease in outrages in Downpatrick and Newry was reported 'doubtless due to the activities of the mobile platoon of Special Constabulary' who were credited, together with internment, with keeping the IRA in check. Probably the most important effect at this time was the direct reinforcement of the RIC by A Specials all over the Province. This strengthened the defence of the larger police stations but also made it possible to reopen many of the smaller stations which had had to be abandoned. In January and February over twenty RIC barracks were reoccupied in Cos Armagh, Tyrone, Antrim and Londonderry alone. This policy, which re-established police control over the whole Province, had the effect of cutting down intimidation, protecting law abiding citizens and preventing Sinn Fein taking over whole areas as they had done in the South. This policy proved superior to that of General Tudor in the South in which, while leaving most small RIC stations empty, he took the offensive with mobile forces against the IRA. His policy certainly led to heavy casualties among the IRA and the arrest of many more. Nevertheless, the extensive use of motor transport by the army and police, which this strategy entailed, gave the IRA opportunities for ambush of which they took full advantage and his control of the country proved spasmodic and temporary.

The IRA had no illusions about the effectiveness of the Special Constabulary. They did their best to intimidate Protestants who joined or were about to join especially in Nationalist areas and near the borders of the six counties. On 5 February Special Constable Lester, who lived at Rosslea, received a threatening letter and on 21 February he was shot at and wounded. Sinn Fein also brought its powerful propaganda to bear not only to manufacture and distort incidents involving the Specials for external consumption but to stir up sectarian feeling against them in the Roman Catholic population of the North. Although it was Sinn Fein that was largely responsible for the failure of Roman Catholics to join the force, they now represented it as 'the wholesale arming of the Orangemen'. Their propaganda was very successful and RIC reports of this time frequently record Nationalist resentment against the Special Constabulary. General Macready, who was against the formation of the Special Constabulary from the beginning, while agreeing that in some parts of the North their work was helpful in the maintenance of order, of other parts said their conduct justified his fears. He cited no examples in his book but presumably was referring to a few incidents which are to be found in the RIC police records of this period. The first of these was on 23 January 1921, when a party of fifteen A Specials of the platoon stationed at Newtownbutler crossed into Co Monaghan and became involved in a battle with the RIC in the town of Clones. It is difficult to establish exactly what happened as there is considerable conflict in the evidence. It is clear, however, that the A Specials under a sergeant drove quietly into Clones in a Crossley tender with only its side lights on in the early hours of the morning. They stopped in Fermanagh Street; sentries were posted and the sergeant and a constable stopped at a licensed premises and shouted to the owner to come down. The owner and a colleague ran out of the back of the house and told the RIC that a burglary was being committed. The RIC turned out and, on arrival, fire was exchanged, none of the RIC were hit but a Special Constable was killed and another in the Crossley seriously wounded. The RIC say they found two Special Constables in the public house who opened fire on them which they returned. The Specials in the Crossley say the RIC opened fire on them without warning – although they shouted that they were police. They did not return the fire and were disarmed and arrested by the RIC and returned under escort to Newtownbutler. Subsequently it was alleged that stolen liquor was found in the Crossley but this was said by the Specials to have been planted after their arrest. Whether this incident was a raid on a public house to steal liquor as alleged in the press or whether they had taken the law into their own hands and were trying to arrest someone suspected of complicity in the murder of two RIC constables the day before, there is no doubt that their presence in Clones that night was unauthorized. A Special patrols did occasionally operate in Co Monaghan and no border was established as yet because the whole of Ulster was still governed from Dublin. Nevertheless, Colonel Wickham, the Divisional Commissioner in Belfast, issued a statement that the public might rest assured that the authorities would take the strongest possible steps to stamp out indiscipline or improper conduct of any kind. Subsequently the platoon stationed at Newtownbutler was disbanded and sent back to the training camp at Newtownards and some of the participants were tried by court martial. There is no doubt that some of the officers of the A Specials were poor. Less than half of them were Ulstermen and the others were from Great Britain and often were slack, too familiar with their men and exercised little control. This seems to have been the main cause of the trouble in the Newtownbutler platoon and the firm action of Colonel Wickham ensured that such incidents would not occur in the future. The majority of A Special Platoons were excellent material, well disciplined and conscientious in their duties.

There were other incidents which General Macready might have had in mind. For instance in Newry, a publican alleged that Specials stole liquor and brandy from him in the middle of January and the RIC charged nine A Special Constables from Belfast. On the night of 18/19 January four B Specials accompanied by a civilian searched ten or twelve Nationalist houses and the owners claimed they lost watches and valuables which were later recovered in the house of the civilian. It appears that this man fabricated a story that he had been fired at in a certain area and the Special Constables carried out the searches on their own initiative and while they were busy the thefts were made by him. It was, of course, easy to make such allegations of theft after a house had been searched and this was why searches were only supposed to be made with a member of the regular RIC present. Nevertheless there was undoubtedly a Sinn Fein attempt at this time to discredit the Specials by this kind of allegation and many of the RIC were very ready to listen. On 15 January a Bessbrook shopkeeper had £99 stolen and alleged it had been taken by Specials. Later he admitted to the RIC that he had no idea who had taken the money. In general, in such a large and hastily organized force, the discipline was good and such infringements as occurred were followed up and investigated by the authorities. Certainly, General Macready had far more serious disciplinary problems to deal with among the forces of the crown in the South.

In the rest of Ireland, the 'troubles' continued and on 1 January 1921 the Government brought into force an Authorized Reprisals Policy. This was, in fact, an admission that they were unable to prevent the 'Black and Tans' and the Auxiliaries from making unauthorized reprisals for IRA murders and outrages. On 4 January, martial law was extended to the counties of Clare, Waterford, Wexford and Kilkenny. In the seven months, January to July 1921, casualties among the security forces were very heavy, 223 police and ninety-four soldiers were killed, while 428 police and 210 soldiers were wounded. At the same time another 466 attacks were made on them which proved unsuccessful. There were more IRA outrages in the South in January and February than ever before and they reached a peak in March. In this month many civilians who had had no contact whatever with the security forces were dragged out of their homes and murdered in cold blood. Many were assassinated because they were Protestants, ex-soldiers of the British Army or suspected of being loyal to the crown. In the period January to April the IRA murdered seventy-three civilians in this way, generally alleging that they were spies and informers.

In the middle of February, there were signs of more trouble in Belfast. On 18 February Protestant shipyard workers were bombarded with stones as they returned from work through a Sinn Fein area. The Protestants returned the stones with interest but the police were able to re-establish control. On 11 March, IRA members from outside Belfast shot at police near the Empire Music Hall killing two constables and a civilian and wounding another. These murders caused further clashes between rival mobs. Five days later a disturbance occurred among rival factions working on an unemployment relief scheme. The Catholics, finding they were superior in numbers, attacked the Protestants using firearms and drove them from the site. This precipitated a number of minor confrontations and disturbances. On 1 April, the IRA tried to stir up trouble in Londonderry and attacked the army and police, killing an RIC sergeant but the security forces took firm measures and the situation was kept under control.

During March, there was a great deal of trouble in Co Monaghan. The IRA 'executed' a member of their own side and the houses of people who gave evidence in the courts were burned. Many Loyalists also had their houses burned and they made reprisals. All this had a very unsettling effect in the adjacent districts of the six counties. In this same month the IRA campaign in the North was intensified. There were four attacks on police patrols and two constables were killed and another wounded. There were three attempts to enforce the boycott, the worst being the burning of Richhill Railway Station and a train standing there. An attempt was also made to hold up a train at Toome. Many more roads were trenched and telephone wires cut and there were another half a dozen

cases of arson. On 21 March a concerted attack was made on
Protestant houses, mostly of members of the Special Constabulary, at Rosslea in Fermanagh near the Monaghan border.
Some fifty to sixty IRA from Co Monaghan appeared at midnight and attacked about a dozen houses simultaneously.
Special Sergeant Samuel Nixon was caught in bed at home and
was shot twice. Nevertheless he got up and returned the fire
until he grew weak from loss of blood when his wife, who had
also been wounded, suggested he surrendered. He did so and
handed over his rifle to the IRA whereupon they shot him dead.
His neighbour, Special Constable William Gordon, returned
the fire of the raiders and wounded one of them but then a
bomb was thrown through the window and killed him. A third
man who was not a Special Constable was dragged out of his
house and brutally assaulted so that he died later. Four more
houses were burned and the arms of the Special Constables
were stolen but in these attacks two IRA men were killed and
five wounded. There were undoubtedly Protestant reprisals
for these outrages by the IRA and it was often alleged that these
had been made by the Special Constabulary. It must be understood, however, that in Northern Ireland, the Protestant population were, in general, on the side of the police and took it as a
blow against their cause when a policeman was murdered, irrespective of his religion. It cannot be assumed, therefore, that
when reprisals were made for the murder of police, it was the
police who were responsible. Sinn Fein propaganda adopted the
view that these crimes were committed without provocation by
the Special Constabulary by orders from superior authority.
Such suggestions were mendacious but were widely believed in
the South and among the Catholic population of the North. It
is, of course, possible that some Special Constables when off
duty were involved but if there had been any evidence that this
was so they would have been prosecuted and if found guilty dismissed from the force. It is probable that most of the reprisals
were made by less law abiding sections of the Protestant population than those who had passed the selection committees,
been vetted by the RIC and had joined the Special Constabu-

lary. General Macready seems, however, to have believed anything adverse that he heard about the Special Constabulary while refuting every allegation against his troops in the South. That he understood the real situation is shown by the following extract from a Special Order of the Day issued by him on 25 February 1921:

'Quite apart from the savagery which has always been a marked feature of the tactics employed by the rebels, there is no doubt but that their crimes are a deliberate attempt to exasperate the troops and tempt them to break the bonds of discipline, thereby providing copy for that scurrilous campaign of propaganda on which the rebel leaders so much rely for sympathy in Great Britain and abroad.'

That some of the Protestant population fell into this trap, though regrettable, is understandable. It is interesting that the British Government's policy of 'authorized reprisals' never had to be used in the North. This policy was a compromise with the aim of preventing the army and police taking the law into their own hands. The security forces in the South were exasperated not only by the murder of their comrades and the difficulty of bringing anyone to justice for these crimes but also because they considered the Government was being weak and failing to support them. In the North the security forces, composed more of Special Constables than anything else, never got out of hand and it never had to be used. The policy was, in any case, a disastrous failure. Obviously an 'authorized reprisal' to burn a house from which the security forces had been fired upon often punished the wrong people. It did not worry the IRA very much, it was the owner of the house who suffered and he had probably been forced at pistol point to allow the IRA to use it. Sometimes the property of Sinn Fein or IRA adherents was destroyed but they retaliated by burning the house of some Protestant or Loyalist as a counter reprisal. The policy did little to defeat the IRA, it impoverished Ireland and made enemies of many people who might otherwise have supported the Government. In April operations against the IRA in the South were slowed down as four battalions of troops were withdrawn to Great Britain as a precaution against a threatened coal strike and another six battalions had to be kept concentrated ready for embarkation. Nevertheless, the army began to make cross country drives to try and round up the IRA. In these drives they used cavalry and armoured cars followed by infantry. They searched every house and interrogated everyone and this policy proved superior to the 'mobility' strategy introduced by General Tudor.

In April Belfast continued in a state of unrest. Two 'Auxiliaries' from Sligo were murdered in Donegal Place and two IRA were murdered as a reprisal. There was rioting and looting after the funerals and the police and army had to open fire wounding five people. Also in April, IRA activity was considerable in Counties Armagh and Tyrone and in the southern part of Down, probably due to the operations of flying columns. There was much cutting of telegraph wires, there were IRA raids on private houses for arms, raids on mails, and more destruction of bridges and trenching of roads in Nationalist areas. The Belfast boycott was continued mainly in the form of burning bread vans. Attacks on the security forces continued, there being some fifteen cases in all in which three were killed and sixteen wounded. On 10 April four Special Constables were ambushed on their way to church by fifteen IRA men at Creggan near Crossmaglen in Co Armagh. They were attacked with bombs and rifle fire and Special Constable John Fluke was killed and two others wounded before the IRA fled on bicycles. On 26 April a bomb was thrown at an RIC patrol in Newry and seven constables were wounded. In Co Tyrone twenty IRA men attacked the house of Albert Hopper, a B Special, and wounded him and his sister. In the same county, a servant girl in the house of a District Inspector had her hair cut off as she refused to give information about him to the IRA. The police, however, also had their successes: a number of IRA were arrested and fifteen firearms were found at Rosslea. The Fermanagh B Specials pursued some men wanted for burning a bread van to an island on Lough Erne and captured them in a small scale amphibious operation. It was due to the initiative of some Co Antrim B-men that ten IRA men were captured at Dunmurry. When the Coalisland RIC barracks was attacked, Very lights were fired as a distress signal and the local Specials helped the RIC to relieve the Station and put the IRA to flight.

In May, the picture was very similar. There was some rioting and looting in Belfast but there would have been much more trouble if it had not been for the vigilance of the army and police. As it was, a District Inspector was wounded and a harbour policeman shot dead by the IRA and they also succeeded in ambushing a Crossley tender. On 29 May 1921, there was a serious attack involving the Specials in Fermanagh. Half an hour after midnight in very stormy weather, a foot patrol on the border at Mullaghfadd was ambushed. All three men of the patrol were hit at close range by a withering fire from about forty members of the IRA. Special Constable Robert Coalter was killed instantly and Special Constables James Hall and John Montgomery were wounded. Hall dragged himself to a farmhouse but the owner, a Sinn Feiner, would not let him in and he died in the road. Montgomery managed to hide behind a hedge and the raiders left him for dead. Captain Brooke, the County Commandant, narrowly escaped as he was making his rounds in his Ford car and spent some time searching for the men on the hill where they had been ordered to keep a lookout. Within an hour the RIC from Fivemiletown and the A Specials from Enniskillen were on the scene and with other B Specials made a thorough search of houses in the area. Three men were later arrested. Although matters in the six counties were bad enough, they were far worse in Counties Cavan, Monaghan and Donegal where there was no Special Constabulary and the many loyalists living there were at the mercy of the IRA. The Unionists in the six counties became incensed by these outrages and tension increased accordingly.

In May too the IRA took the offensive in Dublin burning the Customs House and at the same time they began a series of minor attacks in England. At the end of the month, General

Macready sent in a pessimistic report in which he said that the troops in Ireland could only be expected to go on until October and thereafter the whole army would need to be relieved. No new troops were available for relief on such a scale and the alternatives open to the Government were either to negotiate a truce or to make a supreme effort to defeat the IRA before October. The Government at first decided to adopt the latter policy and nineteen new battalions were despatched to Ireland during June and early July bringing up the total strength in the country to 80,000 men. This left only four battalions of regular troops in Great Britain, the whole imperial reserve now being committed. It was decided that if by mid-July, there was still no sign that order had been restored then martial law would be extended to the whole country. On 3 May 1921, the Government of Ireland Act, which had become law in the previous December, came into effect. In accordance with its provisions, the Viceroy issued proclamations summoning the two Parliaments of Northern and Southern Ireland. The elections were held during the same month and in the South they were a complete farce, not one of the 128 seats being contested: 124 Sinn Fein candidates, mostly members of the IRA, were returned unopposed, no one daring to stand against them. The remaining four seats, also unopposed, represented Trinity College Dublin. In the North the Unionists obtained an overwhelming victory at the polls, winning forty seats to six Nationalist and six Sinn Fein. The election went off quietly and the Special Constabulary were used to help the RIC guard polling stations. On 7 June, Lord Fitzalan, the new Viceroy, swore in Sir James Craig as Prime Minister of Northern Ireland with the rest of his cabinet and it was announced that the King in person would open Parliament later in the month. The Nationalist and Sinn Fein members boycotted the Northern Ireland Parliament as they did the Southern. Consequently the Southern Parliament, in accordance with the act, lapsed. The position of the Northern Parliament was now a curious one. They took over the internal administration of the six counties but were not as yet responsible for law and order. The military stationed in the Province still came under General Macready in Dublin and the police remained subject to General Tudor. On 11 June, troubled flared up again in Belfast, and although the police restored order after four hours, twenty people were injured. Next day after three people had been dragged out of bed and shot, the rioting was renewed and four people including Special Constable Thomas Sturdy were killed. Rioting continued spasmodically for several days and the Sturdy funeral was attacked as it passed a Sinn Fein area. On 13 June, shipyard workers were shot at by the IRA on their way to work. The gunmen entrenched themselves in a Catholic area and a regular assault was required by the army to dislodge them. It was clear that the aim of the IRA was to make the visit of the King impossible and to get the opening of Parliament postponed. A concentration of the army and the police, which included the Belfast Special Constabulary, restored order and frustrated the Sinn Fein designs. The Special Constabulary in the country districts co-operated by taking over local police duties, so releasing regular RIC men for Belfast. On 22 June 1921 King George V arrived in Belfast and opened the Northern Parliament. He received a tumultuous welcome and no trouble of any kind marred the visit. As his cavalry escort of the 10th Royal Hussars returned south, however, their train was blown up near Bessbrook. The train rolled down an embankment and the guard and four troopers were killed and twenty men wounded. In addition eighty horses had to be destroyed.

In June the IRA intensified their operations throughout the whole of Ireland but this was a last desperate effort. During the first half of the year, they had had many casualties and large numbers of them had been interned. Furthermore, except for a few of the new Thompson sub-machine guns, they had been unable to obtain consignments of arms from abroad. Their total casualties since the beginning of the campaign amounted to 752 killed and 866 wounded and there were now over 4,000 men interned in the three camps at Ballykinlar, The Curragh and Bere Island. By the end of June, even the

IRA fanatics were near breaking point. In June and early July, IRA outrages continued in the North especially in Co Tyrone and in the south of Co Down and in Co Londonderry IRA activity was actually increasing. After dark on 5 June, an RIC police patrol at Swatragh, which was in a Nationalist area, was ambushed. Twenty IRA men concealed themselves at the side of the road and arranged for a cottage to shine a light from a window. When the RIC patrol of a sergeant and two constables passed the light, the IRA opened fire at point blank range, killing one constable and wounding the other two. One constable returned the fire and the other crawled to the police station. The IRA then took to their heels and dispersed. The firing was heard two and a half miles away in Upperlands which was the District Headquarters of the B Specials who were at once mobilized by blowing the local factory hooter. They arrived in time to get the two wounded men to hospital and were closely followed by the A platoon from Magherafelt and the RIC from Garvagh. All were, however, too late to catch the raiders. Next day a very large sweep of the area was made and over two hundred Nationalist houses were searched. Little was found but one man who tried to escape out of the back door of a cottage was arrested. The situation in the southern part of County Down was bad where the waterworks at Annalong were damaged. A bread van was burnt and a postman was robbed in Newry and there were a number of other incidents. On 8 June, a patrol of B Specials were ambushed near Newry and one of them was wounded. Reinforcements were sent for and a sweep of the area was made. While searching a house at Corrogs near Newry, Special Constable George Lyness, who had been left outside as a sentry, was shot dead. The rest of the patrol returned the fire and two IRA were killed.[2] Throughout the Province IRA activity seemed to be concentrated on the B Specials. In Co Tyrone B patrols were twice ambushed and two Special Constables off duty were attacked in their homes. On 19 June about forty IRA attacked the house of a Mr Douglas George at Grangemore near Armagh. The owner and his two brothers were all members of the

Special Constabulary and they successfully beat off the attack but their house and a haystack caught fire and were destroyed. Finally, Special Constable Hugh Gabbie was murdered on 30 June in Co Down. The Antrim B Specials had another success on the day of the King's visit to Belfast when they surprised another band of IRA at Dunmurry and captured three of them. At Finnard in Co Down, a patrol was ambushed but succeeded in killing two of its assailants. On the southern border of Tyrone recruiting for the B Specials had not been good and they were seriously under strength. On 22 June 1921, the residence of a Major Stewart near Clogher was surrounded by a large force of the IRA. They ordered everyone out of the house and after looting it, set it on fire. Major Stewart was 'court martialled', but in the end the IRA released him. The house of a Mr A. Todd at Augher was also attacked, but he was a B Special and he opened fire and drove off the raiders. At this point a B Special patrol was approaching and the IRA ambushed it: the rebel marksmanship was bad however and they failed to hit the patrol but the IRA succeeded in escaping over the border.

On 8 July 1921, the order that raids and searches were not to be made by B Specials unless an RIC or A Special Constable was present was reaffirmed. This time the order was that B Specials should not enter houses at all but should remain on guard outside. By the middle of the year, however, RIC police reports cease to emphasize their anxieties and reservations about the Special Constabulary. In April it was reported from Co Down that 'Valuable assistance has been rendered to the RIC by the members of the B Specials in the disturbed areas', and from Belfast 'The Special Constabulary are of very valuable assistance to the regular RIC and their duty is performed with the greatest harmony'. In May it was reported from Co Antrim that the 'B class have started working in several other areas and are of great assistance to the police and are working harmoniously with them', and from Co Down again, 'the organizing of the B force which now numbers 1,700 has had a marked effect on curbing the work of the

IRA. B Specials, A mobile platoons and RIC work well together and co-operate'. In June, the County Inspector of the RIC for Co Londonderry wrote: 'A large number of B Specials have been enrolled and they are now regularly patrolling in all parts of the county at night. I am glad to say that there has been no case of serious indiscipline up to the present and the relations between them and the regular RIC are most harmonious. In some cases the old RIC were inclined to rather throw cold water on the movement, but now they all realize how invaluable a large organized armed force will be in the event of the IRA trying to carry out a campaign of ambushes, etc., in force in this county. The District and Sub-District Commandants have shown a great interest and keenness in organizing their areas and getting things into proper working order'. Behind these somewhat formal commendations lies a story of considerable self sacrifice and courage. The A Specials on whom a great deal of the work devolved were full time paid servants of the Crown who were properly uniformed and armed and equivalent in every way to the regular police and soldiers. The B Specials on the other hand received only a clothing allowance and so were virtually unpaid. They had to do their ordinary jobs as well and missed their night's sleep when on duty. Their main role was guarding, watching and patrolling and they spent a night a week out in all weathers. When on patrol they were always in danger of sudden ambush and could never relax. Even when off duty they were liable to attack in their homes, and unless they had firearms of their own, were without protection. Government arms were scarce and they often had to walk long distances to draw them from the nearest RIC barracks and to return them afterwards. They were often called upon to do extra duties such as acting as guides for the A platoons, who did not yet know the country very well, or helping to guard police stations when numbers were short. Now and again when a large operation against the IRA was necessary they would be called out by day as well. In addition to all this they had their drill nights and sometimes they had to waste a lot of time as witnesses at courts martial.

For such a hastily raised force their discipline was very good. Obviously, their work made them unpopular with the Roman Catholic population, no one likes his house being searched and no one likes being held up in a road block. It was inevitable that most of the searches and inconvenience should fall on the Roman Catholics for it was amongst them that the IRA drew its recruits and its support. There is little doubt that the moderate Catholics suffered far more from IRA intimidation than the surveillance of the Specials. Indeed the Specials gave the Catholic population considerable protection. Yet Sinn Fein propaganda was able to reverse this impression and stir up hatred against them. The temptation to take the law into their own hands when fighting such a brutal, callous and cowardly enemy as the IRA must have been enormous, especially when 'official' reprisals were allowed in the southern part of the country. Yet the number of cases where this was ever alleged in the RIC records, and the RIC was none too friendly, were very small. The Special Constabulary had, in general, behaved with great restraint and the forebodings of Dublin Castle that they would result in civil war were seen to be nonsense. The feelings against them in the Nationalist population were the results of propaganda and not their behaviour. They were more responsible for saving Northern Ireland from anarchy than either the army or the RIC.

Throughout the first half of 1921, there had been talk of trying to stop the bloodshed in Ireland and there had been underground comings and goings by various personages. Dublin Castle were told not to arrest de Valera who had returned from America at the beginning of the year. The steps leading to a truce are very fully described in many other books and it is only necessary here to say that a truce was finally negotiated by General Macready on 9 July and came into effect at noon on 11 July. In this truce the IRA undertook to cease all attacks on the Crown forces and civilians, to cease military manoeuvres of all kinds, to prohibit the use of arms, to abstain from interference with public or private property and to do nothing which might disturb the peace. The security forces undertook to stop all raids and searches by the army and police, to restrict the army to the support of the police in their normal civil duties, to suspend the arrival of reinforcements and to turn over law and order in Dublin to the Metropolitan Police. In addition the curfew was to be suspended. General Macready did not intend the truce to apply to the North of Ireland. Sinn Fein, however, claimed that it did and in order not to prejudice the treaty talks in London, Dublin Castle accepted this interpretation. Although Sir James Craig had been involved in some of the early 'comings and goings' and had, in fact, met de Valera in Dublin in May, the Northern Government was not consulted over the actual terms of the truce. There was some surprise, therefore, when instructions came from Dublin Castle to cease the operations of the Special Constabulary altogether.

The truce was hailed as a victory by Sinn Fein and in the south the IRA came out of hiding, in many cases wearing uniform and carrying their arms openly and they were treated as heroes. In fact the truce came about because both the British and Sinn Fein wanted it. The British were tired of Ireland and its expense and problems and although they believed they could eventually defeat the IRA they were doubtful if public opinion would tolerate the repressive measures which would be necessary. Furthermore, they were not prepared to face up to the problem of keeping order in Ireland indefinitely. On the other side there is no doubt that the IRA were near the end of their tether and the collapse of their campaign was not far off. The new policy of drives by troops had the effect of taking the initiative from the IRA flying columns who spent their time retreating and suffering heavy casualties every time the security forces caught up with them. IRA Headquarters in Dublin was so harassed that they had difficulty in functioning at all. The knowledge of the huge reinforcements of troops that had arrived and that martial law was imminent in the whole country lowered the morale of the IRA leaders. The truce was received with relief in England but with deep suspicion and even disgust in Northern Ireland where it was seen as a sell-out to the rebels. The security forces throughout the country were dumbfounded that it should come just as they were really succeeding against the IRA. The Royal Irish Constabulary in the South never really recovered from the shock and rapidly degenerated into a force awaiting disbandment and more interested in pensions and avoiding trouble than anything else. It was inevitable that this attitude would spread to some members of the RIC in the North.

With the truce, the 'troubles' outside Belfast died down quickly. Throughout the Province the anniversary of the Battle of the Boyne on 12 July was celebrated without disturbances except a minor one in Cookstown when an Orange sash was stolen by some Sinn Feiners. The lifting of the curfew and of restrictions on motor traffic were received by the whole population with relief. Just before the truce there had been serious trouble again in Belfast. On 6 July two police were shot in Union Street and on 9 July a Crossley tender was ambushed in the Falls Road and one constable was killed and two wounded. A large search of the area was made by the RIC and the Specials followed by serious rioting and sniping by the IRA. The army and Specials with armoured cars were in action the whole afternoon. Then Protestant mobs joined in and attacked the Catholic areas burning 161 houses. There were twenty-two killed and seventy-eight wounded on this day alone. With the truce, there was a temporary lull but on 14 July sniping started again and the Protestants, who were almost certainly the aggressors, threw a bomb. Spasmodic rioting continued until 17 July, a number of Catholic-owned public houses being burnt and many arrests made by the police. The troubles then subsided partly because of the appointment of Eoin O'Duffy as IRA liaison officer for the truce, who announced all IRA sniping would cease except in self defence. The calm lasted, except for minor incidents, until 21 August when a bomb was thrown and sniping began all over again, eight people being killed and forty wounded by the end of the month. There was then a pause until 15 September when rioting spread all over the city. On 25 September a bomb killed two Protestants and wounded twenty-seven and they retaliated wounding six Catholics. The IRA in Dublin now announced that, in spite of the truce, they intended to take measures in Belfast to defend Catholics. Throughout the city sectarian bitterness was intense and it was exacerbated by the uncertainty caused by the pre-Treaty talks in London.

During August there were indications of the IRA drilling secretly all over the Province and in September that they had a camp at Torr Head. On 21 September a Special Constable's house was attacked in Cookstown and in October and November there were a number of cases of stealing of arms from B-men and of the burning of their hayricks or outhouses. There were a number of cases of intimidation of Catholics by the IRA and of women having their hair cut off but by and large, outside Belfast, the truce was kept. On 4 September, Michael Collins who had been elected to the Northern Parliament, addressed a political meeting in Armagh and Eoin O'Duffy, the Sinn Fein liaison officer, also spoke and threatened 'to use the lead' against the six counties. As two cars were leaving the meeting, a Unionist crowd hissed and groaned at them, and the occupants of the cars opened fire. The fire was promptly returned from the crowd and one of the Sinn Feiners was wounded. It was fortunate that this affray did not develop into a full scale riot. After his bellicose speech Eoin O'Duffy was relieved of his liaison duties and transferred to Cork by the provisional Government in Dublin. In September, it became essential to use the Special Constabulary again in Belfast but Dublin Castle were very much opposed to this as they were sure it would be taken as a breach of the truce by Sinn Fein and upset the delicate negotiations being made in London. General Macready then agreed that the Specials could be reemployed provided they were under the strict control of the RIC.[3] It was also decided that Colonel Carter-Campbell, commanding the troops in Belfast, should control the police in the city as well as the troops.

In October, Field Marshal Sir Henry Wilson, the Chief of the Imperial General Staff, visited Ulster and conferred with

Sir James Craig. At the time there were some 1,600 A Specials and 16,000 B Specials but there were only arms for about a fifth of the latter. A request for 12,000 rifles and three million rounds of ammunition had been held up by Lloyd George in case it was taken by Sinn Fein as a breach of the treaty and so prejudice the negotiations. Sir Henry Wilson undertook to try and expedite the consignment of arms but he was unsuccessful at this stage. He also expressed the opinion that it should in future be the army's duty to hold the border and for the police to suppress the Belfast riots. This was, of course, the proper division of responsibilities but his advice was not found to be practicable at this stage, mainly because of the weakness of the RIC in Belfast and the reluctance of Colonel Wickham to make a greater use of the Specials. Obviously the division of functions between the Northern Ireland Government and Dublin Castle was undermining the security of Ulster. It was therefore decided to bring into force that part of the Government of Ireland Act which gave the Northern Government responsibility for law and order. The transfer was made on 22 November and the RIC stationed in the six counties was placed at the disposal of the Northern Government for the maintenance of order and suppression of crime. Its administration, however, remained with the Inspector General in Dublin. Opportunity was given to the whole RIC to decide whether they wished to serve in the North or not. A gradual transfer of personnel then took place so that the RIC in the six counties was composed of men who either lived there or wished to continue to serve there permanently. The Special Constabulary which had in fact been controlled from Belfast since its inception, ceased even in theory to owe allegiance to General Tudor in Dublin.

NOTES

1. All official documents and correspondence at this time refer to 'The Special Constabulary' but unofficially the force

was often known as the Royal Irish Special Constabulary.

2. This is the incident quoted in the 'The Easter Lily' by Sean O'Callaghan, in which a sworn affidavit is reproduced which tries to discredit the Specials by alleging that the two IRA members were innocent men murdered by the patrol without cause.

3. This is an example of General Macready's animosity towards the Specials. In Belfast the B Specials had always been under the orders of the RIC and, in fact, had never been used in Nationalist areas at all. The A Specials attached to RIC stations were used in Nationalist areas but they were virtually part of the RIC.

CHAPTER THREE

The 'Troubles' – 1922

On 22 November 1921, when the Northern Ireland Government took over responsibility for law and order the situation in Ulster was serious. In the period 19–25 November, twenty-seven lives were lost and ninety-two people were injured in Belfast alone. There was an orgy of shooting, bombs were thrown at St Matthew's Roman Catholic Chapel in the Newtownards Road, into the Protestant crowd watching and at trams full of Protestant shipyard workers. All this began after sniping in the Ballymacarret area by both sides and it was impossible to say who started it. The troubles died down in the first half of December but started again on 17 December and there were three people killed and twenty-three injured during the next week. These riots were caused to a large extent by the uncertainties about the future which stemmed from the Treaty talks in London but there is little doubt that they were also intentionally fomented by Sinn Fein and the IRA. During the year 1921, no less than 109 people had been killed in the rioting in Belfast.

Early in November, it became clear that the pre-war Ulster Volunteer Force was being recruited all over the Province.[1] Lieutenant-Colonel F. H. Crawford, who had arranged the gun running into Larne seven years before, had assumed command with headquarters in Belfast. The recruiting was being done secretly and was confined to enrolling men and organizing them into units and there were few arms available. The intention was that should there be a general rising of the republicans or an invasion from the South they would offer themselves as a legal force of the Crown. They intended in any case to come into action if the British Government tried to 'sell' Ulster in the negotiations with Sinn Fein. It was realized that the authorities in Dublin Castle would be actively hostile to the scheme but it was hoped that when the Northern Ireland Government took over responsibility for law and order then they would recognize them. The Ulster Volunteer Force was in fact an embarrassment to the Northern Ireland Government and it was feared that it would prove to be a rival for recruiting for the Special Constabulary which was still below strength. Colonel Crawford, however, wished to recruit men from outside the Class B Specials. The Northern Ireland Government believed that the answer was to try and enrol the best of the Ulster Volunteer Force in a new class of C Special Constables to keep them under discipline and Government Control. On 9 November the Divisional Police Commissioner in Belfast sent out a letter to the County Inspectors of the RIC and the County Commandants of the Special Constabulary giving these facts and telling them that such a force was under consideration on a territorial basis to be formed into regular military units of battalion strength. The proposal was that the force would be available for use in grave emergency anywhere in the Province and action was to be confined to estimating the number of battalion areas which it would be possible to form and earmarking battalion commanders.

Unfortunately a copy of the Divisional Commissioner's letter fell into the hands of Sinn Fein, almost certainly through a Republican in the RIC in Ulster, and was published verbatim in their press. The Dublin Castle authorities were alarmed as this action could be construed as a breach of the truce. Colonel Wickham at once explained to General Tudor that the Northern Government was seriously alarmed at the rapid growth of unauthorized Loyalist defence forces which were already known to number 21,000 and had plans to expand to 150,000. They believed that the best action was to try and bring these

men under the Government by enrolling them in the Class C
Special Constabulary. The scheme was to prevent any unauthorized action and above all any reprisals and not, as
claimed by Sinn Fein propaganda, to prepare a force to oppress the Roman Catholic minority. General Tudor had to
admit that when there were rumours of the UVF in February
he had agreed with Sir James Craig that it was better to try
and incorporate these men in the C force rather than to allow
further expansion of an unauthorized formation. He said he
assumed that Sir James Craig would get clearance in London
before going any further.

The 'Wickham circular' as the document came to be called
was used by Michael Collins to embarrass the British Government at the Treaty negotiations in 10 Downing Street on 23
November. Mr Lloyd George told him that Colonel Wickham
had not had authority to issue the document from the British
Government or General Tudor. General Macready had been
summoned to London as he was thought to be responsible. Sir
James Craig also visited London and explained that the circular was a precaution in case the truce broke down. The circular
was, however, withdrawn and he telegraphed back to Belfast
that recruits could be taken as police but not into a military
unit. On his return on 5 December Sir James Craig issued
more detailed instructions about the Special Constabulary.
The enrolment of an additional 700 A Specials was to be begun at once and the B Specials were to be brought up to
strength, which meant the recruitment of a further 5,000 men.
Until this had been done no more C Specials were to be enrolled. General instructions for a force of C Specials much on
the lines of the 'Wickham circular' were also given. This force,
later to be called the C 1 Special Constabulary, was to be
unpaid until called up for service. They were to be armed as
soon as arms were available and were to be trained in their use.
In emergency strength would be unlimited but for the present
was to be kept to about 6,000 men, two thirds of whom were to
be recruited in Belfast and the rest in Lisburn and Londonderry. A number of additional Adjutants and Head Constables

were appointed to the staffs of County Commandants to organize the force and care was taken not to allow these instructions to fall into the hands of Sinn Fein.

The Provisional Government in Dublin was, of course, furious at the suggestion of raising such a force. After the Government of Ireland Act had come into effect in the North, their only hope of a united Ireland was that the British Government would 'sell' Ulster in the Treaty negotiations and would then withdraw the British army. If they could cut down the Special Constabulary and prevent the formation of the new force, they would probably be able to seize the province. Under the Government of Ireland Act, the external defence of Northern Ireland was certainly a Westminster responsibility and the Northern Parliament had no power to raise an army. The device of calling them Special Constabulary was therefore used and the Westminster Government connived at this practice. Clearly, it was a sound move to raise this force which gave confidence to the majority in the province, put a large number of men under military discipline and control and forestalled moves to raise illegal armies such as the Ulster Volunteer Force.

During December 1921 there were two incidents which disturbed the truce. The last casualty to the Special Constabulary during the year occurred on 3 December when an attempt was made to rescue some Sinn Fein prisoners from Londonderry gaol. Special Constable William Lyttle was on duty inside the gaol and he was found dead after being struck on the head and subsequently poisoned. The escape was frustrated by a patrol of Special Constables outside the prison who saw a rope thrown over the wall and fired at one of the prisoners. The second incident was on 19 December 1921 when the young District Inspector at Limavady in Co Londonderry heard that the IRA had captured fifteen Roman Catholics of the village of Feeny whom they considered were insufficiently zealous Republicans. They marched them sixteen miles over the Sperrin mountains to 'court-martial' and make an example of them. District Inspector R. P. Pim,[2] at once obtained the Divisional

Commissioner's permission to take any steps necessary to rescue the men. The problem was complicated as most of the
mountain roads had been trenched or obstructed in some way
and pursuit in vehicles was difficult. Telephone conversations,
even if the lines were intact, were liable to be intercepted by
IRA informers in the GPO, so he motored to Londonderry
and arranged for a strong force of the RIC to be ready to leave
next morning at dawn. From Derry he went on to Omagh to
co-ordinate operations with Colonel McClintock, the Co Tyrone Commandant of the Specials. The Colonel arranged for
three platoons of A Specials to advance from Draperstown and
from Park in a movement which would completely surround
the IRA camp which was believed to be somewhere near the
Cranagh Hall in the Sperrin Mountains. The drive took place
in bitterly cold weather with snow on the ground. Pim's
Londonderry contingent was held up by trenched roads and
was behind schedule and it was Colonel McClintock's Specials
who surprised the IRA which fled, prisoners and all. The pursuit was continued until the IRA made a stand and opened
fire. A sharp action followed, the fire being returned in spite of
the truce. Some of the rebels evaded the trap and got away but
casualties were inflicted on them, five were taken prisoner and
the Feeny men were rescued. In a house near the Cranagh
Chapel a miniature arsenal and bomb-making plant was captured.

On 6 December, a Treaty was signed between the British
Government and the delegates of Southern Ireland. It was
immediately clear that a great many southern Irishmen were
not going to accept the solution. There were two stumbling
blocks, the first was the acceptance of an Irish Free State
within the British Commonwealth instead of a Republic and
the second was partition. Nevertheless, the Dail ratified the
Treaty on 8 January 1922, by sixty-four to fifty-seven votes.
Shortly after the signing of the Treaty, Winston Churchill, the
Secretary of State for the Colonies, took over responsibility for
Ireland from Sir Hamar Greenwood, the Chief Secretary. On
16 January the Government of Southern Ireland was formally

handed over to the Sinn Fein Provisional Government. On 18 February the 'Black and Tans' and the Auxiliary Division of the RIC were disbanded and returned to Great Britain. At the same time the evacuation of the British Army in the South began. This was at first expected to be completed by Easter and the first stage of concentrating the troops in three centres in Dublin, Cork and at the Curragh was begun at once. The Northern Government was at last free of the querulous and uncertain rule of Dublin Castle but the troops in the North, now commanded by Major General A. R. Cameron, CB, CMG, were still subject to General Macready. By far the most sinister effect of the Treaty for Northern Ireland, however, was that beginning on 9 December all the IRA men in the internment camps were released. These men lost no time in resuming the struggle and many made straight for the North or the border.

The new year began with another outburst of rioting in Belfast with the usual sniping and throwing of bombs and on 19 January, Field Marshal Sir Henry Wilson and General Macready visited Belfast to discuss the use of troops to control riots. After the ratification of the Treaty, IRA operations in the North began again and became more methodical. The Northern Government were still trying to observe the truce but it was broken in minor ways by the IRA especially in Co Tyrone. This went unchecked for some time because the Specials were still not allowed to patrol with arms. On 13 January the situation was made much worse when the British Government announced an amnesty for political crimes and released another thousand prisoners who were not just internees but men who had actually been convicted including ninety-six from Belfast and thirty-seven from Derry gaols. All these men were now available for an attack in the North.

Early in January, Colonel McClintock, the Tyrone County Commandant received information that a large IRA training camp had been established two miles from Dromore on the road to Irvinestown. On 6 January he advanced with a large force of armed A Specials, including the platoons from Dro-

more, Omagh and Dungannon. The IRA, who were well
equipped with cars, lorries and motor-cycles, got wind of his
approach and dispersed when he was still a mile away. Nevertheless he succeeded in arresting eleven men and made a large
haul of arms. On 14 January, the A Specials in Co Tyrone
were again active and No 6 Platoon succeeded in capturing a
number of cars with between thirty and forty IRA in them
including the Commander of the 6th Northern Division of the
IRA. Search of the cars revealed that some of the men were
armed and ten of them were arrested. They claimed that this
was a breach of the truce and that they were a Gaelic football
team on their way to Derry to play a match and were armed
for self defence as they had to pass through Protestant areas.
There is no doubt, however, that they were going to Derry not
to play football but to attempt to rescue a prisoner from the
gaol who was under sentence of death for murder which he had
committed during the previous attempted gaol break in December. On 26 January the IRA left no doubt that they had
broken the truce in the North. Twenty of them attacked three
RIC policemen on patrol near Cookstown and captured them.

By January, the rifles to arm the 'B' Specials fully had still
not arrived but with the ratification of the Treaty in the South,
the first consignment was sent to Carrickfergus. By now, with
the need to arm the Class C Special Constabulary too, the
requirement had risen to 26,000 rifles and five million rounds
of ammunition. The distribution of the arms to the whole B
force was made in February 1922 by convoys of furniture vans
escorted by armoured cars of the A Specials. Each man was
issued with a rifle and bayonet, webbing equipment and a hundred rounds of ammunition. At the same time, uniform was
issued to the whole B force. This consisted of 1914/18 type
army tunics, trousers and puttees dyed dark green and with the
appropriate badges and buttons. There were only three sizes,
No 1 Large, No 2 Medium and No 3 Small which accounts
for the somewhat poor sartorial effect of B Specials in many of
the early photographs. In country districts the Special Constables were now allowed to keep their arms in their houses,

giving them protection against attack when at home and also on their way to and from patrol duty.[3]

On 3 February the Sinn Fein Provisional Government, only two weeks after a meeting in London between Sir James Craig and Michael Collins to try and stop the riots in Belfast, issued verbal threats against the Northern Ireland Government. At the same time there were indications that the IRA in the North were making efforts to rearm themselves. In the Dungannon area, twenty-five men of the IRA made extensive raids on Protestant houses for arms. After some success they were repulsed by the owner of a house and his wife with both barrels of a shot gun. Extensive searches of Sinn Fein houses in the area by the Special Constabulary yielded a number of illegal arms and some arrests were made. On the way back from the court martial in Londonderry in which the offenders were tried, three Special Constables were ambushed and seriously wounded, two of them being permanently disabled. On 6 February two Crossley tenders carrying A Specials were ambushed near Newtownbutler and captured with their arms and ammunition.

On 8 February the storm broke and the IRA raided the Ulster border in force, mainly in the Clogher valley in Tyrone and at Enniskillen in Fermanagh. There was widespread cutting of telephone wires and early in the morning a number of cars containing unarmed IRA crossed the border from Co Monaghan into Co Tyrone. Many of these cars were stopped and searched by B Special patrols but nothing suspicious was found. In this way the positions of all the road blocks and patrols on that particular morning were established. A large force of IRA then crossed the border in cars, evaded the patrols and kidnapped some forty Unionists including a former County Grand Master of the Orange Order who was over seventy years of age. They were then driven to Ballybay and subsequently to other places in the Free State. The kidnapping of Loyalists was not so successful in Co Fermanagh. Three cars full of IRA entered Enniskillen at one in the morning but were repulsed by the first two intended victims with their private weapons. The A Specials were at once called out and pursued the raiders towards the border. The B Specials set up road blocks and the RIC captured two cars full of IRA. In all, four cars, fifteen prisoners and a quantity of arms and ammunition were captured and the IRA only succeeded in making a few kidnappings in this area.

This raid led to a considerable strengthening of the Specials on the border. In Tyrone five A mobile platoons were moved up to join the existing platoon at Aughnacloy and were stationed between Clogher and Caledon. The strength of the B Specials in this area was also increased. Similar reinforcement took place in other border counties. All the roads crossing into the Free State were then made impassable by blowing up bridges or digging trenches and were covered by constabulary posts. Only the main roads were left open and on these there were permanent road blocks. These activities in the Clogher valley were opposed by rifle fire from the IRA from the high ground on the Monaghan side of the border. The slightest movement outside the posts drew fire and reliefs had to be brought up in Lancia armoured lorries. As late as 28 March 'most consistent, unceasing rifle fire' was still coming from the other side of the border, and the truce still being in force, not a shot had been returned by the Specials. Nevertheless they held their posts and this demonstrated their discipline and courage. The firing from across the border made farming in the fertile Clogher valley very difficult. Cattle were killed and farmers, both Protestant and Catholic, had to abandon their farms. Starving poultry were fed under fire by Special Constables! Indiscriminate fire from Lifford into Strabane was also common and the bridges across the Foyle had to be guarded by the Special Constabulary. Firing also broke out from Clady south of Strabane and on 10 February an armoured lorry with A Specials was sent to investigate. The patrol left their vehicle and advanced on the village on foot and were heavily fired upon, Special Constable Charles McFadden being killed and two others wounded. The IRA having inflicted these casualties, hastily retired.

On 11 February, a reinforcement of eighteen A Specials left Newtownards by train bound for Enniskillen. They were in uniform but only six of them were armed with pistols which was in accordance with the police regulations in force under the truce. The most direct route was through Co Monaghan changing at Clones and connecting with the train from Dublin to Enniskillen. The British Army had left the Clones area to concentrate in Dublin and the Curragh a day or two earlier. In the circumstances it was foolhardy not to have sent these men by a longer route which kept within the borders of Northern Ireland. At Clones the IRA, who had learned that the Specials were on the train, prepared an ambush. It is probable that their original intention was to make the Specials prisoner. Some of the Specials were in the station buffet, some were on the platform and others had stayed in their carriage. An IRA officer in uniform armed with a sub-machine gun approached and ordered the Specials on the platform to put their hands up and surrender. When the men in the carriage did not immediately comply he fired into the compartment, killing and wounding the occupants. A Special Constable farther down the train then drew his revolver and shot the IRA Commandant dead. Thereupon machine guns and rifles mounted on the footbridge over the railway and in the waiting-room doorway opened fire. Special Sergeant William Dougherty and Special Constables Joseph Abraham, James Lewis and Robert McMahon were killed, eight others were seriously wounded and four taken prisoner. Those who were in the buffet escaped through the kitchen and got back across the border on foot. Several civilian passengers were also wounded by the heavy indiscriminate firing. Subsequently at an inquest in Clones, evidence was given that the Specials were nearly all armed with rifles and that they were the first to open fire. It was also asserted that the IRA had the right under the truce to interrogate the Specials. In fact the RIC were still the official police force in the South and the IRA were bound by the truce to abstain from all attacks on the Crown forces. If they wished to complain about the movement of the Specials through Clones, which they certainly had a right to do, there was ample machinery set up under the truce for this purpose. There is no doubt that the incident, stemming from a mistake in routing, was seized upon by the IRA to try and capture the Specials and this led to a massacre. The survivors, in spite of strong representations from London to the Provisional Government in Dublin, were held prisoner, some in appalling conditions, for several months. On arrival of the train at Lisbellaw, with its wrecked and bloodstained compartments, there was a minor riot.

Trouble in Belfast began again after the Clones Massacre and went on for a number of days. From 12–16 February there was a serious outbreak of shooting with the usual riots and bomb throwing, thirty-one people being killed. However, the kidnapped loyalists began to be released from the South and all were home – thanks to pressure exerted by the British Government – by 16 February. In the rest of the Province, the Specials arrested three IRA officers near Kilkeel and continued to hold the border. On 19 February, Special Constable James McInnes was killed near Kinawley in Fermanagh in an accidental clash between two patrols. Next day Sir James Craig began a tour of the border to visit and encourage the Specials. He started in the Newry area and worked along the whole border ending at Londonderry on 23 February. He visited many units and men on duty, inspected parades and addressed them. On 21 February, the British Government released the 'Monaghan footballers', the ten IRA taken prisoner in January, in spite of the opposition of the Northern Ireland Government. In a telegram of protest about this kind of interference with the course of justice and with the constant allegations against the Specials by the Southern Provisional Government they ended:

'They strongly resent the making of vague charges against the Constabulary, unsupported by any evidence. The Constabulary have behaved admirably under the greatest provocation, but if any individual instance of misconduct is brought to the notice of this Government by responsible persons, accompanied by definite evidence, they will be prepared to make investigations and to take such disciplinary measures as may be proved to be necessary.'

Another consequence of the Clones Massacre was that the Northern Government demanded more troops. At this time, the garrison of Northern Ireland consisted of eleven battalions organized in three brigades, one of five battalions in the Belfast area and the others of three battalions each in South Down and in the west of the Province. It was decided, however, after much discussion and in consultation with General Macready that the Specials should guard the border and that troops should be located at strategic points ready to reinforce them if necessary.

For the last week of February and the very early days of March, Belfast continued to simmer. On 5 March, there was an appalling outbreak of violence and lawlessness. Shooting and bombing occurred nearly every day and troops had to use machine guns against the IRA gunmen in the Falls area. Two RIC constables were murdered and four Specials were wounded. Order was not restored by the police until 14 March, by which time Special Constable Charles Vokes had been killed by mistake when on leave in the city.

By March 1922, it became necessary to be more careful about the exact position of the border. The Old Fort at Belleek in Co Fermanagh which overlooked the town, was actually in Free State Territory and had to be evacuated by its garrison of Special Constables. The RIC barracks at Pettigo, where the border runs through the middle of the village, also had to be evacuated as it was in Free State Territory. The Fermanagh Specials at once sent a detachment to bring away some of their members stationed there. The RIC, however, refused to leave so the Specials disarmed them and brought back all the arms, ammunition and government stores so that they would not fall into the hands of the IRA.

Early in March, Sir James Craig asked Field Marshal Sir Henry Wilson to come over to Ulster and advise him on the military situation. The Field Marshal, who was an Ulsterman, had been relieved as Chief of the Imperial General Staff in February and had been returned unopposed as Member of Parliament for North Down at Westminster. He arrived in the middle of March and rendered his report on 20 March. In a published letter, Sir Henry Wilson said that he expected that the trouble in the South over the Treaty would get worse and that it was essential for Ulster to get Great Britain on her side. He said that he was very impressed with the magnificent way in which citizens had enrolled in the Special Constabulary but he had some suggestions for the reorganization of the police. He also recommended that the law be amended to give greatly increased powers against the illegal carrying, importing and use of arms and explosives. In an unpublished memorandum he pointed out that in Belfast the troops were not being used 'in aid of the civil power' but 'instead of the civil power' and that a larger and better police force must be found to take over this responsibility. He recommended that the RIC in Ulster should be disbanded as soon as possible and be replaced by a new single Constabulary which would embody the Specials. It was to be in three divisions, the A or regular Division,[4] was to replace the RIC and should be 3,000 strong, that is roughly half as big again as the RIC had been in the six counties. He recommended that this force should have a stiffening of regular army officers. The B Division would be part time volunteers very like the B Specials and the C Division would be composed of older men for use in emergencies. He also recommended that this new constabulary should be commanded by a General Officer with a staff who should also act as the Military Adviser to the Northern Ireland Government. At the same time he wanted to see a strong criminal investigation and intelligence department established. General Macready came up to Belfast and agreed with these recommendations. He also arranged for the garrison of Northern Ireland to be increased by two more battalions.

Much of what Sir Henry Wilson recommended was already under consideration. The Special Powers Act to strengthen the law and replace the Restoration of Order in Ireland Act had been introduced in the Northern Parliament on 15 March, and a committee to advise on the police force to replace the RIC had, in fact, been sitting since 1 February. This committee reported on 31 March. It recommended that a new Ulster Constabulary should be formed and should not be more than 3,000 strong and that application should be made for the prefix 'Royal'. It was to be a single force for the Province and not to be raised on a county basis as in Great Britain. In general its pay and conditions were to be similar to the RIC and it was to be armed. One third of the force was to be reserved for Roman Catholics but in this recommendation the committee was not unanimous. Indeed such a reservation could be held to be contrary to the Government of Ireland Act of 1920. The force was to be recruited partly from suitable members of the RIC and partly from the Class A Special Constabulary. The committee also said, 'We take this opportunity of paying a tribute to the services which the Special Constabulary have rendered throughout the six counties. They have proved equal to the special task which has been imposed upon them and by the efficiency they have shown they deserve the thanks of the people of Northern Ireland.' It was the recommendations of this committee rather than those of Sir Henry Wilson which were accepted and the organization of the Special Constabulary was left unchanged. On the same day applications for the new RUC were called for. Sir Henry Wilson's proposal that a Military adviser be appointed was however accepted. On his recommendation Major General A. Solly-Flood, CB, CMG, DSO, was appointed and took up his post on 7 April. This appointment was not received without misgivings in some quarters. It was obvious that he was likely to clash with Colonel Wickham, the Divisional Commissioner of Police and with Major General Cameron, the GOC Northern Ireland District. On 4 April the Royal Irish Constabulary in the South held its farewell parade in Phoenix Park before disbandment.

While these deliberations were proceeding in Ireland, the Government at Westminster began to worry about the expense of the Special Constabulary and the opportunity was taken to review the whole position in a memorandum for the cabinet. It was pointed out that the border between Northern Ireland and the Irish Free State was really now a border of the United Kingdom, but the Northern Ireland Government had had to defend it with the Special Constabulary in the face of attacks by the IRA from the South. The memorandum urged that the British Army should take over the defence of the border as it was their proper function and that there would then be less chance of friction. It also pointed out that unless this was done, it would be very difficult to enforce any revision of the boundary against the wishes of the Northern Ireland Government. There was a danger of the Special Constabulary being used for a purpose contrary to the wishes of Westminster although Westminster was paying for the force. In the memorandum it stated 'The whole of these Specials are Protestants, if only for the reason that Catholics are averse to taking the oath of allegiance.' Nothing came of this memorandum and the Specials continued to defend the border. The reason appears to be two-fold: firstly, Winston Churchill seems to have had complete trust in Sir James Craig and had become sympathetic to the cause of Ulster, and secondly, the army was still under the command of General Macready in Dublin. Its position in the South was not a happy one and it had to guard against an all out attack by the IRA which, as its numbers dwindled, could have been serious. The truce was also nominally in force and the army did not want to do anything that could be construed as breaking it. They were therefore very reluctant to become involved in action on the Ulster border. At the same time, with revisions of the border threatened, and the fear that Westminster might 'sell them down the river', the Northern Government was happy to continue with this responsibility. It is, of course, arguable that as the Specials were doing the army's job for them, it was fair that Westminster should pay.

While these matters of policy were under consideration the troubles continued. On 19 March six people were killed in Belfast and arms were found in St Mary's Hall, the principal

Roman Catholic meeting place in the city, but the troubles now shifted to the country. On the same day a large force of the IRA, mostly from the South, swooped down out of the Sperrin Mountains and attacked the RIC Barracks at Pomeroy in Co Tyrone capturing all the police arms and ammunition. A large force of the RIC and Specials attempted to intercept them but were greatly delayed by trenched and obstructed roads and the IRA got away. Simultaneously 200 of the IRA surrounded the town of Maghera in Co Londonderry, cut off the telephones and the electric light and captured the RIC barracks. They seized seventeen rifles and 5,000 rounds of ammunition and retired taking an RIC Sergeant prisoner. Another group tried to destroy the bridge over the River Moyola and shot dead Special Constable Alexander Kilpatrick who was riding home off duty on his bicycle. They also attacked a Special Constable at Coalisland and took his rifle and ambushed a patrol at Annaghmore which came to his assistance. The raid continued the next day and many buildings were burnt down including mills, sawmills, stables and outhouses especially in Co Londonderry. Burntollet bridge and another bridge near Dungiven were blown up and a shooting lodge on the Glenshane Pass was destroyed. Meanwhile there was heavy firing across the border from Co Monaghan especially in the Ballagh area where the bridge had recently been demolished by the Specials. On 21 March the raid continued in West Tyrone when the IRA murdered Special Constables Samuel Laird and George Chittick in the Trillick area. They were not on duty at the time and were shot down by armed men in cold blood. On the same night a series of raids were made on Loyalist homes in this area, a number of substantial farm houses being burnt down. The A Special Platoon stationed at Dromore was rushed to Trillick but the attacks were simultaneous and so widespread that they failed to intercept any of the raiders that night. Subsequently large scale searches were made in the area by both A and B Specials and a number of suspects were arrested. It seems probable now that most of the raiders came from over the border but a Protestant gang had their revenge by murdering three local Catholics. There was a strong suspicion that B Specials were involved in these reprisals but none of the culprits were ever brought to justice. One thing is certain: if any Special Constables took part in these criminal acts they did so while off duty. Suggestions that reprisals of this kind were official or even condoned by the authorities are without the slightest foundation.

On 21 and 22 March the counter measures by the RIC and Special Constabulary, having been greatly delayed by cut telephone wires and obstructed roads, really got going. A force searched the Maghera area for the kidnapped RIC Sergeant and a larger force of both A and B Specials swept through the Sperrins. At Loughmacrory in Co Tyrone the A Specials outmanoeuvred twenty-five of the IRA who were waiting in ambush for them, wounded five of them and pursued the rest for four miles before they lost them. Most of the IRA had retired into Co Donegal and the Co Londonderry B Specials had to content themselves with a wholesale trenching of roads over the border to try and prevent a repetition of the raid. On 22 March, Special Constables Thomas Cunningham and William Chermside were shot dead in broad daylight in May Street, Belfast. There was spasmodic sniping in Belfast until the next weekend when more trouble broke out and seven people were killed. There were extensive searches for arms by the security forces and heavy firing in the Falls area. The Belfast troubles had by now become, in the words of Winston Churchill 'a foul kind of warfare maintained by the dregs of both religions'. By this time, some of the Belfast Protestants had descended to the level of the IRA and had embarked on a policy of counter assassination. Next day a Protestant murder gang shot seven male members of the MacMahon family, killing four and wounding three, one of them mortally. This horrible deed was perpetrated as a general reprisal against men who do not seem to have been members of the IRA. Sinn Fein propaganda, predictably, tried, without a shred of evidence, to place responsibility for this atrocity on the Special Constabulary. The IRA had their revenge on equally innocent people when on 31

March a bomb was flung into a Protestant house wounding Francis Donnelly, killing two of his children and wounding two others. As if this was not enough, on 18 May IRA gunmen murdered three Protestants in a cooperage in Little Patrick Street.

On 29 March the IRA became active on the southern border of the Province. At Cullaville in South Armagh they crossed the border and ambushed a police patrol killing an RIC Sergeant and Special Constable James Harper. In this raid they used some of the uniforms they had taken from the prisoners at Clones. At Newry they derailed a goods train and fired at a Crossley tender on patrol on the road to Omeath. The worst incident was at Belcoo in Co Fermanagh where fifty of the IRA seized the RIC Station and captured twenty-two rifles, twenty-one revolvers and 5,000 rounds of ammunition. They also took the whole complement of sixteen policemen prisoner including eight Special Constables. In this attack the RIC put up no resistance and treachery was suspected. On 30 March Special Constable David Allen was killed in an ambush in Kilmorey Street in Newry and at about the same time the Ulster Bank at Ballycastle was robbed of £7,000. On 31 March a sharp action was fought at Dungate in Co Tyrone, when a mixed force of A and B Specials surprised a band of IRA four times their strength in the act of destroying a bridge. The Commander of the A Platoon, an ex-naval officer of twenty-two years' service, was seriously wounded and the need to get him medical attention delayed the pursuit and the rebels again escaped into the mountains. Two of them later died of their wounds.

On 30 March an agreement was signed between Sir James Craig representing the Government of Northern Ireland and Michael Collins representing the Provisional Government in Dublin. It was a genuine effort on the part of the Northern Government to end the 'troubles' in Belfast and on the border. Among many subjects covered, there were a number of points about the police which are of interest. In return for a complete cessation of IRA activity in the six counties, it was agreed that Roman Catholics should join the Special Constabulary and be responsible for order in Nationalist areas. In mixed areas, the Specials would be half Protestant and half Catholic. Searches were only to be carried out by police of both denominations with the military in attendance. All arms were to be kept in barracks and all police on duty were to be in uniform and be numbered. An advisory Committee nominated by the Provisional Government in Dublin would select the Catholic candidates for the Special Constabulary. All this was a big pill for the Northern Government to swallow. They were very anxious that the trouble in Belfast should end and were prepared to go to almost any lengths to stop the riots. They were happy for Roman Catholic Specials to be used provided they were loyal, but to allow the Southern Government to choose the selection committee was asking a very great deal. Nevertheless it was the Northern Government which had to exert pressure to get the agreement implemented. Sir James Craig had to 'hasten' Michael Collins twice and it was a month before he nominated the Committee. The Committee consisted of twelve members, to be presided over by the Roman Catholic Bishop of Down and Connor (Dr McRory). It included moderate Roman Catholics but also others who were undoubtedly connected with the IRA. There was some argument over the place and date for the first meeting and it was 16 May before the Committee got together. Only seven of the twelve members then attended and the Bishop was not among them. General Solly-Flood, Colonel Wickham and Mr Gelston, the City Commissioner for Belfast, were there to represent the police. The General welcomed the Committee, said the aim was to restore order in the city impartially and it was therefore important to build up a force of Roman Catholic Special Constables. It was clear, however, that some of the members were more interested in obtaining information about the police than recruiting Catholics and the meeting made little progress. A second meeting was held on 31 May when only five members attended and it was obvious that the extremists were not going to allow Catholics to be Special

Constables at all. At a final meeting on 7 June there were only three members present, two having been arrested, and most of the time was spent in recriminations. General Solly-Flood reiterated that he was trying to suppress outrages irrespective of creed and trying wholeheartedly to secure Roman Catholic police, but the sinister hand of the IRA was determined to prevent it and the committee never met again. There were other parts of the agreement of 30 March which need not concern us here. It will suffice to say that nothing came of them and by midsummer the agreement had become a dead letter. The principal reason for the failure was that the IRA never stopped operations in the six counties, the northern Catholics tacitly refused to recognize or co-operate with the Government of Northern Ireland and the IRA had no intention of permitting any Catholics to join the Special Constabulary.

In spite of the agreement between North and South, throughout April there were a number of incidents both in Belfast and the rest of the Province. The month began with a bad weekend in Belfast and a Protestant mob went berserk after an RIC Constable had been shot. On 2 April ten platoons of A Specials totalling some 500 men from Cos Tyrone and Londonderry made a huge sweep to try and clear the IRA from twenty square miles of country between Cookstown, Greencastle and Draperstown. They detained some 300 men for questioning but only four of these were found to be in the IRA. The rest of the IRA evaded the net probably being safe in Co Donegal. On 6 April a foot patrol of six A Specials was ambushed near Garrison in Co Fermanagh by seventy IRA who opened fire with a machine gun. Special Constable Joseph Plumb was killed and three others wounded. Reinforcements in a Lancia armoured lorry failed to intercept the raiders before they were able to cross back into the Free State. About the same time a Crossley full of Specials was ambushed at Wattlebridge, five of them were wounded and their vehicle and arms fell into the hands of the IRA. On 9 April a B Special patrol was attacked by bombs and rifle fire at Charlemont in Co Armagh, a Sergeant and a Special Constable being wounded. In a subsequent house to house search, five members of the IRA were arrested. In the middle of the month the IRA were seen to be massing on the southern borders of Fermanagh and the 'B' Specials in that area were called up for full time duties. On 11 April two 'B' Specials were attacked near Newtownbutler and one was wounded and on 16 April a patrol on the Keady-Ballbay road in South Armagh was ambushed by the IRA using machine guns and another Special Constable was wounded. Three days later there was heavy sniping in the Ballagh Bridge district. In Belfast, Specials in a Lancia lorry were ambushed on 13 April and four of them were wounded, Special Constable Nathaniel McCoo mortally and events there gradually deteriorated until there was a serious day of disorder on 20 April, followed by looting and terrorism. A B Special patrol was also ambushed at Albert Bridge and in all, four more Specials were wounded.

On 31 March Royal assent was given to the Free State Bill which became the new Constitution of the South of Ireland but by 7 April there were rumblings on a small scale which presaged trouble. A week later, irreconcilables seized the Four Courts in Dublin and the split which resulted in the civil war in the South came into the open. On 7 April, the Special Powers Act came into force in Northern Ireland for a period of one year. Under it the Minister of Home Affairs was given wide powers 'in respect of persons, matters and things ... to take all such steps and issue all such orders as may be necessary for preserving the peace and maintaining order'. It specified severe punishment for the carrying and possession of arms or explosives and for arson and malicious damage and in some cases even the death penalty. It gave wide powers of arrest to the army as well as the police and under the act it was possible to make orders for detention without trial.

As far back as May 1921, Sinn Fein had declared that they were 'out to smash the Ulster Parliament, and if it cannot be smashed in this election, it will have to be smashed otherwise'. There followed the bellicose speech by Eoin O'Duffy at

Armagh in September in which he threatened to 'use the lead'. On 27 March 1922, a Mr Joe McGrath publicly called for volunteers to fight on the border. On 18 April, an IRA order was issued saying that the aim was to make Ulster part of a Free State Republic by force and on 26 April the Provisional Government of the Free State virtually broke off relations with Ulster: the organized conspiracy of violence being intensified in May 1922. Sinn Fein policy was to try and make the government of Northern Ireland impossible by using the same methods as they had used in the South. By assassination, arson, fomenting riots, intimidation, kidnapping and boycotting they hoped to impoverish the Province and create a weariness of the 'troubles' which would force the North into accepting Sinn Fein rule. They had, however, seriously underestimated the determination of the majority of the people of the Province who had no intention of submitting. It was in the Ulster Special Constabulary that that determination was given practical effect and it was more from the existence of that force than anything else that they drew the courage to resist. This was the reason that Sinn Fein and the IRA hated the Specials and did their best to discredit them by propaganda in any way they could.

The full strength of the IRA in March 1922 was 112,650 and it had used the truce to reorganize and train itself. Arms had been supplied in considerable numbers by the British and it had now to be considered a very formidable force. Fortunately for the North, at its convention on 26 March it split into two factions which were for or against the Treaty or 'Free Staters' and 'Republicans'. The IRA who actually lived in the North numbered about 8,500 and were practically all of the anti-Treaty faction. Michael Collins therefore had little control over them. A great deal of the trouble on the border was also caused by irregulars who were not under the control of the Provisional Government. Dublin was, however, sometimes able to exert some influence on them and on 10 April they secured the release of the last of the Clones Specials. There is little doubt, however, that both pro- and anti-Treaty forces were prepared to co-operate in an attack on Northern Ireland. Michael Collins was personally involved and seems to have welcomed this co-operation as a way to unify the IRA in the South and prevent it splitting into two factions. He was very anxious that the arms supplied to him by the British should not be used on the border and some reshuffling took place to ensure that this did not happen. In the circumstances it is hardly surprising that the agreement of 30 March came to nothing and by now even the truce had been forgotten. All the Specials were armed at all times and fire was returned when necessary. In the border areas of Co Tyrone, where there had been unopposed sniping for so long, machine guns were issued to the A Specials and this particular nuisance was soon brought under control.

Early in May a flying column of the 1st Northern Division of the IRA from Co Donegal attacked again in Co Tyrone and Co Londonderry. As usual telephone wires were cut all over the area probably by the local IRA. The RIC barracks were attacked at Bellaghy, Draperstown and Coalisland. At Bellaghy there was a sergeant and three constables of the RIC in the station as well as a Special Constable who was barrack orderly. One of the constables went outside the barracks late at night, and left the door unlocked when he returned. The IRA burst in, shot one constable dead and wounded the sergeant and another constable. The Special Constable however was behind the door and returned the fire driving out the IRA and saving the barracks. Patrols of B Specials hurried to the scene and captured three of the assailants. At Draperstown, too, the IRA were repulsed at the cost of two constables wounded and at Coalisland only slight damage was suffered by the station. Elsewhere, the IRA committed other outrages, they tried to derail a train between Derry and Strabane and murdered four people in various parts of the Province. In Limavady which had hitherto been quiet they burnt a number of buildings, mills and factories and the B Specials were at once called out to patrol the town and district. On 19 May as a result of the IRA activities there was a serious reprisal at Desertmartin in

Co Londonderry. Four Roman Catholics were murdered by masked men and half a dozen buildings owned by Roman Catholics were burned down. The few B Specials who were on duty in the village opened fire on the gang but had difficulty in summoning assistance as the telephone wires had not been repaired after the IRA had cut them. By the time Specials had arrived from neighbouring districts, the buildings were burnt to the ground. Houses were searched but the perpetrators were never found. On 2 May 1922, information was received that a quantity of arms had been smuggled over the border into Co Tyrone. A number of searches were made in Nationalist areas leading to skirmishes with the IRA but it was not until six months later that a large force of Specials found a cache of forty-eight weapons in a well concealed dugout. Early in the morning of 3 May 1922, the IRA attacked a house near Coalisland and set it on fire. Two B patrols at once investigated and one of these was ambushed, Special Constable Robert Cardwell being killed instantly. It took half an hour's heavy fighting to drive off the raiders and the subsequent search was delayed by cut telephone lines so that the IRA were able to escape. On the same day an A mobile patrol in the Sperrins was held up at a bridge which had been destroyed and their Crossley tender was then riddled by rifle fire and a Special Constable was seriously wounded. Reinforcements were sent but the IRA were again able to escape to the mountains. In Co Tyrone, the cutting of roads to reduce the mobility of the A Special mobile platoons became serious especially in the northwest of the county which was strongly Nationalist. The B Specials, however, succeeded in surprising the IRA destroying a bridge just west of Omagh and the miscreants were brought to justice. Furthermore a Nationalist working party was forced to repair the bridge. On 7 May 1922, the IRA attacked several houses at Castlecaulfield in Co Tyrone. Their aim seems to have been to murder an A Special Constable who was on leave. The owners of the houses put up a stout resistance but Special Constable Samuel Magilligan, aged eighteen, of the B Specials was killed as well as one of the civilians, before the

assailants were driven off. B Specials were often singled out
for attack when off duty. A Special Constable's house was
attacked near Augher; he drove off his assailants with his rifle
but every window in his house was broken. A young Special
Constable riding home on his bicycle to Cookstown, off duty
and unarmed, was ambushed, brutally assaulted and thrown
into a drain. There were also three ambushes of B Special foot
patrols at Moy, Enniskillen and Cookstown but no casualties
were reported. All this was accompanied by border sniping
especially in the Ballagh area.

In Belfast after comparative peace since the end of April,
sniping began again on 7 May and a bomb was thrown at
Protestant workmen in a tram on 11 May. On 14 May there
was serious disorder again and heavy firing in York Street. At
the same time a B Special patrol was ambushed near Lurgan
by a large number of the IRA and four Specials were wounded. There was peace on 15 May but fierce fighting broke out
again on 17 May after a Protestant funeral was attacked,
mostly between the army and gunmen and lasted all week.
On 18 May Musgrave Street Police Station was attacked
and on 21 May fourteen people were killed in an orgy of
shooting.

Simultaneously with these Belfast eruptions, on 19 and 20
May the IRA launched a widespread and intense attack from
the Glens of Antrim and the Mountains of Mourne as well as
from across the border from the South. In Co Antrim forty
men of the IRA burned Shanes Castle, the home of Lord
O'Neill, and set fire to Ballymena Railway Station. Five other
railway stations were burnt in this area as well as a number of
post offices. They attacked Martinstown RIC barracks, east of
Ballymena and when the B Specials from Clough came to the
rescue there was a desperate battle lasting three hours during
which the A Special platoon from Ballymena was ambushed.
Ballycastle RIC Station was also attacked but was relieved by
the Specials from Ballymoney. In the Glens of Antrim the
RIC barracks at Cushendall, Cushendun and Carnlough were
attacked, the first by 150 of the IRA who were engaged in a

four-hour battle with the police. Crebilly Castle and Glen-mona House were burnt but the fire was extinguished at Drumnasol House. Post Offices, banks and garages were raided or burnt in this area too. Farther east Loyalist homes were attacked in Cloughmills and a railway bridge between Killagan and Dunloy was blown up cutting the main northern counties line. In Co Down, 'Old Court' at Strangford, home of the de Ros family, was burnt down and a wide area was obstructed by trees felled across roads. Attacks on Castle-wallan and Ardglass RIC barracks were beaten off but a B Special patrol was ambushed south of Banbridge.

On 22 May Mr W. J. Twaddell, a member of the Northern Ireland Parliament and a Belfast City Councillor was mur-dered in Garfield Street in Belfast and on this day the Govern-ment acted. Under orders made in accordance with the Special Powers Act, they arrested some 400 of the IRA and Sinn Feiners all over the Province and interned them. To accom-modate so many prisoners they had to use a ship, the *Ar-genta*, moored at first in Belfast Lough and later off Larne. There was at once a mass exodus of the IRA over the border to the South and others went 'underground' in the Glens of An-trim and other Nationalist areas. At the same time the Gov-ernment proscribed Sinn Fein, the IRA, the Irish Republic Brotherhood and other organizations such as Cumman na mBan. In the days following, trouble continued in Belfast and on 25 May Special Constables James Murphy and George Connor were murdered, the first in the Falls area and the sec-ond in the Cromac district. On this day the curfew was ex-tended to the whole of Northern Ireland. For the next few days arson became the main terrorist weapon in the city and there were a great many fires. Outside Belfast a patrol of A Specials was ambushed in the Glens on the Parkmore Road and the battle lasted two and a half hours, two IRA being shot dead. Three more large houses, Garron Towers in Co Antrim, Kilclief House in Co Down and Hawthorn Hill in Co Ar-magh were burnt down. Police were ambushed at Dromara and an unsuccessful attack was made on the Ballagh Bridge

B Specials in 1921 before uniforms were issued

B Specials at Westminster Abbey, 1921

An A Special Constabulary mobile platoon

The Premier of Northern Ireland addressing Special Constables:
Sir James Craig (*right*) during his tour of the Ulster border

Two of the Rolls-Royce armoured cars that escorted Sir James Craig

A tree felled by raiders half a mile within the Ulster border. Farmers ask the County Commandant to break down the Ballagh Bridge over the Blackwater, the boundary river between Tyrone and Monaghan

A Specials in an ambush exercise in 1922

An A Special church parade in 1922

B Specials soon after the issue of ex-British uniforms dyed green, 1922

A Lancia armoured lorry used by A Specials

Under canvas at the Coagh Camp

Children play while a patrolling armoured car enters Cavour Street

post held by the Specials. There was a great deal of sniping all along the Tyrone–Monaghan border and finally Tobermore RIC barracks was fired on.

On 24 May the Constabulary Bill (Northern Ireland) was introduced which gave effect to the recommendations of the Committee which had reported at the end of March. It also gave new rules for recruitment to the Special Constabulary which became the Ulster Special Constabulary. On 9 June the RIC was finally disbanded in the North and the RUC came into being, Colonel C. G. Wickham being appointed Inspector-General. Only 1,100 of the old RIC were accepted into the RUC, 400 of whom were Catholics. The Catholics were however being subjected to intense pressure and this number was tending to dwindle rather than increase.

Towards the end of May 1922, the Irish papers were full of rumours that the IRA was preparing for a large scale attack across the western borders of the Province. Reports came in of the massing of the IRA all along the borders of Co Fermanagh and Co Londonderry. The loyalists in the Pettigo-Belleek triangle had been making requests for protection to the Government of Northern Ireland for some time. The Divisional Commissioner had already, on 26 May, directed Sir Basil Brooke the County Commandant, to send a force of Specials to their assistance. The so-called Pettigo-Belleek triangle lies at the western end of Lough Erne and at its eastern end is cut off from Enniskillen by the Free State border which at this point comes down to the lough shore. It can only be reached by land by crossing Lough Erne at Enniskillen and following the road to Belleek along the southern shore of the lough and even this route passes through Free State Territory for a few yards. To comply with the Divisional Commissioner's order, a mixed force of A and B Specials, some fifty strong, was sent by boat across Lough Erne on 27 May and occupied Magherameenagh Castle. A patrol from this force into Belleek was attacked by a strong force of IRA early on 28 May and this patrol and a relief party which had been sent from the castle was ambushed on its way back. The detachment extricated itself from the ambush but the Specials were now virtually besieged in Magherameenagh Castle by strong forces of the IRA. A force of A Specials from Garrison was sent to their assistance in three Crossley and two Lancia tenders. On approaching Belleek this force was heavily fired upon by the IRA from the old fort in Free State Territory. Special Constable Albert Rickerby, driving the leading vehicle, was killed and his Lancia ran into a ditch blocking the road. The Specials then had to abandon their vehicles and retire on foot. At this point, Sir Basil Brooke ordered a general mobilization of the Special Constabulary in Co Fermanagh, calling the whole of the B force to full time duty. That night the A Specials returned to Belleek and recovered the Crossley tenders but had to leave the Lancia in the ditch and it fell into the hands of the IRA. The force at Magherameenagh was however reinforced by another forty men including ten from the regular RIC who were sent in by Crossley tenders from the South. During the day large numbers of IRA took possession of Belleek and Pettigo and 'invaded' the triangle, the Protestant residents of the area abandoning their homes and fleeing towards Enniskillen. Colonel Barton, a resident at Waterfoot, having sent his family away by boat, put up a spirited resistance with the help of a Corporal of the Rifle Brigade who was on leave, and three B Specials. Nevertheless the situation was so serious that the County Commandant, who had been unable to procure reinforcements of A Specials from other parts of the Province, decided to evacuate the triangle. The garrison of Magherameenagh was taken off by water, mainly in the pleasure boat *Pandora*, an operation which the IRA nearly frustrated by opening sluices and lowering the level of Lough Erne. The Specials withdrew to Rough Island and took up a defensive position there.

Sniping then became general all along the borders of Fermanagh and Tyrone and the village of Garrison in Fermanagh was virtually surrounded. On the Free State side of the Tyrone–Donegal border, the IRA evicted all Protestants from their houses which were close to the border and commandeered them as barracks and frontier posts. These Protestants flocked across the border in a steady stream and were met by the Specials and sent to Castlederg in their transport. Some big move by the IRA seemed imminent in this area too and reinforcements of A and B Specials were rushed to the scene. All the border roads were made impassable and were guarded day and night and a reserve of thirty A Specials and a hundred B Specials was billeted in the Castlederg Orange Hall for four days. It is certain that some large raid had been planned but the IRA changed their minds either because of the failure of an attack they made on Strabane on 30 May, which was repulsed by B Specials, or because they got wind of the concentration of the Specials at Castlederg.

The seizure of the triangle caused a stir in London but the British Government were anxious that nothing should be done to upset the negotiations over the Constitution of Southern Ireland then in progress. No moves to recover the territory were therefore made for some days. The Irish Provisional Government, however, denied that the attack was anything to do with them and claimed that the IRA concerned were irregulars operating independently. Winston Churchill, who seems to have had complete authority for Irish affairs, then ordered the triangle to be reoccupied by the army. General Macready was reluctant to do this and imposed restrictions which, while rightly laying down that the army was not to enter Free State territory unless absolutely necessary, also said that the army was to undertake the whole operation and not to work with the Special Constabulary. The task was entrusted to General Cameron who decentralized again to the 17th Infantry Brigade. The Brigade first retook Pettigo and then advanced in two columns one on each side of Lough Erne. The northern column consisted of the 1st Battalion of the Lincolnshire Regiment with some armoured cars and the southern column of the 1st Battalion of the Manchester Regiment with more armoured cars and some howitzers. The IRA did not resist this show of force seriously and the triangle was soon reoccupied. The IRA however had to be driven out of the old Fort at Belleek by artillery fire. The army had only one soldier slightly injured but Special Constable Thomas Dobson, who had been lent to the army as a driver, was killed by a sniper firing across the border from Co Donegal. The IRA suffered a number of casualties and fifteen of them were taken prisoner and held as hostages for the return of some of the Specials who had been kidnapped. Mr Lloyd George was not at all happy about the troops being used in this way as he feared the talks with the Provisional Government might break down but fortunately he did not hear that the army had orders to advance until too late to stop the movement. The use of the army on this occasion at least showed that the Westminster Government was not going to allow the territorial integrity of Northern Ireland to be violated in this way. The area could have been recovered by the Special Constabulary but it would probably have meant calling up the C 1 Specials for the purpose.

Recruiting for the C 1 force had continued slowly during the first quarter of 1922 and in April another battalion had been authorized for the Lurgan–Portadown area. In May it was decided to separate the C 1 force from the rest of the Special Constabulary and to appoint Lieutenant-Colonel W. R. Goodwin, CMG, DSO, as its Commandant.[5] Local C 1 commanders were enjoined to co-operate if necessary with County Commandants of the Special Constabulary. The new C 1 force was quite different from the C force, which remained in existence. The C force was simply a reserve for the police, mostly of elderly men, and would only be used in a very static role close to their homes. The C 1 force was, in fact, a Northern Ireland Territorial Army. They did no police work except as static guards and were organized in military units for service anywhere in the Province. They were not necessarily elderly men and were expected to do training periods, drills and musketry. In mid 1922 they were about 7,500 strong, organized much as an Infantry Division with Headquarters in Belfast and a School at the Balmoral Show Grounds. The Brigades were called Groups and there were three of them, the 1st and 2nd (Belfast) Groups and the 3rd

(County) Group. Each group had four battalions or districts, each of four companies.

While the battle in the Belleek-Pettigo triangle was in progress, the trouble in Belfast continued almost without a pause. Special Constable John M'Garrity was killed by a sniper in the Falls area on 29 May and two days later there was an appalling outbreak of violence in the City, ten people being killed including Special Constable Andrew Roulston. Many buildings were burnt and there was a long battle between the army and the IRA. This sort of trouble continued into early June. Elsewhere outside Belfast the B Specials frustrated attempts to burn Ballyscullion House near Bellaghy and Killeleagh Castle in Co Down, but a Roman Catholic Magistrate was murdered in Newry by the IRA. Belfast was relatively quiet for the rest of June but there were a few murders, and arson and looting continued on a small scale. There were a number of incidents outside Belfast, the worst being on 18 June when four Protestants were murdered in the Newry area by bands of IRA from over the border, some disguised in police uniform. Special Constable William Russell was killed in an ambush between Newry and Forkhill on the same day and Special Constables William Mitchell and Samuel Young were ambushed three days later and shot dead when cycling to join their patrols near Keady. On 23 June, a motor patrol of A Specials from Ballymena ran into an ambush in Cushendall but they extricated themselves and killed four of the IRA. The unsettled state of the Glens was remedied by moving a half platoon of A Specials into Cushendall.

On 22 June Field Marshal Sir Henry Wilson was murdered in London by two members of the IRA as he was returning to his home after unveiling a war memorial at Euston Station. Sir Henry Wilson had visited Ulster again in the middle of April, where he found General Solly-Flood installed and making progress, and yet again in May. His advice was for firm government and for law and order to be applied impartially. He was even worried that no Roman Catholics could be found for the Special Constabulary. To the IRA, on the other hand, he represented the arch enemy. His murderers were London members of the IRA but there seemed little doubt that members of the Government in the South were implicated.

In midsummer 1922 Winston Churchill sent over Mr Stephen Tallents,[6] a civil servant, to make an on-the-spot investigation in Northern Ireland. Mr Tallents was sent mainly to report on why the agreement of 30 March had broken down but his comments on the appalling rioting in Belfast during the first half of the year are of great interest as they can be taken as impartial as it was possible to be in such troublous times. Altogether there were 236 people killed and 346 injured in the City between 6 December 1921 and 31 May 1922. Of the killed, sixteen were casualties among the security forces, two of whom were soldiers, eight Special Constabulary and the rest RIC, five of whom were Roman Catholics. Of the civilians seventy-three of those killed were Protestants and 147 Roman Catholics but this disparity is not repeated amongst those injured, the figures being 143 Protestant and 166 Roman Catholic. These figures were quoted at the time by the Provisional Government in the South to try to prove that the Roman Catholics were the victims of pogroms by the Protestants. Mr Tallents, however, pointed out that many of the Roman Catholic casualties were caused by indiscriminate firing by the IRA in their own areas. Mr Tallents gave the uncertainty of the future of the six counties as the principal reason on the Protestant side for the riots including the failure in the South to establish order especially in Co Donegal in which there was anarchy. There was fear about the outcome of a boundary commission too. At the same time there was an organized conspiracy of murder and violence by Sinn Fein against the Northern Government in close collaboration with the South and this was met in many cases by counter outrages and reprisals. He said that the Northern Government had taken over security successfully under quite exceptional difficulties and with a regular police force far too small for the purpose.

Mr Tallents included in his report some comments on the Special Constabulary. He said that the reputation of the B

Specials was 'disquieting' but that Sir James Craig would hear 'nothing to their detriment'.[7] He does not say why and quotes no evidence but it is clear that he obtained this impression mainly from the Roman Catholics[8] he consulted who fed him with the usual hostile Sinn Fein propaganda. He also consulted General Ricardo[9] who had been against the Special Constabulary from the beginning. It is clear that the General did not like a part time force such as the B Specials and complained of lack of discipline. In this it seems that he meant the kind of discipline that one expects in a regular soldier. The B force never pretended to be like the Guards but in fact their self-discipline was second to none and absenteeism or neglect of duty were very rare. Of the A force he says that they had too much pay and, except when the IRA were very active, too little to do and consequently were liable to pass the time drinking. He thought the control above platoon level was too loose. Undoubtedly his criticisms applied to a few units but he himself agreed that the majority of the A Specials were good. When he complained that the Special Constabulary were soldiers rather than police, he was probably on firmer ground, as he was when he pointed out that there was insufficient co-ordination between the RUC, the A Specials, the B Specials and the army. Nevertheless there were few complaints on these scores from the officers who actually controlled the operations, and it does not seem that Mr Tallents consulted anyone who really knew what was going on below the Inspector General of the RUC. General Ricardo continued to harp on his point that B Specials, who worked in their own areas and 'against' so to speak their Catholic neighbours, would cause local feuds which might last for generations. Whereas the RUC or the A Specials who were always employed in areas other than their own were less likely to do so. He said nothing of the great advantages that the local knowledge of the B Specials gave them. Not only did they know their area well but also the people in it and they could distinguish the sheep from the goats. They knew at once if a stranger arrived to stir up trouble. If feuds were being started, it was the IRA with their brutal and callous sectarian murders and outrages that caused them. Because of the way they intimidated and forced the Catholic population to co-operate with them, it was inevitable that counter measures by the police should inconvenience them more than their Protestant neighbours. The rift was made wider by Sinn Fein propaganda which made out that IRA gunmen were heroes and their unspeakable acts were patriotic deeds. At the same time it painted the forces of law and order as monsters and the Catholic population believed them.

It is very understandable that moderate Nationalists should become irritated by the searches, the road blocks and the restrictions and should blame all this on the Special Constabulary who had to put it all into effect. On 20 June and on other occasions Cardinal Logue's car was stopped and searched and it must have been exasperating for a high personage to suffer such an indignity. It was, of course, essential to make sure that the Cardinal's car was not being used for smuggling arms or other illegal purposes by his servants without his knowledge or by those who could easily have been intimidated by the IRA. In June, too, some priests at Crossmaglen complained of being searched and on 29 May the Catholic Mayor of Londonderry was furious when he was searched as he returned from Co Donegal. These people were believed by the police to be supporters of Sinn Fein and had little cause for complaint and the Special Constabulary would have been guilty of a grave dereliction of duty if they had not searched them. Some of the complaints would have been justified in a country which was at peace but in the situation brought about by IRA terrorism such searches were inevitable. In the state of the country at that time, the idea that murderers caught red-handed should have been treated with the courtesy shown to someone who had committed a minor traffic offence is palpably absurd. Irritation was caused by other actions. For instance in Co Fermanagh it was found that the IRA used bicycles a great deal to increase their mobility. A large number of Sinn Feiners' bicycles were therefore commandeered for the Special Constabulary whose patrols became thereafter more mobile. When the IRA forced local Nationalists to trench roads or break down bridges, the B Specials requisitioned their labour to repair the damage again. Such measures were effective but did not increase the popularity of the force among the Nationalists. On occasion Roman Catholics were able to express their abhorrence of the IRA and even to applaud the action of the Special Constabulary. In February a resolution in the Town Council at Portadown congratulating the Special Constabulary was seconded by a Nationalist who said 'The action of the Specials had been greatly appreciated by his co-religionists generally'. There is plenty of evidence to show that Sinn Fein's hatred was not because of what the Specials did, but because they were the answer to a terrorist campaign of the type perpetuated by the IRA. They therefore used propaganda ruthlessly to restrict the operations of the Specials in any way that they could.

The Special Constabulary had cost £1,500,000 in 1921–22 and the estimate for 1922–23 was £2,700,000. This had to be borne mostly by the British taxpayer and it was natural that they would wish to be assured that the money was being spent wisely and economically. In midsummer they sent over General Vesey to investigate and make a report. He pointed out that it had been necessary to organize the Specials in great haste and that this had led to the imposition of the classes A, B, C and C 1 upon one another without a definite allocation of responsibility and with some lack of overall control. He said that the HQ Staff was not excessive in the present conditions but would have to be reduced when the situation returned to normal. General Solly-Flood had already come in for some criticism from Mr Tallents. It was pointed out that he was a soldier without police experience and had no very great standing in Great Britain. His schemes, which seemed to be more concerned with the external defence of Northern Ireland if the British Army was withdrawn than the suppression of internal troubles, had not been subjected to treasury control or tested by any kind of government criticism. If his target strengths were reached then one in four of all Protestant men of military age would be in some branch of the Special Constabulary. On the other hand he pointed out that there was a lack of transport organization for the C 1 force. In general the Specials came out of this investigation very well and in retrospect it cannot be denied that they were cheap at the price. By midsummer the establishment and strength of the Special Constabulary was:

	Establishment	Strength
Class A	8,250	5,500
Class B	22,000	19,000
Class C 1	15,000	7,500
	45,250	32,000

There was also a large number of Class C, who were seldom used but by enrolling were allowed to keep arms in their houses. When it was realized that the RUC had only 1,100 of its establishment of 3,000 at this time, it can be seen how much depended upon the Special Constabulary.

By the summer of 1922, the Special Constabulary had emerged as a formidable force. The A Specials formed the main police force of the Province being five times the size of the infant RUC. Some of them had been policemen for eighteen months or more and all were fully uniformed, armed and equipped. Over half the men at police stations throughout the Province were A Specials and there were now some fifty mobile platoons. The B Specials, too, nearing twenty thousand were fully uniformed, armed and equipped. As they did one patrol a week, this meant that there were normally only 3,000 or so available for duty at a time but in emergency all could be mobilized for a short period. Behind the As and Bs stood the C and C 1 Specials, the latter equivalent to two brigades of infantry. When up to strength the C 1 force would be the same size as the British Regular army of sixteen battalions stationed in Northern Ireland and so could replace them if they were withdrawn.

As one reads the long list of widespread and varied IRA activities one is bound to ask how it was that they were not prevented by the security forces. The list of positive successes against the IRA seems small. The problem, however, was a very difficult one as at one moment the IRA were apparently peaceful citizens and at another vicious and ruthless gunmen, generally operating from cover with their targets uniformed and conspicuous, and then within minutes private citizens again. This way of operating relied heavily on the support of a proportion of the population, in whose houses they could hide and be supported or at least conceal their weapons. They used unarmed and apparently innocent people, often girls or children, as scouts to give them warning of the approach of the police or of the positions of their road blocks or patrols.

The problem which faced the security forces could be divided into three major aspects. The first was the control of the urban guerrilla operations of the IRA in Belfast and its frequent eruption into riots, reprisals and counter reprisals, looting and incendiarism. The second was the suppression of the indigenous IRA in the rural areas of the Province and to try and prevent them carrying out a campaign of intimidation, murder and arson. The third was to hold the border to prevent the southern IRA infiltrating into the Province, to prevent the smuggling of arms to the northern IRA, to prevent raids across the border and to intercept wanted men escaping to the South.

The first of these threats was met by the RUC in Belfast reinforced by a substantial number of A and B Specials, who guarded valuable buildings and people and carried out foot patrols. The A Specials also patrolled in armoured cars and lorries and stood ready to reinforce the police at any trouble spot. The 15th Infantry Brigade stationed in the Belfast area were frequently called upon to control riots and to compete with the continual sniping in the city.

The second problem of the IRA in the countryside was, of course, partly dealt with by the RUC with their substantial reinforcement of A Specials, but mainly by the mobile A platoons and B Specials. The A platoons patrolled their areas in their vehicles as ordered by the Area Commandant[10] of the

Special Constabulary and stood ready to proceed to any trouble spot. They did most of the work by day when the B Specials were about their normal occupations. The B Specials operated mainly at night and were used to guard important points such as telephone exchanges, power stations, bridges, railway lines and the houses of important people. They were also used to set up road blocks which searched vehicles for arms and ensured that the curfew regulations were enforced and as bicycle or foot patrols on the roads. All of them, with their arms and uniform at home, were ready at any time to deal with emergencies. When off duty too they kept their eyes open and provided a first class intelligence system in their areas, where their knowledge of the local people proved invaluable. The C 1 force also helped with guard and protection duties where necessary.

The third problem of guarding the border was a difficult one. The border was some 250 miles long crossed by 175 roads. In places it followed no natural boundary and it was not easy to recognize its precise location. Since the border raids of the first half of 1922, all the minor roads had been trenched or obstructed in some way and only the major roads were left open. By day as much of the border as possible was watched by A Special platoons who had fixed sandbagged posts and who patrolled along roads close to the frontier. These platoons lived in requisitioned temporary quarters close to the border which were heavily sandbagged and defended like minor fortresses. When necessary the A Specials were reinforced by calling up B Specials for full time duty. At night B Specials reinforced the border guards and patrols. Behind the Special Constabulary stood the British Army in reserve in its barracks some distance from the border, its strength outside the Belfast area being some ten battalions totalling 6,000 men.

All that can be said of these operations was that they made the task of the IRA very much more hazardous. Movement at night was difficult and they never knew when they might meet a patrol or a road block. An outrage in an area meant that there would be an intensive search of houses putting them and their weapons in great danger of discovery. There is no doubt that the Special Constabulary had a firm grip on the whole country and were far more effective than the security forces had been in the South before the truce. Of course they had the great advantage that two thirds of the population were loyal and on their side but it was their presence which prevented intimidation and kept them that way. It was the Ulster Special Constabulary that held the breach while the transition from the disintegrating RIC to the new RUC took place and while the British Army had, so to speak, largely contracted out of the Irish problem. Sinn Fein and the IRA knew that they had defeated the RIC in the South by a policy of murder and intimidation and hoped they could do the same to the new RUC. They felt, quite wrongly, that they had also defeated the British Army and that they had little to fear from the remnant of it left in the North with its uncertain political direction from General Macready and Westminster. With the Special Constabulary, however, it was very different. Here was a well armed force rapidly improving in efficiency which they could not infiltrate or intimidate and which was composed of men implacably opposed to Sinn Fein and all that it stood for.

NOTES

1. It had actually been reformed in the middle of 1920 under Colonel Sir Wilfred Spender.

2. Later as Sir Richard Pim to become Inspector General of the Royal Ulster Constabulary.

3. They were instructed to keep the bolt separate from the rifle so that if their home was raided by the IRA when they were out, they would find it difficult to capture the rifle intact.

4. Sir Henry Wilson's A, B and C were different from the A, B and C used at that time for the Special Constabulary.

5. He was relieved as County Commandant in Antrim and Belfast by Lt-Col A. J. Vernon, DSO, MC.

6. Mr Stephen Tallents had been Private Secretary to the Viceroy of Ireland and later held the appointment of Imperial Secretary in Northern Ireland until 1926. He was knighted in 1930.

7. Replying to an assertion in the *Observer* at about this time, Sir James Craig said 'there is no religious test in the Ulster Special Constabulary. I am glad to say that Roman Catholics have joined the Special Constabulary, and that that force deserves the greatest credit for the high discipline which it has maintained in spite of the greatest provocation and intimidation which have been specially directed against it by the IRA. I regret to say that I have just heard that five members of this force have today been foully murdered in different parts of Ulster.' The number of Roman Catholics in the B Specials was very small, but there were more, mostly ex-soldiers, in the A Specials.

8. Cardinal Logue went as far as to make the astonishing assertion that the Special Constabulary were the cause of all the trouble in Belfast. The B Specials were very seldom used in Nationalist areas of the City and one of their main occupations was guarding Roman Catholic public houses situated in Protestant areas. Three incidents were mentioned; Cushendall, Hawkhill and Edenappa. The last, in which an army sentry shot two girls who failed to answer a challenge, was nothing to do with the Special Constabulary. Hawkhill was a reprisal murder of a member of the IRA in which an A Special Constable was suspected of complicity. Cushendall was the ambush of A Specials on 23 June in which four IRA were killed. The Sinn Fein allegation was that the A Specials had simply entered the town, pulled the four men out of bed and killed them. There was a Commission of Enquiry held but it was never published. There is little doubt that an ambush took place and that the men who were shot were in the IRA and high on the wanted list.

9. Brigadier General A. St Q. Ricardo, CMG, OBE, DSO, is answered in some detail simply because he committed his criticisms to paper and they have been preserved in the Public

Record Office. As a senior retired officer and a Protestant with no republican or Sinn Fein connections his adverse criticisms are worthy of respect. It is a pity that the comments of more of the officers who actually commanded the Specials have not been preserved as they were the men who really knew what was going on. General Ricardo does not seem to have been asked for his comments but volunteered them. He was for a short time a B Special Constable in Co Tyrone where he had considerable differences of opinion with Colonel McClintock, the County Commandant, on how to use the force. General Ricardo had unorthodox ideas on how to compete with the IRA. At one time he put forward a scheme for a secret armed police who would operate in plain clothes! It seems odd that someone who was so keen to comment was not used more in the Special Constabulary, where he would seem to have been ideal for a high position. Possibly this thought may be the key to his readiness to criticize.

10. In the summer 1922, the operational control of a county was found to be too much for a County Commandant. Area Commandants were full time and they controlled the A platoons and the B Specials in their area. District Commandants were part-time and only looked after the B Specials.

CHAPTER FOUR

Order Restored – 1922–5

On 28 June, the Provisional Government of the South ordered the Free State Army to attack the IRA which was in occupation of the Four Courts. Using artillery hastily purchased from the British Army in Southern Ireland, they captured the building after a siege lasting three days. The civil war which had been simmering for months now began in earnest. The 'troubles' in the North at once died down and the incidents during July were few. On 2 July a force of Specials had to be rushed to the border at Carrigans outside Londonderry as 'Free Staters' and 'Republicans' were fighting each other near to the other side; and on 5 July a bomb was thrown into the barracks of the A Platoon at Ballymena but little else happened. On 14 July General Eoin O'Duffy, the Chief of Staff of the Free State Army, wrote to Thomas Barry, a high IRA Officer then in Mountjoy Gaol, and asked for a meeting to arrange combined action against the North, but little seems to have come of this. The 'Twelfth' celebrations held all over the Province on 12 July were not attacked and were peaceful. The previous day, four battalions of the 1st (Belfast) Group of the C 1 Specials, then mobilized at Balmoral for their annual training, marched past Sir James Craig. According to the Press they made a brave show and were fully armed, uniformed and equipped and had a high proportion of ex-soldiers in their ranks. On 19 July the British Government agreed to a grant of £2,850,000 to maintain the Special Constabulary and announced that an army garrison of sixteen battalions would be kept in Ulster. The defence situation in the Province was therefore now healthier than ever before. There is no doubt that the relative tranquillity of the Province was mainly due to the Civil War in the South which took a great deal of pressure off Northern Ireland. From then on it was only the indigenous IRA in the six counties, of some 8,500 men, which gave trouble as the 100,000 IRA in the South split and began to tear each other apart. In spite of the fact that the IRA originally outnumbered the Free State Forces by four to one, they were soon driven out of Dublin to the south west of a line from Waterford to Limerick.

In midsummer the Inspector General had time to clarify the relations between the County Inspectors of the RUC and the County Commandants of the USC. In a memorandum dated 27 June he emphasized that the RUC and USC were parts of the same force doing the same duties and they must co-operate closely. Subject to this they had to work on their own initiative. The County Inspector was the senior police officer in the county and with the RUC and attached A Specials would attend to ordinary law and crime and would bring all offenders to justice. In consequence the RUC should normally be free from military guards and patrols. The A Special platoons and the Specials should do the patrols and take all the military measures to guard the border and protect important places and people. They should also take counter measures against outrages by the IRA; prepare plans for counter attack and make raids for arms. In short, the County Inspectors were responsible for police measures and the County Commandants for para-military action against the IRA. In Belfast and Londonderry there was a slight difference and the Police Commissioner controlled the A Special platoons stationed in the city rather than the City Commandant.

In midsummer the Inspector General received predictable complaints against the police alleging thefts during searches for arms. He issued firm instructions that searches must be carried out by the regular RUC and that B Specials were on no account to make searches on their own. He also had complaints of discourtesy and about the discipline of the Special Constabulary and drew attention to the need for smartness and proper behaviour on duty. At this time too the Special Constabulary received some technical improvements the most important of which was the introduction of wireless for communications. The cutting of telephone and telegraph wires had made the reaction of the security forces to outrages slow with the result that the IRA often escaped. A Wireless Platoon was formed in the A Specials and detachments were with every A Platoon by November. One of the many duties of the A Specials was the security of the *Argenta*, the ship in which the IRA were interned. Prison officers were on duty inside the ship herself but the A Specials were responsible for guarding her externally.

By the end of July the Free State Forces, now 60,000 strong, had thrown the IRA out of Waterford, Limerick and Tipperary and in August they took Tralee and Cork by seaborne landings. By the middle of the month the IRA had ceased trying to hold territory, and had reverted to the tactics of ambush, assassination and arson and had gone underground again. In the North the first three weeks of August were quiet but on 22 August, the post held by the Specials on Magilligan Point was fired at across the Foyle from Co Donegal. On 24 August a bomb was thrown in Belfast and on 27 August a soldier was shot and wounded. The next day a patrol of B Specials was attacked at Castledawson in Co Londonderry and a B Special post at Enagh on the Co Donegal border fired at three men tampering with the railway line and dispersed them. These were minor incidents but on 29 August shots were fired in the Crumlin Road in Belfast and a bomb was thrown wounding eight people. This might well have escalated into full scale rioting but no serious disorder resulted.

On 12 August, Arthur Griffith, President of the Dail, died in Dublin and ten days later Michael Collins was shot dead in an ambush in Co Cork. Winston Churchill said of him, 'He was an Irish patriot, true and fearless', and no one could deny that, but for once the Special Constabulary in the North agreed with General Macready when he said, 'Michael Collins was, and must for ever be, the embodiment of a campaign of ruthless murders carried out by men styling themselves soldiers of the Irish Republic, but who systematically ignored every condition of warfare recognized among civilized nations'. Sir James Craig records that his relations with the Irish Free State greatly improved when Mr Cosgrave took over the leadership. The obsession of Michael Collins that all the troubles in Belfast were started by unprovoked pogroms on the Catholic minority made him very difficult to deal with. He refused to recognize that they were more often begun by attacks by IRA gunmen on soldiers and police and that these led to reprisals and counter reprisals.

Although the bill for the Specials had been met by the British Government in July, it had been a struggle to get them to make this payment and it was clear, as soon as the situation eased, that drastic economies would have to be made. It had already been arranged that the engagements of all classes of the Special Constabulary would end on 30 September and on 10 August recruiting for Class A was stopped. With the improved situation in August it was decided that considerable reductions in strength would have to be made before the end of the financial year. Reduction of the A Specials was planned to start on 1 October and continue until January. From this date the engagements of A Specials were to be on a monthly and the B Specials on a three-monthly basis. Mobilized B and C 1 Specials were to be reduced to 300 by 1 September and a hundred by 15 September. Rather than pay off too many A Specials at a time of high unemployment, their pay was reduced from £3 10s. a week to £2 9s. This allowed about 1,000 men of the force to be kept on the books who would otherwise have had to be discharged. To save man-power the protection afforded to important people was drastically reduced and the troops were warned that they might have to do more. In September it became clear that these measures were having an unsettling effect on the A Specials, and there was talk of mass meetings in Belfast and deputations to see Sir James Craig. They were, however, reassured when they realized they were not to be disbanded altogether.

In September Belfast began to simmer again and on 3 September there were several small shooting and bombing incidents. On 8 September a Special Constable was wounded in the Short Strand area and on 15 September a bomb was thrown and nine people were injured. Two days later there was further sniping but then the trouble died away and on 22 September the City had become sufficiently quiet to shorten the curfew by half an hour. Outside Belfast there was sniping on the border in the Ballagh area; a week later two border posts were attacked and on 21 September two Special Constables off duty in plain clothes were shot and wounded at Markethill in Co Armagh. On 25 September some Free State troops crossed the border by mistake near Clones. They were at once detained by the Newtownbutler A Specials and later shown their way back and released. This action was in striking contrast to the way the Specials had been treated by the IRA in Clones eight months before.

The Civil War dragged on in the South throughout the autumn. The Free State Government took progressively harsher measures which amounted to a campaign of counter-terror. When the IRA began to murder members of the Dail, the Free State Government, without a suggestion of legality, took four members of the IRA who were in prison and shot them as a reprisal. This ferocious act, something which the Government of Northern Ireland had never even contemplated, was effective and no more members of the Dail were attacked. In October, the Roman Catholic hierarchy condemned the IRA and in a Pastoral, Cardinal Logue said:

'They carry on what they call a war, but which in the absence of any legitimate authority to justify it, is morally only a system of murder and assassination of the National Forces ... the guerrilla warfare now being carried on by the Irregulars is without moral sanction, and, therefore, the killing of National soldiers in the course of it is murder before God, the seizing of public and private property is robbery, the breaking of roads, bridges and railways a criminal destruction, the invasion of homes and the molestation of citizens a grievous crime.' This Pastoral referred, of course, to the operations of the IRA against the Provisional Government in the South. It expresses exactly, however, how the Government of Northern Ireland had felt about the IRA from the beginning and this is what they used the Special Constabulary to counter.

In Belfast in October, a woman was shot by a sniper on the Newtownards Road on 5 October and an extensive haul of arms was found three days later in the same area. At the end of the month a regular arsenal was discovered in the Falls Road, thirty-seven rifles, ten revolvers and 6,000 rounds of ammunition being captured. In general, however, the city was quiet. On the border there were a few incidents, on 14 October there was a shooting affray when a B Special patrol surprised some IRA near Bessbrook and the next day there were skirmishes at Belcoo and Garrison in which shots were exchanged. Two Specials were wounded when their patrol was attacked near Keady but they killed one of their assailants. On 31 October when addressing a parade, Colonel Wickham said,

'... in places where it was once thought unsafe to put a regular constable the Bs were now regarded with respect. He was thinking of a case in which they had the most strenuous opposition from a number of residents when it was proposed to remove a certain unit from the Falls Road. All this went to justify the formation of the Special Constabulary and to show that they carried out their duties impartially.'

On 24 October Lord Fitzalan, the Viceroy, who, under the two rather curious interim constitutions, still reigned in Dublin and had responsibility for Northern Ireland, visited the Province. He arrived from Great Britain at Larne and stayed until 26 October visiting Belfast and Enniskillen. He was received by ceremonial guards, one hundred strong, of all classes of the Special Constabulary at various places. B Specials provided the guards at Larne and the York Road Station in Belfast, A Specials at Enniskillen and C 1 Specials on his departure.

On 19 October, Mr Lloyd George resigned and the Coalition Government collapsed. General Macready records that this was received with satisfaction among the British troops still in the south of Ireland. It was also welcomed in the North and the new administration under Bonar Law was very much more sympathetic to Ulster and its problems. Nevertheless by 22 November, A platoons had all been reduced to a strength of thirty-six men and there were calls for further reductions and for standardization of the organization of the B Specials throughout the country so as to exercise the utmost economy. Nevertheless the Inspector General's suggested strength for the following year was given on 11 December as:

RUC	3,000
A Specials	5,000
B Specials	25,000
C 1 Specials	12,000
Total	45,000

In November there were few incidents in the North, one bomb, which failed to explode was thrown in Belfast and the sentry at the barracks of the A platoon at Ballycastle was fired on. On 19 November Colonel Wickham again referred to the state of the Province. He said the situation in Northern Ireland had greatly improved and they were now passing through a period of normal quietness and were living under settled and reasonable conditions. This was due to all classes of the Constabulary co-operating in the one firm resolve that law and order should be established and maintained. At the end of the month Sir James Craig set off on another tour of the Specials in the border areas. On his return he sent this letter to all members of the Constabulary:

'I wish to place on record my high appreciation of the splendid bearing and discipline of the Officers and Men of the different Branches of Constabulary whom I have had the honour to inspect.

It has been an unqualified pleasure to me to observe a material increase in efficiency and a continued fine attendance on Parade, which testify to the loyal spirit animating all Ranks. . . .

. . . The Government of Northern Ireland thoroughly understands its indebtedness to the Constabulary Forces and I am glad to avail myself of this opportunity of placing it on record and, at the same time, of thanking *you* personally for your services and of tendering you all good wishes for the New Year.

Xmas 1922   James Craig'

The British troops in the South were now concentrated almost completely in the Dublin area, Cork having been evacuated in May. In December the final evacuation took place by sea and on 17 December General Macready sailed for England in HMS *Dragon* from Kingstown. An armoured car company which covered the final embarkation then turned and in two hours safely crossed the border into Northern Ireland. General Cameron now answered for the Northern Ireland District direct to the War Office. The army left in Northern Ireland consisted of twelve battalions of infantry and a few howitzers and armoured cars with a total strength of only 6,529. In December too the army withdrew from the Pettigo and Belleek area which they had occupied since they had recaptured the triangle in June. They were replaced by the RUC and Specials. There was no trouble in Belfast or on the border during the month although the IRA raided Blacklion just on the Free State side of the border which caused some tension.

On 12 December the Duke of Abercorn was sworn in as Governor of Northern Ireland and a permanent guard of A Specials was provided at Government House. When Parliament was prorogued on 14 December, His Excellency said,

'I am gratified that the measures adopted for restoring law

and order in the province have been crowned with success, in achieving which both the Royal Ulster Constabulary and the Special Constabulary have to be congratulated, they have won the confidence of all classes of the community.'

On 20 December the appointment of Military Adviser to the Northern Ireland Government was abolished and General Solly-Flood returned to England. His staff were dispersed and Lieutenant-Colonel J. Sargent, DSO, OBE, was transferred to the headquarters of the Inspector General to deal with all matters to do with the Special Constabulary. The General's exit from the Irish scene went practically unnoticed. Undoubtedly he had been considered by many as a fifth wheel to the coach and when money was short he and his considerable staff were an obvious economy. Certainly the Special Constabulary never looked on him as their leader but put their faith in the Inspector General. The Minister for Home Affairs publicly credited him with obtaining £850,000 worth of arms and equipment free from Great Britain but this was all. In September, General Solly-Flood had put forward a detailed scheme for replacing the A, B, C and C 1 classes of the Specials with what he called a Territorial Special Constabulary which he visualized as a permanent force in Northern Ireland. He pointed out that the A Specials were very expensive and a large number had to be available even when a region was quiet. The B Specials cost £250,000 a year but were not organized in military formations and were immobile. The C 1s were less expensive but came mostly from the cities but they had a degree of mobility. General Solly-Flood considered that the A, B and C 1 Specials should all be replaced by a single force of 30,000 men organized in three Divisions which would be a cross between the Bs and the C 1s. He believed it would cost much less and be available both as a Territorial army to oppose external aggression and as a police force to deal with internal trouble. The scheme evaporated with the General. In any case it was wildly beyond Northern Ireland's pocket and, of course, external attack was properly the responsibility of Westminster.

With the withdrawal of the British Army from the South and the continuation of the civil war, it was clear that plans would have to be made to defend the Province from an organized overt attack from that direction. This was really the business of the British Army but on 9 November 1922, the Inspector General had ordered County Commandants to prepare and submit defence plans to him. On 5 February 1923 he called a conference to bring these plans into line with each other and directed that counties should check their schemes in the near future by twenty-four hour test mobilizations. In these plans it was necessary to be prepared to repel a full scale attack from the South instead of merely trying to prevent infiltration. The defence schemes therefore visualized the mobilization of the whole B force for full time duty and the calling up of the C and C 1 forces. In these plans it was also necessary to continue with as many of the internal security duties as possible and the C Specials were to be utilized for this purpose. The defence of the border was to be undertaken in depth. Close to the frontier would be a zone or line of observation provided by B Special posts and reconnoitring patrols. Further back would be a line of supports provided by the A platoons reinforced by B Specials. Finally reserves of B and C 1 Specials would be concentrated behind the line of supports. The B Specials were to be called up in three stages. 'Preliminary Mobilization' of a part of the B force would enable the A platoons to be reinforced, guards to be provided for RUC stations and some roads, railways and important places. 'Additional Mobilization' involving a substantial proportion of the B men would enable guards for all the above to be increased, and finally 'Complete Mobilization' of the whole force would allow mobile reserves to be formed and the C Specials to be used for many of the patrols normally done by B Specials.

The scheme of defence varied considerably for each county. In Fermanagh, for instance, with eighty-three miles of border, a high proportion of the men were to be stationed on the frontier, some were to be kept back for road and railway protection, but none were to be provided for the protection of

RUC barracks and the reserves did not amount to more than
three companies. In Co Tyrone, although there were two sections of frontier to be held, the rest of the county was able to
mobilize two full battalions. Co Londonderry too was able to
mobilize a battalion known locally as 'The Derry Borderers'.
As an example the disposal of B men in the southern area of
Co Down was planned as follows:

Frontier protection	262
RUC barracks reinforcements	60
Railway, public works and road protection	236
Reserve	107
	665

In the Londonderry City area, the border was guarded by two
A platoons and 196 B men who lived in that area. If there was
a serious attack they had orders to act as scouts and fall back
to a line held by the B Specials of the City. The City B
Specials, 1,251 strong, were to keep back some 370 men to
guard vital points in the City itself and the rest were organized
into a battalion of four companies, 906 strong, which would
move up to hold the defence line.

In the defence schemes for the C 1 force it was visualized
that it might be required either to hold the border or to support the RUC and Special Constabulary in disaffected areas.
For local defence and the maintenance of law and order the A
and B Specials would be mobilized first and the C 1 force
would only be used if they could not compete. It was not
expected that the C 1 Division would be required to man-
oeuvre as a single military formation but the battalions or
companies would be moved to the vicinity of the border or
other trouble spots or to relieve military garrisons for active
operations. Plans were made to accommodate them in various
places from which they could operate, mostly in the border
areas and in the west of the Province. These defence schemes
were completed early in 1923 and were tested by exercises as

instructed by the Inspector General, that in Fermanagh being held in February. The order to mobilize was given without warning and was passed at 7 PM from Enniskillen by wireless. The B Specials living near the border quickly took up their posts and claim that all roads from the Free State were closed within a quarter of an hour. Behind them the A platoons, mobile in their Crossley tenders and reinforced to full strength by B men were ready and kept contact with the scouts on the border by cyclists. Behind were the reserves, in this exercise represented by token forces. The County Commandant toured the area and pronounced himself well satisfied. Thereafter the schemes were kept up to date and ready for use throughout the years 1923 to 1925.

Looking back on this period it is astonishing how little interest the Westminster Government took in its undoubted responsibility for the external defence of Northern Ireland. Throughout the period covering the civil war, there were large forces available in the South and a temptation to unify the two sides by an attack on the North, but the War Office steadily decreased the army garrison of Ulster. It seems that they did not take the threat from the South very seriously and history has proved them to have been right. At the same time they were quite happy to abide by whatever a boundary commission decided even if it meant the ceding of large parts of Northern Ireland to the South. The Northern Ireland Government had, however, adopted a policy of 'not an inch' on the border. Sir James Craig had said as early as January 1922, 'I will never give in to any rearrangement of the boundary that leaves our Ulster area less than it is under the Government of Ireland Act'. There is little doubt that this was behind their readiness to defend the border with the Special Constabulary although of course they had good reason to fear a renewal of the troubles if the large number of men in the internment camps in the South were released. The Westminster Government seems to have accepted this argument as they continued to pay for the Special Constabulary and the Northern Government made no attempt to conceal its composition and organization from them. The result of these policies was that what was wholly the business of British soldiers was being done by the Northern Ireland Special Constabulary. The force available to defend the border was equivalent to two divisions. The 5,000 A Specials were well trained and efficient and up to the standard of first class troops but they had no higher organization than a platoon. The B Specials were by now well trained in musketry but apart from the fact that about half of them were ex-soldiers they had no practise in military tactics and their organization was static. Their strength was their availability and readiness; 23,000 men could be mobilized in a matter of hours. The C 1 force was not so well trained in musketry but was better organized in military units, was more mobile and had some elementary tactical training. The command structure was probably the weakest part. The Commander-in-Chief was the Inspector General of Police with an inadequate staff. It is true that all the senior officers down to Area Commandants were ex-soldiers, but none of them had held a rank higher than Lieutenant-Colonel.

On 11 January 1923 the C 1 force was reorganized and military nomenclature used for the units. The Groups became Brigades and the Districts became Battalions. As before two brigades of eight battalions were raised in Belfast and one brigade of four battalions in the rest of the Province. Civilian transport was organized to move the force when necessary. Each battalion had a strength of twenty-five officers and 800 men and the whole Division had a strength of 10,593. The force was armed mainly with rifles but there were sixteen Lewis Guns for each battalion. Apart from a summer camp, however, training had been very sketchy and, in the absence of any pay, the number of men who attended drills was small. After Sir James Craig had stated publicly that the force was in a good healthy condition and training was proceeding well during the winter months, the battalion commanders wrote a letter of protest. They said they were starved of funds and had the feeling that the Government had lost interest in the force. A committee was formed to remedy matters and £100,000 was allocated in the financial year 1923–4. The committee recommended reducing the force to eleven battalions to provide incentive bonuses for training. Full provision was recommended for the training of five battalions in camp each year. With these proposals the conditions were improved but it is doubted if the force reached the standard of efficiency of the Territorial Army in Great Britain.

There were few incidents to report in the early part of 1923. Tension was increased in February when IRA Irregulars in the course of the civil war attacked the town of Ballyconnell just over the border, and many Protestants there suffered. Nothing could be done about this but when a member of the IRA who lived in the Sperrin Mountains became disillusioned and resigned he needed protection. He was assaulted and his house wrecked by nine armed IRA men. He had the courage to go to the police and brought a case of malicious damage in the Crown Court, made possible by mounting a strong guard of B Specials at his house for many months. With the falling off of incidents it became possible to devote more time for training. In January 1923, authority was given for 170 full-time Sergeant Instructors to be appointed to the B Specials and these were recruited mainly from the ranks of redundant A Specials. An annual musketry course, basically the same as that used by the army, was undergone by the whole force. It included the firing of thirty rounds with a 0.22 rifle on a miniature range, fifty rounds with a 0.303 rifle on a thirty-yard range and sixty rounds up to 400 yards on an open range. Similar annual courses for Lewis Guns and revolvers were laid down. Instructions were given in May for the Ulster Special Constabulary to be trained in accordance with the army 'Infantry Training Vol I 1922', and to drill in the same way as Infantry of the line. In October County Commandants were told by the Inspector General that they should inspect every platoon and sub-district quarterly and that Area Commandants should visit them unofficially more frequently. In November an Officers' course was held at Newtownards for Area Commandants.

In March the British Government grant of £1,500,000 for

the Special Constabulary was less than the estimated expenditure. The difference had to be found by the Northern Ireland Government and on 24 March the Inspector General demanded a strict economy drive. On 1 April the approved strength of the B Specials was:

Belfast	2,200	Londonderry	3,800
Antrim	2,950	Fermanagh	3,200
Armagh	3,350	Tyrone	4,300
Down	3,350		
			23,150

On 1 April new conditions of service were issued. In future B Specials were to be signed on for six-month periods and pay was to be according to the duties performed. The sum of 2s. 6d. was to be paid for each night patrol and 1s. 6d. for each training drill attended. The sum of 5s. was to be paid on satisfactorily completing the annual musketry course and 5s. per day during the twelve days of the annual Summer Camp. When mobilized for full-time service, pay would be 7s. a day.

From 7–10 April, the Earl of Derby, Secretary of State for War, came over to Northern Ireland to make a tour of inspection. He visited Newtownards Camp and inspected a large parade of A, B and C 1 Specials from Cos Antrim, Armagh, Down and Londonderry at Lisburn on 7 April. He attended a church parade of Belfast A, B and C 1 Specials next day. On 9 April he inspected the Fermanagh Specials under Sir Basil Brooke drawn up at St Angelo near Enniskillen organized in four battalions. From there he went on to Omagh and inspected the Tyrone Special Constabulary drawn up in five battalions under Colonel McClintock and here he presented the efficiency cup to Fintona Sub-District. Throughout the tour he was accompanied by Sir James Craig and the Inspector General. Presumably his aim was to satisfy himself on behalf of the British Government that the Special Constabulary was worth the money being spent upon it. From the speeches which he made on this tour and reported in the Press he seems to have been well satisfied.

During the winter of 1922–3 and spring of 1923 the civil war had continued in the South until in April a number of leading men of the IRA were killed or captured. By March the IRA in the South had been reduced to 8,000 men. Faced with great provocation and the same ambushes and murders as had been suffered by the British and later the Specials in the North, the Free State forces were more ruthless and followed a policy of fierce reprisals. On 7 March at Ballyseedy in Co Kerry they secured nine men to a land mine and blew them to pieces and this was by no means an isolated incident. By May the Free State Government had interned and imprisoned the staggering total of 11,316 men and had executed seventy-seven others. On 24 May, de Valera finally capitulated but he did not surrender. The order he gave was to stop fighting and dump arms until a better opportunity occurred. With the ending of the civil war, the Free State Government did not at once release the internees. They were afraid that they would dig up the dumped arms and start again. There was some trouble trying to reduce the size of the Free State Army. The reduction planned was substantial, from 60,000 to 20,000, and the majority of those disbanded faced unemployment. Many of the soldiers felt that the army should not be demobilized but should be used against the North. This explains, to some extent, the reluctance of the Northern Government to reduce the size of the Special Constabulary in spite of the improvement in security in the Province. Throughout 1923 the Special Constabulary maintained its patrols and the curfew remained in force.

In October, conditions in Belfast were reported to be peaceable and orderly: good relations were said to exist between all factions. There was no open IRA activity but some attempts were clearly being made to reorganize and keep the army together. On 9 October shots were fired across the border by Free State soldiers at Carrickaduff in Co Armagh, killing a cow. Although warnings of increased IRA activity on the border had been received this was an isolated incident probably caused by alcohol. Otherwise the whole Province had been quiet for the best part of three months. During this period many demobilized Free State Army soldiers returned to their homes in the North and it was learnt that the Free State Army Headquarters had a large relief model of the whole border area which was disquieting. In November, however, a start was made to repair many of the bridges across the border.

In October it was learned that the British Government grant for the Special Constabulary for the next year would be cut to £1,000,000. The Inspector General recommended that the saving should be made by cutting down the A Specials and mobilized B-men. He proposed to reduce the A Specials working with the RUC in police stations and to cut not only the number of A platoons but the strength of each platoon to thirty men. In Belfast it was proposed to dispense with all mobilized B Specials and to cut the strength of the force from 2,200 to 1,750, the saving being effected gradually by wastage. On 6 November recruiting for the B force was suspended temporarily until these problems could be settled.

The year 1924 was peaceful both in Belfast and throughout the Province. At the end of January, the Inspector General said that patrols could be decreased in many places without risk to security. At the same time he fixed the maximum strength of the B force at 20,000 and as Westminster finally allowed an additional grant of £1,250,000 it was not found necessary to insist on another heavy demobilization of A Specials. By working out new conditions of service for the B Specials which came into force on 1 April 1924, it was possible to keep within this amount. Some of the new conditions were at the request of the B Specials themselves and there was a return to the annual bounty system. Engagements were to be for quarterly periods again and three categories were introduced – Full Patrol, Half Patrol and Reserve. The annual bounty was fixed at £10, £7 and £3 for these categories respectively. All categories were required to carry out nine drills each quarter and in the full- and half-patrol categories, one patrol in every ten nights and one patrol in twenty nights had to be performed in addition. If mobilized the pay remained at 7s. a day. No districts were reduced to the Reserve category as yet but patrolling was cut down and many districts were reduced to the half-patrol category. The strength of the various counties was fixed as follows and recruiting was allowed again within these limits:

Armagh	3,200
Antrim	2,420
Down	2,750
Fermanagh	2,700
Londonderry City	1,350
Co Londonderry	2,150
Tyrone	3,630
Belfast	1,750
	19,950

In one direction the Government decided to spend more money when on 7 February they introduced a new pension order which provided better pensions for members of the USC wounded in the execution of their duty and allowances for widows and children of men who had been killed.

Throughout the year there was continual political tension over the redrawing of the border. It was part of the treaty between the British Government and the Free State that the boundary should be reconsidered but Northern Ireland clung to its policy of 'Not an inch', and refused to nominate a member of a commission to consider the matter. There was now a Labour Government in Britain under Mr Ramsay MacDonald and many meetings between Sir James Craig and Mr Cosgrave were held to try and resolve the problem. On 19 September the Irish Boundary Bill was passed at Westminster setting up a Boundary Commission followed by another Bill empowering Westminster to nominate a member if Northern Ireland declined to do so. On 7 October Sir James Craig made his position quite clear when he declared that if the Boundary Commission was unfavourable to Ulster, by which he probably meant the cession of the whole of Fermanagh and Tyrone, he would resign as Prime Minister and take any necessary steps to defend territory which had been unjustly taken from Northern Ireland. There seems little doubt that this was an added reason for the retention of some 40,000 men in the Ulster Special Constabulary. The Specials never had to be used for this purpose but there is no doubt that their very existence exerted a powerful influence during the negotiations.

In the South the most significant feature in 1924 was the steady release of IRA prisoners and internees. Of the 10,000 detained in the autumn of 1923, less than 2,000 remained in April and 600 by the end of May. In July the total was about 200 and on 16 July de Valera himself was released. Everywhere there were signs that the IRA, which had been totally defeated in the Civil War, was trying to reorganize itself, harrassed however by the Free State Authorities with their powerful Public Safety Act. The growth of the IRA was stunted by the fact that large numbers of the internees had 'signed out' or given an undertaking for good behaviour in future and the IRA would not have any of these men back.

The Free State Army, many of whom had been in the IRA during the struggle with the British, was by no means a stable organization. In March there occurred what was to become known as a 'Mutiny'. An ultimatum was presented to the cabinet by the dissidents who included a major general and a colonel which accused them of failing to move towards a Republican form of government. It wanted the present Free State Army Council dismissed and demanded that demobilization should cease. The Cosgrave Government surmounted this crisis which involved the resignation of a minister and most of the Free State Army Council. There were disturbing features, however, including the desertion with their arms of a number of Free State Army Officers and an attempt to stir up trouble with Great Britain by machine-gunning British troops on leave from the forts on Spike Island in Cork Harbour: one was killed and twenty-three wounded including five civilians. This and a number of other shootings in the South during the year showed that there was a continuing threat of violence and that if there was a *coup d'état* the Free State might well invade the North. Such an invasion would be bound to fail if the British Government honoured its responsibility for external defence: there was always the fear that they would procrastinate until the Free State had seized substantial parts of the country and would then talk instead of throwing them out again. With a Labour Government in power this was considered possible and it was by no means certain that they would repeat Winston Churchill's action at Pettigo and Belleek in 1922. This therefore by itself gave the Northern Government a good reason to keep the Special Constabulary in being.

There are many indications in the police records of the period that the Province had returned to normal. In March long and involved questionnaires were sent out calling for information about the commandeering of bicycles so that compensation could be paid. In the same month the popularity of the A Specials suffered a set-back when they were authorized to act under the Illicit Distillation Acts! In April there was talk of Constabulary golf meetings and in May of the Constabulary sports at Balmoral. In July the Government directed that the curfew was to be enforced leniently so as to cause the least possible inconvenience to the public. On 22 July at Ballywalter a motor cyclist was wounded by a B Special patrol when he failed to stop after curfew. A very different view was taken of this incident than would have been taken at the height of the troubles. The Inspector General minuted, 'The shooting in this case was quite unjustifiable and you must impress on the men under your command the folly of such reckless use of firearms'. Towards the end of the year there was talk of Constabulary Xmas cards and farmers were allowed their shot guns again. On 19 December the curfew was suspended over the Christmas and New Year periods with such happy results that on 30 December it was cancelled altogether.

At the end of October, in a general election the Conservatives under Stanley Baldwin came to power and Westminster became sympathetic to Northern Ireland again. In the election the disputed counties of Tyrone and Fermanagh returned

Unionists with large majorities. They had been able to do this partly because of a split between Sinn Fein and the National- ists, but it was clear that many Roman Catholics had voted Unionist and this greatly strengthened the case of Northern Ireland in the boundary question.

In January 1925 Sir James Craig held a meeting with General Cameron to discuss defence and co-operation between the Special Constabulary and the army. The army had by this time been reduced to one brigade of five battalions with a battery of howitzers and an armoured car company, the whole amounting to scarcely 3,000 men. General Cameron said that he hoped to be reinforced at once in emergency with a second brigade headquarters and another battery of artillery. If re- quired a second brigade of four battalions would probably be forthcoming. General Cameron said that he did not expect the army would be required unless the Free State Government itself took part in hostilities and that the Special Constabulary would be able to deal with any lesser danger. As the Special Constabulary was so much larger than the army, he felt that it was better to leave the two commands separate. If the Govern- ment of Northern Ireland wished the GOC to take command of both forces, this would, of course, be possible but the ad- ministration of the Special Constabulary would have to remain under the Inspector General.

During 1925, the underground IRA in the South was hounded and kept in subjection by the Free State Authorities using the Treasonable Offences Act. Increasingly, Republicans turned to political action rather than force. In the North the Province, including Belfast, remained quiet. The patrols of the B Specials were continued on a reduced scale and they had orders only to stop people and vehicles acting suspiciously. Attention was called to the serious risk under the Common Law of the unjustifiable use of firearms by the police. The Inspector General pointed out that even under the Special Powers Act, fire could only be opened if there was no other means of making an arrest and that an offence must actually have been committed and not merely suspected.[1] There was

concern that the police should be seen to be impartial at all
times. In May the Inspector General said that he had heard
that a policeman had officiated as referee at a football match
and that this was not to occur again unless both teams were
police.[2] Police correspondence was increasingly concerned
with economy. In February the Inspector General wrote, 'Now
that the conditions in the Province have reached a more normal state ... it is desirable that all ranks ... should review
critically all items of expense ... and to institute every possible economy'. In February the services of B Special Orderly
Officers at the City Commandant's headquarters were dis-
pensed with and the strength of the City B Specials was reduced to 1,300. There was a great deal of attention paid to
training. County Commandants were told to see that the training of A Special Platoons was continuous and not confined to
intensive training periods. The training of B Specials was to
emphasize field duties, minor tactics, fire control and use of
ground and was to be carried out up to platoon level. The C 1
force carried out simple tactical exercises from time to time.
On 6 March 1925 a typical exercise was carried out at
Ligoniel by one of the Belfast Battalions. The battalion was
divided into two forces, 'White' acting as the rearguard of a
force retiring to the north-west was overtaken by 'Green'.
White force took up a position covering the road and forced
Green to deploy and attack. Green then took the position and
formed an outpost line and White retired in good order. The
battalion then reformed and marched back to barracks with a
band.

The cost of the Special Constabulary was, of course, a matter of continual concern to the British and Northern Ireland
Governments. With the return of normal conditions there was
strong pressure to cut down the force and save money. Sir
James Craig still wished to keep the Specials in being for the
threat from the Free State and the IRA could not yet be dis-
counted. The main Free State Army had now been reduced to
a strength of 20,000 which was slightly larger than that allowed by the Treaty.[3] The Free State Army had cost

£7,000,000 in 1924 out of a total revenue of £26,000,000 which was a severe burden to them, and further reductions were inevitable in the near future. Sir James Craig gave September 1926 to the British Government as the date on which he could begin to disband the Specials and until then it was estimated that they would cost about £2,250,000 of which Westminster were reluctant to contribute more than £500,000.

On 3 December 1925, a Boundary Agreement was signed in London by the British Government and the Governments of Northern Ireland and the Irish Free State. It set aside the report of the Boundary Commission which had awarded the largely Roman Catholic parts of Cos Fermanagh and Armagh to the South and Protestant east Donegal to the North, and agreed to leave the border unchanged. The immediate result was a great improvement in relations with the Irish Free State and a Special Constabulary of some 33,000 could no longer be justified. Sir James Craig therefore agreed to start to wind them up and to accept a final payment of £1,200,000 from the British Government after which whatever Special Constabulary was retained would have to be maintained by Northern Ireland without any assistance from Westminster. The British Government also wrote off an outstanding bill of £700,000 for arms, ammunition and equipment.

The most expensive part of the force were the 3,553 men of the full time Class A Special Constabulary and it was clear that, with the RUC now on its feet and in full control, they would have to go. Also with the border settled the maintenance of the C 1 force could no longer be justified. It would be too much to hope that the IRA was dead forever and some force would need to be kept which was within the pocket of the Northern Ireland Government. On 9 December when the details of the boundary settlement were given to the Westminster Parliament it was announced that the Ulster Special Constabulary would be disbanded in due course and that a final payment of £1.2 million would be made. Next day Sir James Craig announced in the Northern Ireland Parliament that the A and C1 forces would be disbanded at once but the B force would be kept in a modified form. Most of the £1.2 million promised by Westminster was already committed and the A Specials could not be given more than two months' full pay on disbandment. Sir James said he hoped the employers of Northern Ireland would be generous to these men and that they would do their best to absorb them into employment. He went on to say that the Bs were to all intents a voluntary force already and would not prove too expensive in the future. 'Night after night they have patrolled the roads and guarded the lives and liberties of the people without regard to class or creed', and it would be most unwise to disband them altogether.

Disbandment came as a shock to the A Special Constabulary who did not realize that it was even in the wind. Some of them had been policemen for five years and they had come to look on their jobs as practically permanent. During the next few days the more militant members, backed, it is suspected, by a few of the officers, held meetings and on 14 December the contingents in Londonderry and at Ballycastle openly showed their opposition to disbandment. They kept their discipline and continued with their duties but they put their officers under open arrest and placed a guard on their arms, stores and equipment. Their opposition to disbandment was partly that they felt it was unsafe for the country to dispense with their services and partly that they were almost certain to go 'on the dole' when disbanded and were dissatisfied with the conditions of discharge. They already had in fact some slight grievances about differences in their pay compared with the RUC, but they could have no possible legal claim for a demand which they seemed to be making for a substantial bounty. They had earned a bonus instead of pension but this had already been paid out to them quarterly at their request. During the next few days the 'strike' or 'work in' as it would probably now be called, spread to Belfast and some other platoons in the country. The Class A Special Constables attached to the RUC were unaffected as were most of the platoons on the border. The officers were then allowed to come and go as they pleased but were not permitted to exercise authority. Strict discipline was, however, still maintained. On 16 December after a meeting of the representative body of the force in Belfast, a demand was put forward for a £200 bounty free of tax in return for which they undertook not to claim unemployment benefit for a year. Next day the Inspector General offered to meet the men to discuss their grievances if they would return to duty.

On 18 December, the Minister for Home Affairs issued an ultimatum, 'These terms have been adopted as the result of much care and deliberation, and I am authorized to state, with the full concurrence of every member of the Cabinet, that they are final and conclusive. In saying this I have in mind the fact that some members of the A force, and I am glad to say that the number is not considerable, have during the last 48 hours been adopting an attitude which certainly is not in keeping with that spirit of loyalty which they have hitherto shown. The Government are willing to attribute this improper attitude which they have adopted to a want of consideration on their part or it may be to unwise advice, but to whatever cause it may be due the Government now wish to make it plain that the terms which have now been decided upon cannot be augmented, and if after the publication of these terms ... any officer or man displays any indication of insurbordination he will thereby render himself liable to immediate dismissal and will forfeit any of the benefits which the Government's proposals offer.'

By next day the 'strike' had collapsed. The officers took over again and things returned to normal. The Strike committee accepted the Government's terms after making one more unsuccessful attempt to get three months' pay instead of two. On 22 December 700 men were paid off in Belfast and 500 to 600 in Co Tyrone and the whole force had been disbanded by Christmas except for a rearguard to dispose of the stores and move out of the temporary barracks all over the Province in which they had been accommodated. It was sad that a force which had done so well should have ended like this. The way in which the news was broken to them was a contributory cause. They heard the news and the terms second-hand from Parliament through the Press without explanation and a similar mistake six years later led to the mutiny of the fleet at Invergordon. Who are we in these days of redundancy pay, much higher employment and the welfare state, to blame them?[4]

The 'troubles' of the twenties in Ireland which began in 1919 were now definitely at an end and it is appropriate at this point to assess the part played in them by the Ulster Special Constabulary. Winston Churchill, referring to partition and the Government of Ireland Act of 1920 says, 'From that moment the position of Ulster became unassailable.... Every argument of self-determination ranged itself henceforward upon their side.... They were masters in their own house, and small though it might be, it was morally and logically founded upon a rock'. This then was the justification for Ulster defending itself against Sinn Fein and those who wished to bully it into a united Ireland by force. Ulster loyalists have never felt that they were partitioned off from the rest of Ireland but rather that they have remained part of the United Kingdom and that it was the South which seceded. The key factor in their successful defence was the existence of the Special Constabulary. The A Specials arrived in the nick of time to reinforce the disintegrating RIC and to re-establish the rule of law throughout the Province. The B Specials, working voluntarily for practically no reward, gave confidence to the majority of the people to resist Sinn Fein. They established a grip on the country which the IRA was never able to break. In the campaign of 1921 and 1922, forty-nine of them were killed and many more wounded. These figures do not begin to tell the tale of endurance and bravery needed to fight a savage enemy. Without them it is doubtful if Great Britain would have had the will to defend Ulster. Far from being 'the agents of imperialism' or the instruments of British power in Ireland, they were the bulwark of the vast majority of the people of the Province. As Tim Pat Coogan has said in his history of the

IRA, they were 'the rock on which any mass movement by the IRA in the North has inevitably foundered'.

NOTES

1. It was an offence for a person to refuse to halt when called upon by the police but it had to be certain that they had heard or seen the order.

2. It is as well the Inspector General had not heard of an incident at Strabane during the Truce with the South when an IRA officer who had entered Northern Ireland was under arrest. He was released to officiate in place of a referee who had failed to turn up for a football match between two teams of B Specials!

3. The Treaty stipulated that the Irish Free State should not keep an army larger than the British in proportion to the population.

4. One can almost hear their political opponents saying, 'There you are, I told you they were undisciplined!' but the London Metropolitan Police went on strike in 1918 and no one could say they were undisciplined.

CHAPTER FIVE

The Struggle for Existence

The new year 1926 left the B and C Specials as the only surviving parts of the Ulster Special Constabulary. On 26 January all recruiting for the B-men was closed until further orders, the aim being to reduce the size of the force. On 4 February recruiting for the C Specials was also stopped and this branch gradually withered away. The need to save money was still paramount and the drive for economy was greater as the IRA in the North was quiescent. The IRA in the South, however, had again reached a strength of 20–25,000 but was engaged in a great deal of political haggling and they had not made up their minds on the future direction of their policy. They were handicapped by lack of funds, American contributions having dried up. On 16 March the salaries of Area Commandants were decreased and the whole of the B Force was ordered to revert to the Reserve category by 1 April. This meant that they were reduced to a £3 a year bounty for which drill periods only would have to be attended. From this date the B Specials ceased to make patrols and to be an active police force. On 19 April the Inspector General laid down that no B-men would be demobilized solely for the purpose of reducing the strength of the force. Dismissals would be made only for inefficiency, failure to attend drills or other irregularities and the force reduced solely by normal wastage. The Public Accounts Committee was, however, close behind him and complained that the expenditure on the police was still too high. They cited the misuse of vehicles, excessive mileage claims and excessive postage, telephone and telegraph charges as fields in which further economy could be made.[1]

In April the reorganized Ulster Special Constabulary took shape. Under the Inspector General, who also commanded the RUC, was Lieutenant-Colonel J. Sargent, DSO, OBE, with the title of Chief Staff Officer. His staff consisted of three staff officers and three civilians and was divided into three sections. The first dealt with administration and finance; the second with training and the third with stores and accommodation. Some matters such as arms and ammunition were dealt with by a single department shared with the RUC. In each county there was a permanent full-time staff of from fifteen to eighteen headed by the County Commandant at a salary of £450 per annum. There were from two to four Area Commandants at £400 per annum and an Accounts Officer at £250 per annum. In the non-commissioned ranks there were eight to nine Sergeant Instructors, an armourer and two clerks. The half dozen or so District Commandants and the forty odd Sub-District Commandants in each County were part-time and paid £50 and £15 per annum respectively. The whole force, now about 15,000 strong, cost approximately £100,000 a year to run. On 23 June the number of training periods required each quarter was reduced from six of one and a half hours' duration to four of two hours. Throughout the rest of the year the force settled down to a routine of drills, rifle meetings and social occasions. In November the need to retain the force was emphasized by the IRA attacks in the South on twelve Garda barracks in which two policemen were killed.

In March 1927, the Northern Ireland Government gave another turn of the financial screw. The strength of the Ulster Special Constabulary by this time was 14,900 and had cost £94,347 during the previous year. The Ministry of Finance now demanded that expenditure on the force be reduced to £50,000 a year. After an agonizing reappraisal the appointments of the nineteen Area Commandants were terminated with one month's notice and they were replaced by eight Adjutants, one for each county. The Sergeant Instructors were reduced in number from fifty-eight to thirty-eight and the clerks from fourteen to seven. The County Commandants had their 'locomotory' allowance cut and the Sub-District Commandants had their pay reduced. At the same time new conditions of service were brought in for the main body of the force. The Reserve category was divided into Sections A and B. Section A was much as before but the training periods were reduced to two instead of four and the annual bonus from £3 to £2. Section B was a new category which was to be optional. It required no drills but simply attendance at one parade a year at which all uniform and equipment had to be produced in good condition. Subject to this the reward would be the princely sum of 5s. per annum. This scheme was not a success financially as by June only 101 men had transferred to Section B of the Reserve.

In the middle of 1927, the strength of the Ulster Special Constabulary was:

Full-time	6	County Commandants
	8	Adjutants
	7	Accounts Officers
	37	Sergeant Instructors[2]
	6	Armourers
	7	Clerks
	7	Mobilized Special Constables
Part-time	25	District Commandants
	325	Sub-District Commandants
	2,053	Sergeants
	12,317	Special Constables

The County Commandants at this time were:

Belfast and Antrim	Colonel H. R. Charley, CBE
Armagh	Captain C. R. Ensor, OBE
Down	Major D. Ker, OBE
Fermanagh	Captain Sir Basil Brooke, Bt, CBE, MC
Londonderry	Lieutenant-Colonel F. S. N. Macrory, DSO
Tyrone	Colonel J. K. McClintock, CBE, DL, ADC

During the year the North remained quiet but on 10 July 1927, the Minister of Justice in the Free State was murdered by gunmen. In August the Free State Government passed the Public Safety Act which gave the police more power. They continued to harass the IRA, who were not very dangerous at the time and whose effort was mainly devoted to holding their organization together. In 1928 a detective was shot in Dublin but the Government felt able to repeal the Public Safety Act. Nevertheless the southern authorities continued to make life difficult for the IRA and in the North the RUC kept a watchful eye on them.

The B Special training continued to emphasize musketry and there were competitions between Sub-Districts, Districts and Counties. An example of the standard achieved in Belfast and Antrim is as follows:

	Co. Antrim Rifle	Belfast Revolver
Marksmen	119	131
1st Class Shots	271	290
2nd Class Shots	438	401
3rd Class Shots	319	248
Total who fired	1,147	1,070

During 1928 the B Specials were used only twice. Two hundred of them were called up to reinforce the RUC during the first Ulster Tourist Trophy Race and one hundred were used as a ceremonial guard for a visit by the Princess Royal. With no recruiting, by the end of the financial year total strength was down to 14,166 but still only 219 had transferred to the Class B Reserve. The force had therefore cost £56,000. In July the Ministry of Finance began to say that it was desirable to bring the cost of the force down to £30,000 a year. The Inspector General believed that it was not possible to economize any more without large scale compulsory retirement, which the Prime Minister had promised would not happen. In the end there were no reductions and in March 1929 the estimates were approved on the same scale as the year before. With recruiting at a standstill and the consequent wastage reducing the size of the force, there were many undesirable results. The belief was engendered that the Government intended to let the force die out by degrees and this was bad for morale. At the same time the average age was rising. The older men stayed on to keep the strength up when it is probable that if recruiting had been resumed, they would have retired and made room for younger men. The waste too was found to be uneven. Some units such as the District in the Petigo-Belleek triangle were seriously under strength while the other less important units had not even been reduced to their establishment. The Ministry of Finance was perturbed that half the money available was being spent on the small permanent staff and felt that this was disproportionate. On 2 September 1929 the total establishment of the force was lowered by 20,000 to 12,187 but the reduction was still to be achieved by wastage. Recruiting was however allowed whenever a unit was below the new establishment.

On 12 May 1929, Captain Sir Basil Brooke, the founder of the Special Constabulary in Co Fermanagh and its County Commandant from the beginning, retired to enter politics. He was relieved by Lieutenant-Colonel H. S. Richardson and on leaving he was appointed an Honorary County Commandant. The Inspector General was required to convey to Captain Brooke 'an expression of the Government's appreciation of the most valuable services rendered by him to the Special Constabulary since its inception, and of the regret which they feel at the impending retirement of Sir Basil from active participation in the work of the Special Constabulary'. Captain Brooke had been awarded the CBE in 1922 for his services to the Ulster Special Constabulary.

At the beginning of 1930, new conditions of service were issued and the number of patrols required in the Full and Half Patrol categories was decreased. The only difference which affected the force, which was all in reserve, was that the number of drills required was raised to one a month. The categories were again altered and the force divided into Section A, composed of active personnel and Section B of the Reserve. Section A was subdivided into Full Patrol, Half Patrol and

Drill categories. The majority of the force were now therefore in Section A Drill category instead of Section A of the Reserve category which was just a change of name. There was criticism in Parliament as well as in the Civil Service that roughly half the cost of the whole force was spent on the permanent staff and there was pressure to reduce County Commandants' pay. The County Commandants were understandably indignant. They pointed out that they had to administer 2,000 men which included their training, discipline, pay, clothes, arms and equipment. They had to do a great deal of work in the evenings and at weekends visiting their units. They pointed out that their pay had been halved since 1925, that they were not entitled to a pension and their terms of service compared very unfavourably with the Territorial Army. These objections seem to have been accepted as they staved off any reduction for a year.

By the beginning of 1931, the strength of the Ulster Special Constabulary had fallen naturally to its establishment. The strength in the various counties in January, with the names of their commandants, was:

County	Active (A) (Drill Category)	Reserve (B)	Commandant
Antrim	1,411	4	Col H. R. Charley, CBE
Belfast	1,066	—	Col H. R. Charley, CBE
Armagh	1,664	2	Capt C. H. Ensor, OBE
Down	1,861	2	Col H. Waring, MBE
Fermanagh	1,745	53	Lt-Col H. S. C. Richardson, DL, ADC
Londonderry City	921	27	S. W. Kennedy Esq
Londonderry County	1,171	49	Lt-Col F. S. N. Macrory, DSO
Tyrone	2,062	112	Col J. K. McClintock, CBE, DL, ADC
	11,901	249	

Total 12,150

In March 1931 in the Great Depression, the financial situation necessitated drastic reductions in the expenditure of every department of Government. The Ministry of Finance decreed that the most that could be spent on the Special Constabulary was £20,000 a year, a reduction of £34,000. The Inspector General decided at once 'to meet the practically unanimous desire of the members of the Force to remain as a live organization with full opportunities for maintaining efficiency', not to disband any of the men but to put them all into Section B Reserve, that is to do one parade a year with equipment for a bonus of 5s. This was done on 1 April 1931. Any training would be voluntary and unpaid and it was decided to make a generous allowance of ammunition, of which there was plenty in stock, to allow weapon practices to continue. Obviously considerable cuts in the permanent staff were also necessary and, while something was worked out, all the full-time staff were given a month's notice. In the end it was decided to reduce the headquarters staff to one permanent Staff Officer, a clerk and a typist. In the counties the Adjutants and Accounts Officers went and only one permanent organizing officer was left, in most cases the County Commandant himself. Instructors were cut to twenty-four[2] and armourers to three and three mobilized B-men were sanctioned to help out. The pay of these officers and men was cut by 7 per cent. In the interim financial year 1931/32 this still cost £31,340 but the estimates for 1932/33 were £21,413, subdivided as follows:

Pay of Permanent Staff	£9,874
Bounties of B-men	£3,047
Ammunition for practice and hire of Ranges and Drill Halls	£3,348
Miscellaneous	£5,144

From that time the rifle meeting became almost the sole activity of the B Specials. They still kept their weapons in their homes and maintained them themselves. In winter they practised with 0.22 rifles on indoor miniature ranges but in summer they used their own 0.303 rifles in open ranges. Shooting competitions were frequent and most of the photographs of the Specials of this period show successful rifle teams and cups being presented by various dignitaries.

The activities of the IRA in the North during this period were confined to participation in labour disputes and 'red' political activity. In the South they had been involved in attempts to intimidate juries and a juror had actually been shot in 1929. The situation was brought under control by the Free State Government's Juries Protection Bill, but in January 1929 a Garda was killed by a booby trap. Early in 1931 they shot a detective and also killed one of their own men whom they had branded as a police informer. In 1931 the annual procession to Wolfe Tone's grave at Bodenstown, a great Republican occasion, was banned by the Free State Government. The ban was defied successfully and 15,000 IRA attended. In July another witness was assassinated and the Government responded by writing a Public Safety Article into the constitution. Under this they banned the IRA and eleven other organizations and military tribunals were set up. The IRA responded by causing a riot on Armistice Day but in general the Free State Government seemed to have the situation in hand. In February 1932, however, the Free State general election returned de Valera and the Fianna Fail party to power. This was the political party which had grown out of the Republican or IRA side in the civil war. The IRA had actively canvassed for it and the new Minister of Defence had fought as an IRA Divisional Commander against the Free State Army over which he was now to preside. This new Government at once suspended the orders made under the Public Safety Article of the Constitution; the police were ordered to cease harassing the IRA and in a case where the police shot two IRA men they were taken to task. As a result the IRA began to expand again and is estimated to have been some 30,000 strong at this time.

These upheavals south of the border were bound to worry the Northern Government just at a time when they had for financial reasons to reduce the Special Constabulary to its nadir. Some 150 B-men had been mobilized for a day to reinforce the RUC for the celebrations of the Royal Black Perceptory at Newry but the training and organization of the force except in shooting practices, had suffered by the lack of money. In July the Government of Northern Ireland decided to bring 3,200 B Specials in the border areas to a higher state of readiness. The conditions of service had again been altered on 1 July 1932, the Half-Patrol Category was abolished and the active (Section A) of the force was now divided into simply a Patrol Category and a Drill Category. It was Section A Drill Category to which these men were advanced. Four part-time officers had also to be enrolled in addition to nine more Sergeant Instructors and a clerk. The annual cost of this increased preparedness was £15,000. There had been some minor sectarian trouble in Belfast and several towns in 1931. In 1932, there were disturbances among the unemployed of both religions and some sectarian incidents in which Protestants were undoubtedly the aggressors, but all of these were dealt with by the RUC in their stride. Nevertheless the Belfast City Commandant of the Specials began to worry and to bring his orders up to date. He complained that it was difficult to find out what had happened in the bad troubles of 1922, ten years before. The Belfast force was still in the Reserve category and its strength stood at 1,029 which was seventy-six below establishment. Although voluntary training had been well attended and the revolver practice of the vast majority was up to standard, the organization was inevitably somewhat rusty. After consultation with the City Commissioner of the RUC, who emphasized that the role of the City Specials was to work closely with the regular police, a plan was drawn up. It was assumed that it was unlikely that the Specials would be required at very short notice and that their function, unlike the country forces, would be to work entirely as a reserve for the RUC. In what was called an anticipatory period, detailed planning would take place. In a precautionary period the whole B force would be placed in the Active Patrol Category (Section A). Finally, if mobilization was ordered all the B-men would be called up for full-time service. Normally action would be initiated by the City Commissioner who would ask the City Commandant for assistance. In emergency any regular RUC officer, however, had the power to call on his attached Special Constables for help.

In the periods when the Opposition at Stormont deigned to take their seats, they did their best to get the Specials disbanded. In 1932 Mr McAteer asked, in view of the very favourable reports of judges as to the state of the peace, whether the Government should not disband the B Specials and hand their arms over to the RUC. This was a theme which continued to the end. There is no doubt that a great many of the Catholic population resented the fact that this force existed. It gave them a sense of insecurity to feel that their political opponents were uniformed and armed. At the same time Republican political circles and propaganda played upon this fear and, in spite of the fact that the Specials were not used for any purpose at this time, tried to dub them as some form of political police which was, of course, nonsense.

In the South the years 1932 and 1933 saw the emergence of a popular anti-IRA movement of a fascist type called the Blueshirts under General O'Duffy who had been dismissed as Commissioner of Police. Throughout 1934 there were clashes between these groups which were suppressed by the Gardai. The military tribunals sat again and handed out sentences to both sides. During this period the only trouble in the North was the murder of two members of the RUC by the IRA. By 1935 de Valera's government had become totally disenchanted with the IRA and in March, because of its intervention in trade disputes, the split opened. The police, especially the S-branch which was now mostly composed of ex-IRA men, acted and by April, 104 of the IRA were in prison. In May a Garda was shot and the situation became similar to that which persisted during Mr Cosgrave's Government.

In July 1935, Belfast erupted again. On 3 July some shooting began but the real trouble started on 12 July when an orderly Orange procession was fired upon on three separate occasions resulting in serious rioting in which three members of the RUC were shot and two civilians were killed and fifty wounded. The RUC did its best to keep the sides apart and erected barricades. By 15 July three more people had been killed and another twenty injured. On this day the City Commandant wrote to the Inspector General enquiring if the B Specials were not going to be used. He asked what was the use of training the men for so many years, if they were not to be called up when the situation was so serious. Two days later, the RUC, still trying to compete with serious rioting, arson and sniping, were feeling the strain; the army were asked to assist[3] and the whole of the City B Specials were placed in the Active Patrol category (Section A). A curfew was imposed but the troubles continued into August especially in the York Street–Queen Street area. The Church of Ireland Dean of Belfast described the position from 12 July: 'In that and the following days horrible events took place ... sectarian-political passions in Belfast have a low explosive point. The mobs on both sides broke loose. To describe the shooting and evictions as a one-sided programme is absurdly unjust.' The RUC, backed up by the army and the City B Specials, struggled against this disorder. By the time the situation was brought under control, eleven people had been killed and 574 injured. There were 367 cases of malicious damage and 133 cases of arson. Over 300 families belonging to both sides were evicted and a wholesale polarization of the community took place. As the Specials were simply used to reinforce the RUC, it is impossible to single out any particular incidents in which they were involved. They were used to replace regular police in routine duties and for guarding barracks rather than active suppression of the riots. Often they were simply used to replace the RUC in quiet areas so that the riot areas could be reinforced. The Specials were called on at short notice in the holiday season and the response was very satisfactory. In spite of their long period in reserve their assistance was invaluable. They were kept in the Patrol category until the end of the year and received one half of the £10 bonus for which they had to do one night's work a week. If they were fully mobilized they were paid 6s. 6d. a day. A problem arose as some of the Specials were unemployed and when put in the Patrol category they lost their unemployment benefit. After much negotiation the Assistance Board agreed to ignore 50 per cent of their income so that they did not lose by serving. Subsequently the Inspector General wrote 'It is satisfactory to record that during the whole period of their active employment they (the Specials) have maintained that high standard of discipline which is the hallmark of all good police forces and have preserved throughout the confidence of the public, the Royal Ulster Constabulary ... and those responsible ... for the maintenance of law and order'.

A sinister move was made in April 1935, when the IRA convention carried a resolution to attack in the North in the next six months. Preparations were made and a plan to use an IRA Active Service Unit from Cork to raid the military barracks at Armagh was evolved. Just as it was about to be put into execution, the IRA believed that the operation had been compromised and it was called off. There is, however, no indication that the RUC knew about it as their contact in Belfast had been shot by the IRA. Certainly the B Specials were not ready. Even in the border areas they were still in the Drill category and were making no patrols. After this, however, IRA policy changed again and no more action against the North was planned for the time being.

In December 1935, the IRA, having been very active in the riots during the summer, decided to raid the armoury of the Officers Training Corps at Campbell College in Belfast. The raid was a disaster, the RUC intercepted the raiders and after a lot of shooting captured some of them. In April 1936, the RUC had another success and captured the whole northern leadership of the IRA, with two officials from the headquarters in Dublin for good measure. They were engaged at the time in a 'court-martial' in Belfast. It was obvious that RUC intelligence in both these cases was based on inside knowledge and a witch-hunt ensued within the IRA.

In February and March 1936, the IRA murdered three

people in the South, one of them being Admiral Sommerville, a retired officer living in Castletownsend, Co Cork, who was accused of recruiting for the British Services. In May and June the Southern Government really clamped down on the IRA. A large number of them were arrested and the organization was again proscribed. The annual march to Bodenstown was not only banned but the ban was enforced. Mr de Valera believed that now he was in power, everything for which the IRA had fought in the civil war would be achieved in due course. The IRA therefore had no purpose and should disband itself. In the middle of 1936 the situation was to a certain extent eased by the departure for Spain of numbers of both the Blueshirts and the IRA to fight on opposite sides in the civil war.

In fact the IRA was so disorganized by regular police action north and south of the border that they were very little danger for nearly two years. During this time the Northern Government continued to economize on the Specials but the force was kept in a remarkably virile state by voluntary effort. In 1935 the City Commandant was asking for more permanent staff as he said that the amount of voluntary training being done was now greater than the compulsory training before the force was put in reserve. In April 1936 the purse strings were slightly eased and an allowance for meals at shooting competitions was authorized but was only 9d. a head for teams of 'not more than eight'! In the following month, however, the 1931 cuts in pay were restored and Special Constables in the Reserve Category had their bonus doubled from 5s. to 10s. a year. New conditions of service came out in July 1936, with minor alterations to the number of patrols and drills to be done in various categories. In May there had been a Parliamentary question from the Unionist side objecting to the appointment of a retired regular army officer as County Commandant in Co Down instead of promoting someone who had been in the Specials for years. The Minister for Home Affairs' answer is interesting. He said the duties were largely of a military nature and experience of training, command of men and administration was required. The officer concerned was also a native of Co Down and no member of the B force had the same qualifications. The B Specials had, as a glance at the names of the County Commandants will show, always been commanded by ex-regular soldiers of the British Army. Only one civilian had reached the rank of County Commandant since their inception. The same had been true of Area Commandants when they existed but the majority of District and Sub-District Commandants were civilians or sometimes ex-non-commissioned officers. The age distribution of the Belfast Specials in 1937 has been recorded and is of interest:

Age Group	Number	Percentage
Over 50	180	17·6
46–50	100	9·8
41–45	118	11·6
36–40	199	19·5
30–35	184	18
Under 30	240	23·5

Early in 1937, Colonel McClintock, who had been the County Commandant of Co Tyrone since the beginning of the Special Constabulary, died. He had been awarded the CBE in 1922 for his services and was a great loss. He was succeeded by Lieutenant-Colonel M. F. Hammond Smith, MC, who retired from the army to take up the appointment. In July 1937, King George VI and Queen Elizabeth visited Ulster after their coronation. Detachments of B Specials were mobilized for three days and sent to Belfast to line the streets. A year later in July 1938, the Co Londonderry Specials saw action when several hundred IRA and their sympathizers suddenly swooped on the town of Maghera and tried to burn the Orange decorations put up for 12 July. This started a major riot in which the few RUC available were completely overwhelmed. An attempt was also made to burn the RUC barracks. The shooting was heard three miles away at Upperlands and in a very short time the local B Specials were mobilized: they rescued the RUC several of whom were injured, and restored order in under twenty minutes just as the RUC from Magherafelt arrived.

The District Commandant and three others were commended for their prompt action by the Inspector General. It is to be noted that the B Specials were in the Reserve category at the time.

In April 1938, the leadership of the IRA changed and it was decided to prepare for a bombing campaign in England. The IRA was by no means unanimously behind this policy and many felt that the plan was foolhardy. Nevertheless preparations went ahead for six months or so and it was then decided to have a trial run in the North. In November an attempt to blow up customs posts at Clady and Strabane in Co Tyrone ended in disaster and a premature explosion killed three IRA men. Other customs posts were, however, successfully blown up the next night. The RUC at once increased their pressure on the IRA in the North and on 22 December they arrested and interned a number under the Special Powers Act. At the same time the whole B force was placed in the Active Patrol category. On 12 January 1939, the IRA sent an 'ultimatum' to Lord Halifax, the British Foreign Secretary, to withdraw all armed forces from the north of Ireland or war would be declared. On 16 January the bombing campaign began with explosions in London, Manchester and Birmingham and continued for the next few days. On 25 January the Inspector General in Northern Ireland warned that although there had been no further explosions in the Province, the police must assume that there would be. He emphasized that the best antidote was irregular offensive patrolling and to be prepared for attack. He warned B Specials that they must be particularly careful not to have their arms stolen and to realize that after their long period of inactivity they needed a lot of training. There were often complaints that the B Specials were very quick on the trigger at their road blocks. The fact of the matter was that when they ordered a vehicle to stop, they meant STOP. If a car tried to bluff its way through, fire would indeed be opened. If this policy had not been adopted then the IRA would simply have ignored the road blocks. On 25 March 1939, a car drove fast through a road block at Tamlaght in Co

Derry. The Specials had little time to act and fired a warning shot in the air as instructed. As this had no effect they fired a second shot right through the near side front wheel bursting the tyre and bringing the car to a halt. The occupants of the car were both embarrassed cousins of the local District Commandant and said that they thought the red light signal to stop was a bicycle! The B Specials at this road block had to think very quickly on this occasion and displayed first-class marksmanship. They were rightly complimented by the District Commandant and his cousins were told not to drive so fast. In June the IRA started posting bombs in letter boxes in England and in the south of Ireland the annual Bodenstown march became a riot. De Valera was furious at the IRA bombing campaign in England which wrecked his plans for a political solution to the border. On 14 June he brought in the Offences Against the State Act including military tribunals again. In July the British Government after there had been 127 explosions, which had killed one person and wounded fifty-five, brought in the Prevention of Violence Bill. This allowed arrest on suspicion, control of immigration, and the deporting and restriction of movement of Irish Nationals. The bombing campaign in England did not, however, spread to Ulster but went on throughout the year being particularly bad in May. In July there were explosions in left-luggage rooms and then in August an explosion in a crowded shopping area in Coventry killed five people and wounded sixty. In general, thereafter, the counter measures by the police in Great Britain under the Prevention of Violence Act were gradually more successful and by the end of the year the campaign had died away. Counter measures in England were, of course, much easier than in Ireland. In England the Irish stood out among the population, who were not afraid to inform on them, and they had no sanctuaries, such as the Catholic areas of Belfast, where they could hide. At the same time it was much easier to control traffic across the Irish Sea than across the border. There were sixty-six convictions by September and later two of those implicated in the Coventry explosion were tried and executed. In August with the threat of war with Germany, with whom the IRA were known to be already in contact, the B Specials were ordered to guard vulnerable places in addition to their patrols.

On reflection the survival of the B Specials in this period of financial stringency from the end of the 'troubles' to the opening of the Second World War was remarkable. It was more due to the men themselves than the Northern Ireland Government. The B Specials existed literally on a shoe-string and were almost entirely a voluntary organization. This is the more commendable when it is recalled that this was a period of appalling unemployment. The men seemed to know instinctively that the IRA was not dead and that they would be required again. The Government concentrated on weapon efficiency which being a sport, the men were happy to take part in for no reward. The opposition politicians knew how important the B Specials were for the defence of Northern Ireland and never missed an opportunity to snipe at them. Throughout the period they were very seldom used and when they were their conduct was exemplary.

NOTES

1. These strictures applied mainly to the RUC but the B Specials were included.

2. It is of interest that the 'nationality' of these Sergeant Instructors was twenty-three Ulstermen, twelve Englishmen and two Irishmen, these last two presumably from the South. All were Protestants.

3. It is of interest that the assistance of the troops 'in aid of the civil power' needed only a request from the Inspector General of Police to the GOC Northern Ireland District. The Governments at Stormont and Westminster knew what was going on but that is all.

CHAPTER SIX

The Wartime USC, 1939–45

The outbreak of war on 3 September 1939, found the Ulster Special Constabulary fully occupied in precautions against the IRA during its bombing campaign in England. It could not relax for one minute for there was ample evidence that the IRA intended to seek the help of the Nazis. As early as 1 February 1939 a German agent was in touch with IRA headquarters in Dublin, and in August they had contacts with the ABWEHR, the main German Intelligence organization. The IRA had a radio transmitter in Belfast on which they broadcast anti-British propaganda and in May they had incited crowds in the Nationalist areas of Belfast to pile up and burn the civilian gas masks which had been issued as an air raid precaution. After the outbreak of war they even got them to ignore the blackout regulations.[1] With the added security precautions by the Specials the IRA found it increasingly difficult to cross the border and so they established a 'Northern Command' which became virtually independent of Dublin and included Co Donegal. The Governments north and south of the border interned a considerable number of the IRA soon after war was declared: some sixty were arrested in the North with the intention of keeping them in prison for the duration of the war. By such measures the IRA was kept in check and rendered little more than a nuisance. The situation was, however, made no easier by the refusal of the Nationalist Party or the Roman Catholic Church to support the war effort. Recruiting in

Nationalist areas was therefore poor. At the same time the Ulster Special Constabulary lost from 30 to 35 per cent of its younger members who left to join the British forces.[2] Recruiting was opened to refill the ranks and to expand the force and this was done without difficulty and a number of B Specials were mobilized for full-time duty to help the RUC.

The IRA had been seriously weakened in arms, money and men. In Tyrone at this time their two 'battalions' had only twenty men between them armed with weapons which had been buried since 1922. In the South the IRA used a radio set to establish contact with the ABWEHR in Germany with the aim of getting them to send in arms and money. On 1 December, as a result of a High Court decision fifty-three of the IRA who had been interned were released. Three weeks later the IRA raided the magazine fort in Phoenix Park in Dublin. This operation was a remarkable success and they captured thirteen lorries full of arms and ammunition which constituted practically the complete reserve of the Irish Army. The IRA organization for disposing of such a quantity of arms was poor and the Irish Army and police succeeded in getting practically all of it back. Some of the ammunition, however, got across the border into Co Tyrone where it was recaptured by the RUC and returned to the Irish Army. The Gardai also began to have its successes. At the end of the year it found the IRA radio transmitter in Dublin severing the movement's communications with Germany. An agent who landed from a U-boat on the west coast in February was also captured almost at once. The Eirean Government then introduced the Emergency Powers Act so that the IRA could be interned again, this time at a special camp at the Curragh. The members of the IRA in the South still at liberty were then hard put to it to hold the organization together. In the North the IRA at liberty now numbered between 300 and 400 but they were short of arms. They were busy collecting intelligence about the British forces in Northern Ireland which they were ready to pass to the Germans. Some of the IRA enlisted in the British Army and in the spring of 1940 there were five of them stationed in Ballykinlar Camp. With their aid an arms raid on the camp was made stealing 200 rifles. In the South the IRA did their best to make contact with the Germans again. They sent an agent through England and Belgium to suggest joint operations of some kind against the North. At the same time another German agent parachuted into Southern Ireland but he was promptly captured by the police. On 17 May 1940 the Inspector General of the RUC issued a memorandum pointing out that in the past months the IRA had demonstrated its widespread organization and power to commit outrages in England and in Eire and that there was little doubt that they were in touch with the Germans. Serious outrages had been committed over widely distributed areas which showed that the organization extended throughout the whole of Northern Ireland. He said that the B force had to be particularly on the alert and work closely in its patrols with the RUC. In the middle of 1940 the RUC caught the IRA organizers of Co Tyrone at a conference and captured them after a gun battle at Carrickmore. An important IRA document was captured in Cookstown at about the same time setting out information to be collected by its members about the army in Northern Ireland, the RUC and the B Specials. The work of the B force was dull and monotonous and consisted of patrols, road blocks and guards, mostly at night. New conditions of service were issued on 30 September 1939, which made provision for Active and Reserve Categories. The B Specials were, of course, all in the Active Category, with a bounty of £10 a year for which they were required to do thirteen patrols each quarter. For those mobilized for full-time service the pay was slightly better and was now 9s a day.

These operations of the Specials in Northern Ireland were, of course, puny compared to those of the huge mechanized armies then locked in battle in Northern France. Alarmed by the effectiveness of the airborne troops used by the Germans in their invasion of Holland, the British Government announced on 22 May 1940 the formation of Local Defence Volunteers primarily to compete with this menace. The early LDVs in

Great Britain had no uniform except armbands and their weapons consisted of sporting rifles, shot guns and private pistols and often only pikes or clubs. Compared with these the B Specials were like seasoned regulars. After Dunkirk Winston Churchill, doubtless recalling his own part in its formation, remarked that the only properly armed and disciplined force left in the United Kingdom was the Ulster Special Constabulary.[3] It was decided therefore that the role of the Local Defence Volunteers in Great Britain should be undertaken by the RUC and Special Constabulary in Northern Ireland. Instructions in their additional duties were at once issued by the Inspector General. The object was to oppose invaders landed by air or parachute and to deal with fifth columnists.[4] The Inspector General went on to say that a German air landing was possible south of the border in co-operation with the IRA. The B Specials were told to organize rapid concentration points in case of emergency and that they must know where the nearest military forces were stationed and how to communicate with them. Finally, it was pointed out that the new LDV in Great Britain was unpaid and any extra work falling to the B Specials from this added responsibility would also be unpaid and must be taken as part of the war effort of the men concerned. It soon became clear that the B Specials, 13,000 strong, were too small a force to cope with these added duties. There were plenty of rifles available which had been stored at the RUC Depot at Sprucefield since the 'troubles' in the twenties. On 29 May recruiting was authorized for a new class of the Special Constabulary, the Local Defence category, to an establishment of 11,342. At the same time difficulties with international law became apparent because police are civilians and are not supposed to engage in hostilities. On the other hand the Government of Northern Ireland had no power to raise a fighting force. The compromise arrived at was in emergency to declare by proclamation the whole Ulster Special Constabulary, both B Special and Local Defence categories to be part of the forces of the Crown when they would come under the command of the GOC Northern Ireland District. They would then wear khaki battle dress. The Local Defence Category in fact always wore khaki battle dress.[5] They were attached to the B Special Districts and Sub-Districts and were trained by them. They did no police patrols and so, like the Local Defence Volunteers in Great Britain, were unpaid.[6] Until the proclamation both categories were administered by the Inspector General of the RUC and the County and District Commandants of the USC. At the end of May a conference of County Commandants was called to consider the best way to deal with parachutists. It was decided to continue with road blocks and to man observation posts of likely landing areas. Instructions were issued to fire at the parachutist not the parachute and try to kill them on the way down. Particular warning was given not to shoot RAF aviators by mistake. The capacity of the B Specials was greatly stretched by these new duties and it was laid down that they should not be asked to do more than one night in four on duty. Approval was however given to mobilize a number of B Specials for full-time duty in country districts to man road blocks round the clock. On 21 June the establishment of the Local Defence category was increased by another 7,400. Recruiting had to be temporarily suspended on 1 August, however, because there were no more rifles available and already there were many unarmed men. On 24 August the title Local Defence Volunteers was changed to Home Guard in Great Britain and to the Ulster Home Guard Section of the USC in Northern Ireland. At this time, with Norway and France in the hands of the Germans, the British Chiefs of Staff were seriously worried about an airborne landing in Ireland. The Prime Minister, however, refused to allow them to send a first line army division across until the army in Great Britain had been built up to a greater strength.

In Belfast the B Specials and the Ulster Home Guard, although both administered by the City Commandant, were quite distinct organizations. The B Specials were generally required to help the RUC and had no time for Home Guard duties. The Ulster Home Guard, while it still came under the

City Commandant was organized in battalions. By March
1941 the UHG in Belfast had an establishment of 8,975. The
B Specials in the country were taken up a great deal with their
patrols and had little time for army training. The Ulster
Home Guards made no patrols and so were able to concentrate
on training for which they received no reward. Reading between the lines it seems that they did not get on with each
other as well as all that. Nevertheless the UHG quickly
achieved a reasonable standard and it owed this almost completely to the help given by the B Specials. During the year
the units throughout the country improved steadily in efficiency. Instructions were issued on many subjects among others
about ringing church bells in emergency and methods of putting petrol pumps out of action to prevent their use by the
enemy.

In 1941 the IRA began to rob banks to obtain funds for its
operations. On 5 July 1941, soon after 1900 hours, six armed
IRA men attempted to raid a bookmaker in Belfast for money.
The manager rushed back into his office and broke a window
with his fist. The sound of breaking glass was heard by Special
Constables Adam McCappin and Hugh Foreman who were on
patrol protecting post offices. They drew their revolvers and
entered the bookmaker's shop. Special Constable Foreman
found three armed men in the passage and ordered them to
drop their revolvers, two did but the third made as though to
fire and Foreman shot and wounded him. Special Constable
McCappin entered the office and saw three men concealed behind a partition. He ordered them to come out and drop their
revolvers, again two did so but the third made a dash for a
door to the street and escaped; McCappin fired at his legs but
missed him. The prisoners were then secured with the assistance of two more off-duty B Specials who had heard the shooting. Both Special Constables McCappin and Foreman were
subsequently awarded the King's Police Medal for gallantry.
The IRA had a certain amount of internal trouble about this
time and suffered from a lack of leadership and purpose.
There were many cases of vicious intimidation in which IRA

men were shot in the legs as punishment. They continued to gather intelligence in the North which was smuggled to Dublin where there was a new radio transmitter brought in by another German agent. It is of interest that the Eirean government also made use of intelligence about the British forces gathered by the IRA in the North. In midsummer the IRA was rent by what became known as the Hayes affair in which the 'Chief of Staff' was accused of being a traitor. By the autumn the IRA, North and South, had lost all purpose. The Germans treated them with contempt and would not help and they became simply a number of independent fugitives. In the heavy air raids on Belfast in April and May 1941, three Special Constables lost their lives. William Howe and John McCombe on 16 April and James Thompson on 5 May 1941.

Towards the end of 1941 the Army considered that the Ulster Home Guard required reorganizing so that it would fit better into the military plans and so that its training could be done in proper military formations. The Ulster Home Guard was also under strength and it was believed that its association with the Special Constabulary might be one of the reasons. Very few Roman Catholics had joined the Home Guard and it was hoped to tap this source of manpower. There was some discussion about separating the Special Constabulary altogether from the Ulster Home Guard but this could not be done for, as the War Office pointed out, they had no power to administer the Ulster Home Guard until action stations were ordered and the GOC took control. In any case it would have been a great waste of trained manpower to restrict the B Specials solely to a police role, in which, by international law they could not help to repel an invasion. After some consultation between the Inspector General and the GOC a new organization was brought into force on 5 January 1942. Its aim was to bring the force into line with the army so that the whole could be trained as soldiers ready to take their place in an invasion. It was hoped that the new organization would give the force a more military status, strengthen its command structure and at the same time help recruiting. Except in Belfast where the City B Specials were to remain police, the whole Ulster Special Constabulary, both B Specials and Ulster Home Guard, was to be combined in platoons, companies and battalions. Area Commandants[7] were to command battalions, which were to be grouped under the former County Commandants so as to fit the military areas rather than the counties. All officers were to wear military insignia and would receive army commissions in the same way as the Home Guard in Great Britain when action stations were ordered. The result by February 1942 was a force of twenty-nine battalions totalling some 38,000 men in eight groups for administrative purposes under the County Commandants. The whole force was administered, as before, by the Inspector General of Police and those members who were also B Specials had to do police patrols as before for which they were paid the annual bonus. The rest of the force was, as before, unpaid. The order of battle was as on page 146.

The reorganization of the Ulster Home Guard came at a time when the military garrison of Northern Ireland was substantial. It consisted of a whole army corps of three divisions. In January 1942, however, two of the British divisions were relieved by two US divisions which were the first American troops to cross the Atlantic to the European theatre. They were sent to Northern Ireland at the request of the British Prime Minister with the full consent of the Northern Ireland Government in order to release British troops for Great Britain and operations overseas. The US troops were not fully trained and it was hoped they could continue their training in Northern Ireland. Both the Government of Eire and the IRA objected to the stationing of foreign troops in Ireland without their being consulted and it is of interest that the US General made contact with the IRA through his Roman Catholic Chaplain to say that he was not going to get involved in any IRA versus the British trouble but that he was prepared to talk about it. Fortunately the IRA ignored him, for any such conference would have caused a major political upheaval with the Northern Ireland Government, especially as the

ORDER OF BATTLE ULSTER HOME GUARD, 23 February 1942

Group	Battalion	Headquarters	Commanding Officer
Antrim/Derry (Ballyclare) Col R. S. Hanson, MC	1st (Antrim) Bn	Ballymoney	Lt-Col V. Unsworth
	2nd (Antrim) Bn	Ballymena	Lt-Col H. O. N. Chichester, CBE
	2nd (Derry) Bn	Garvagh	Lt-Col W. Murland
	3rd (Derry) Bn	Magherafelt	Lt-Col W. L. Lenox Conyngham, HML
Armagh (Armagh) Col C. H. Ensor, OBE, DL	1st (Armagh) Bn	Lurgan	Lt-Col J. Morton
	2nd (Armagh) Bn	Portadown	Lt-Col L. S. Edgar
	3rd (Armagh) Bn	Bessbrook	Lt-Col H. A. Whiteside
	4th (Armagh) Bn	Armagh	Lt-Col R. J. Tamplin, DSO
Belfast (Belfast) Brig Gen M. Kemp Welch, DSO, MC	2nd (UHG) Bn	Belfast	Lt-Col J. D. Nicholl, OBE, MC
	3rd (UHG) Bn	Belfast	Lt-Col I. D. Stanley-Dream, MC
	4th (UHG) Bn	Belfast	Lt-Col J. N. Fulton
	5th (UHG) Bn	Belfast	Lt-Col The Rt Hon H. G. N. Mull-holland, DL, MP
Down (Newcastle) Col J. E. Blakiston-Houston	3rd (Antrim) Bn	Carrickfergus	Lt-Col J. A. McFerran
	4th (Antrim) Bn	Muckamore	Lt-Col A. C. Herdman, OBE
	1st (Down) Bn	Newtownards	Lt-Col J. Bagwell, MVO, MC
	2nd (Down) Bn	Crossgar	Lt-Col J. A. Jaye
	3rd (Down) Bn	Newry	Lt-Col A. Turkington
	4th (Down) Bn	Banbridge	Lt-Col M. W. Edmunds, OBE, TD
Fermanagh (Enniskillen) Col H. S. C. Richardson, DL, ADC	1st (Fermanagh) Bn	Irvinestown	Lt-Col R. J. Clifford
	2nd (Fermanagh) Bn	Lisnaskea	Lt-Col H. C. Butler, MBE
	3rd (Fermanagh) Bn	Enniskillen	Lt-Col G. E. Liddle
Londonderry City (Londonderry)	1st (Derry City) Bn	Whitehall	Lt-Col R. B. W. Irwin, MC
	2nd (Derry City) Bn	Killaloo	Lt-Col W. J. I. McLaughlin
North West Londonderry Col S. W. Kennedy, OBE, DL (Limavady)	1st (Derry) Bn	Limavady	Lt-Col F. S. N. Macrory, DSO, DL
Tyrone (Omagh) Lt-Col Hammond Smith	1st (Tyrone) Bn	Castlederg	Lt-Col R. H. Todd, MBE
	2nd (Tyrone) Bn	Omagh	Lt-Col W. H. Fyffe, MBE
	3rd (Tyrone) Bn	Cookstown	Lt-Col R. A. Darling
	4th (Tyrone) Bn	Dungannon	Lt-Col W. J. Hall, MM
	5th (Tyrone) Bn	Augher	Lt-Col W. A. McKay

IRA's involvement with the Germans was beyond doubt.

In November 1941, the IRA in the South had revived sufficiently to form a new headquarters staff and a decision was taken to operate against the North again. On 25 March an IRA 'Northern Council' convention also decided to start operations in the North. Before they could do anything, however, they needed both money and arms. Some £4,200 were obtained by a raid on the Air Raid Precautions Headquarters in Belfast in which they seized the weekly wages. With some of this money they hoped, so they said, to buy arms from British soldiers. On 4 April the IRA shot two RUC policemen in Dungannon killing one of them. Next day the IRA hoped to score a propaganda victory by staging an Easter commemoration and to do so decided to cause a diversion. They therefore fired a few shots at an RUC patrol car and in the subsequent gun battle, although an RUC Constable was killed, six of the IRA were arrested, tried and condemned to death. An IRA man who was stopped for questioning on the bridge at Strabane shot and wounded an RUC constable but was also captured. During the summer the IRA in the South evolved a plan to help the campaign in the North. They decided to collect the arms concealed in dumps all over the South and to take them to the North. They had vague plans of operating as Commandos in the North without any clear idea of what they were trying to achieve. On 30 August they succeeded in smuggling two lorry loads of arms and explosives across the border near Newry and concealed them in a barn. The RUC by following known IRA men found the dump, captured the munitions and shot a member of the IRA dead. After the execution of an IRA man in Belfast who had been involved in shooting a policeman in April, the IRA both North and South were determined to make reprisals. On 2 September a lorry containing twenty IRA crossed the border near Culloville in Co Armagh. It was intercepted by an RUC patrol car with only three men in it but a gunfight developed. One man on each side was hit but the IRA managed to disarm the other two police and escape back across the border. On 5 September an RUC Constable

and Special Constable Samuel Hamilton were shot dead at
Clady in Co Tyrone and another Special Constable was
wounded. On the same day an RUC Constable was wounded
in Belfast but four IRA were captured. In addition to these
incidents there had been some sixty armed attacks in the three
months from August to October and on 10 October a curfew
from 2030 hours to 0600 hours was declared in the Nationalist
areas of West Belfast. Shortly afterwards a bomb was thrown
at Donegal Pass Police Station and in the ensuing gun battle
Special Constable James Lyons was mortally wounded.
Gradually the situation was brought under control, which involved intensive use of the B Specials throughout the Province
with their usual road blocks, guards and patrols. In the South
too, pressure on the IRA was continuous and by the end of the
year they were so disorganized that they were incapable of
further operations.

For the rest of the war the Ulster Home Guard continued
its training. It was not intended to be a mobile field force but a
static defence force each battalion remaining in its own area:
it was not therefore trained above Company level. Mobile
military operations would be conducted by the regular field
force. The UHG relied on civilians to feed it, civilian transport where necessary and the civilian telephone system. Its
communications were, however, backed up by despatch riders,
bicycles, runners and homing pigeons. The GOC's orders
visualized two states of increased preparedness. The message
'Stand to' meant prepare for action in every way except that
the men would not actually move to their assembly stations. At
'Action Stations' the Governor of Northern Ireland would
make the proclamation declaring the UHG to be part of the
forces of the Crown and the GOC would take command which
he would exercise through his three Sub-District commanders.
There were three types of attack which might be expected: an
airborne landing; a seaborne landing on the coast or an attack
across the border after a landing in Eire. In his operational
instructions the GOC visualized four main roles for the UHG.
These were the defence of airfields, the defence of river cross-

ings, the defence of 'resistance centres' and the ambushing of enemy columns passing through Home Guard areas. The UHG would be ordered what to do according to the circumstances. If there was a general parachute landing, the UHG were to try and wipe out the parachutists at once before they could organize themselves on the ground. The defence of airfields was a formidable task: there were by this time twenty-one airfields in Northern Ireland, some of which were still under construction. The personnel of the airfields were also available for defence and the purpose was to protect them for the use of our own aircraft and to deny them to the enemy at all costs. The defence of the border was no new task to the men of the B Specials and, if ordered, would be undertaken by all the UHG Battalions in the border areas. An example of the defence of a river line was the Bann north of Lough Neagh which had only five bridges across it and which, if defended, cut the north of the Province in half. It was planned that there should be three main 'centres of resistance' and these were Belfast, Larne and Londonderry, the largest ports in the Province through which reinforcements were expected from Great Britain. The UHG were kept busy studying the ground and making detailed plans for all these contingencies.

Annual camps were held by the various battalions which in general seem, from press reports of the time, to have been pleasant social occasions too. It was remarked that more was learnt in these camps than in all the drills in a year. There were of course many incidents throughout the Province during this period of planning and training. On 29 July 1942, a course of UHG officers was attending a regular army battle school. What was known as a battle inoculation exercise was in progress in which a machine gun was fired to 'near-miss' the students and accustom them to being fired upon. One machine gun was badly aimed and wounded Lieutenant-Colonel Hammond Smith, the County Commandant of Tyrone, and three other men. Lieutenant-Colonel Hammond Smith's wound was mortal and he died the next day. On 16 May 1943, men of the 2nd (Tyrone) Battalion were practising throwing live grenades. A pupil under instruction threw a grenade badly and it landed in a bay occupied by an officer under instruction and his instructor, Sergeant William Anderson. The officer crouched where he was – 'frozen' and incapable of moving. Sergeant Anderson, although the grenade was due to explode, re-entered the bay and lifted the officer bodily and thrust him behind a traverse, falling on top of him as the grenade went off. This very prompt and gallant action undoubtedly saved the officer's life and having performed it Sergeant Anderson continued his instructional duties unperturbed. He was subsequently awarded the British Empire Medal for Gallantry.[8] On 20 February 1944, a Sunderland flying boat from the base at Castle Archdale on Lough Erne, hit some overhead electricity cables and crashed in a field near Ballinamallard in Co Fermanagh. Sergeant Henry Lunny of No 1 (Fermanagh) Battalion of the Ulster Home Guard, who lived nearby, ran towards the wreck which had caught fire. He entered the burning plane three times and with the help of two members of the crew saved four other wounded men. The plane was burning furiously and ammunition was exploding. Sergeant Lunny was also awarded the British Empire Medal for Gallantry.

Throughout 1943 there were few incidents with the IRA. In January four important IRA men escaped from Crumlin Road Gaol and in March, twenty-one more tunnelled out of Derry Gaol and escaped across the border.[9] In April the IRA pulled off a propaganda stunt by seizing the Broadway Cinema in Belfast, reading the 1916 Declaration of a Republic and an IRA policy statement and after a two minutes' silence for those killed in the 1916 rising, they decamped. By June the organization of the IRA, both North and South, had collapsed again. With most of their members interned or in gaol and with contacts with Germany cut and with no funds from America, due to the activities of the FBI, they were a spent force. On 21 November, Hugh McAteer, one of the men who had escaped in January was recaptured in Belfast. He was the last hope of any reorganization of the IRA and they were of no further danger for the rest of the war. Their defeat was brought about by relentless pressure by the police north and south of the border and by internment. The ubiquitous B Specials with their road blocks, patrols and guards had played their part. Their monotonous work continued, however, to the end of the war.

By August 1943, the invasion of Ireland by the Axis powers became much less likely. The operational role of the UHG then became to increase its efficiency to the maximum extent so that regular troops could be released for offensive operations. They were also, of course, to continue to prepare for any incursion by the enemy into the Province and to inflict the maximum damage upon him if he did so. In December 1944 the Ulster Home Guard stood down. Both the B Specials and UHG categories of the USC were subsequently made eligible for the award of The Defence Medal providing they had served for a period of three years.

NOTES

1. These infringements of the blackout ceased abruptly with the German air raids on Belfast in 1941!

2. It has been difficult to produce exact figures. An example is the Armagh City Sub-District which did particularly well. Out of a strength of ninety-five, they sent ten to the Royal Navy (two killed), twenty-nine to the Army (two killed) and fifteen to the Royal Air Force (one killed).

3. Conversation with Sir Richard Pim, at that time in charge of the Prime Minister's map room.

4. In discussing the defence plans of the British Local Defence Volunteers, Winston Churchill remarked that there was no need to worry about a fifth column in Great Britain as it did not exist. Unfortunately the same was not true of Northern Ireland.

5. To be accurate, there was a short period at the very begin-

ning when the local defence category wore civilian clothes with black arm bands. Then they were issued with locally manufactured black denim battle dress. A few months later when the legal complications were appreciated, they were issued with khaki battle dress.

6. They could, under certain conditions, be compensated for loss of earnings.

7. Area Commandants had been instituted again on the outbreak of war.

8. Sergeant Anderson later joined the Royal Ulster Rifles and after the war became a Sergeant Instructor with the B Specials. He is now serving as an officer in the 6th (Tyrone) Battalion of the Ulster Defence Regiment.

9. All the Derry prisoners were recaptured in Eire and interned in the Curragh.

CHAPTER SEVEN

Post World War II, 1945–56

At the end of the war the IRA was at a very low ebb. Most of its members were no longer interested in violence although some of the fanatics began to try and reorganize when they were released from the internment camps. For two years, however, they were no danger and most people, north and south of the border, thought that they were finished. With the standing down of the Ulster Home Guard, the Ulster Special Constabulary became a police force again. There was the usual pressure to economize: in 1943–4 the UHG had cost £559,312 of which the Home Guard part needed £108,788 and the B Specials, who were in the patrol category and 13,000 strong, £132,421. The force retained its pre-war strength of 11,250 and also its pre-war organization. After considerable discussion with the Ministry of Home Affairs, it was decided to retain two permanent officers in each county, the County Commandant and an Adjutant. The temptation to reduce one or both of these officers to part-time status was resisted as it was felt that the Districts and Sub-Districts would quickly lose interest if they were not regularly visited by officers from County Headquarters. In January 1946 new conditions of service were published. Age limits from eighteen to sixty were laid down with extensions permitted up to sixty-five in certain cases; enrolment was to be for yearly periods. There were to be two categories, Patrol and Non-patrol with annual bounties of £10 and £6; when mobilized pay would be the same as the regular RUC. The training periods required were two each month and the number of patrols performed when in the patrol category would be as ordered. The whole force was, however, put in the Non-Patrol category. This cost £165,291 in the financial year 1946–7. In January 1946, the disciplinary regulations for the force were made the same as for the regular RUC. The only activity in the period immediately after the war was the royal visit on 19 July 1945. The Belfast USC members were indignant that on this occasion they were all mixed up in the lining of the streets with the RUC and were not paraded under their own officers as a separate force. In Londonderry, however, they provided a ceremonial Royal Guard, one hundred strong.

For two years all was quiet but in a general election in Eire in February 1948, Fine Gael, the descendants of Cosgrave's 'Free Staters', were able to form a coalition with Labour and a new militant Republican party, Clan na Poblachta, and this combination ousted de Valera and Fianna Fail by seventy-five votes to sixty-eight. The new Prime Minister was Mr Costello and the one major issue on which this heterogenous coalition was agreed was to end partition. As when de Valera came to power in 1932, the remaining internees were released and the police were ordered to cease harassing the IRA. The next year Mr Costello's Government introduced the Republic of Ireland Act which claimed sovereignty over the whole of Ireland including the six counties of Northern Ireland. After a general election in Northern Ireland which overwhelmingly demonstrated that the Province wished to remain part of the United Kingdom, the British Government in an Act of Parliament of 4 May 1949, recognized that the south of Ireland had ceased to be part of the Commonwealth and that the twenty-six counties would in future be referred to as the Republic of Ireland. The Act went on to state, however, that Northern Ireland would remain part of the United Kingdom and 'in no event will Northern Ireland or any part thereof cease to be part of His Majesty's dominions and of the United

Kingdom without the consent of the Parliament of Northern Ireland.'

In 1948, too, an IRA organization began to take shape and by 1949 its aims became clear. The policy was not to take part in politics, certainly not 'red' politics, and was that they would not act against the Government in the South. 'The aim of the Irish Republican Army is simply to drive the invader from the soil of Ireland and to restore the sovereign independent Republic proclaimed in 1916. To that end, the policy is to prosecute a successful military campaign against the British forces of occupation in the six counties', said one of the principal speakers at Bodenstown in 1949. The same speaker pointed out that, 'The Republican movement is divided into two main bodies – the Military and the Civil Arms, the Irish Republican Army and Sinn Fein. Each has an important task to do. In the final analysis the work of either is as important as that of the other.'

Clearly the time had come to check that all was in order in the Special Constabulary. In March 1949 the Inspector General proposed that a force of Class A Special Constables, 1,000 strong should be raised for 'With the ever increasing volume of propaganda against the partition of this Island and the frequent threats and innuendoes that force is the only solution of the problem, it is quite possible that, contrary to the stated policy of the leaders of the Government and Opposition in Eire respectively, the IRA may take matters into their own hands'. It was proposed that the new force should be full-time and mobile and it was considered to be necessary because the RUC was under strength and could not be increased sufficiently by normal recruiting. At the same time an increase in the size of the B force, although this would be possible, would not provide the answer. The new force was required to operate in Nationalist areas where there was no B force and where one could not be raised. The new force was to consist of fifty-six officers and 928 men organized in eight companies and twenty-four platoons and would cost £326,000 a year. The Ministry of Home Affairs was not so sure that the time had come to spend so much and kept the matter under consideration for the best part of a year. Also, in March 1949, an up to date patrol scheme was drawn up by the Fermanagh County Commandant, on his own initiative, to meet any sudden emergency. At the same time the Inspector General ordered a check to be made on the security of all USC arms and ammunition to ensure that they could not be stolen.

In October a recruiting drive for the USC was begun as the strength of the force was 9,919 which was about 1,000 below its establishment. This at once caused an uproar in the Northern Parliament, the Opposition doing their best to prevent the force being built up again. At the time there was a shortage of men for the Territorial Army in the United Kingdom as a whole. The Opposition asked why Northern Ireland had 10,000 Specials and only 1,603 men in the Territorial Army. If the Specials were disbanded then the Territorial Army could be brought up to strength and if the Unionists were really loyal this is what they should do. In fact there were only 51,175 in the Territorial Army in Great Britain and so Ulster's contribution was the same in proportion to its population. Shortly afterwards the Government made it clear that there was no objection to a member of the USC belonging to the Territorial Army as well.

On 31 August 1948, Colonel Sargent, the staff officer to the Inspector General for the B Specials since 1922, retired owing to ill-health. Although not concerned at the very beginning he was thought of by many as the 'father' of the B Specials and they were sorry to see him go. At the age of sixty-six, however, he could not have stayed on very much longer. Colonel Sargent had first had anything to do with the Specials as the Deputy Director of Training to the Military Adviser in 1922. In 1938 he had been awarded the OBE in recognition of his services to the Ulster Special Constabulary. To everyone's sorrow he died the year after he retired. He was relieved by Brigadier F. Y. C. Knox, DSO.

In 1950 preparations for trouble continued and in February, the Inspector General asked for Bren guns to be supplied for the USC and the Ministry of Supply was requested to deliver sixty of them. The guns did not arrive until the middle of 1951 and training in their use was much delayed. In April the Inspector General said that he assumed that all County and City Commandants were prepared to change to the patrol category at short notice. From Co Antrim came the reply that they were ready to assume patrol category at six hours' notice and from Co Down that no difficulties could be foreseen. At the end of the month the Inspector General issued co-ordinating instructions to bring the counties into line with each other. The new Staff Officer did not support the earlier method of allowing District Commandants to operate the patrols on their own and required detailed plans for the positions and times of all patrols to be produced in the form of operation orders and to be under the control of the County Commandant and his permanent staff.

Brigadier Knox, the new Staff Officer, was something of a 'new broom', he was accustomed to tour the Province frequently to inspect Sub-Districts on their drill nights and to visit the rifle ranges during practice. Generally his visits came as a surprise. From the correspondence of the period, in which he reported his findings to the County Commandants, it is obvious that they did not like this prowling round their counties. One County Commandant complained to the Inspector General: 'For many years it was the custom of members of your staff to notify County Commandants of their intention of visiting Counties and I consider that that custom should be revived'. It is also clear from the letters of the period how short funds were and that the USC was still run on a shoestring. Sometimes Brigadier Knox was pleased: 'This was a well-attended parade, turn out was excellent'; 'Weapon training record showed 67 marksmen in 6 sub-districts'; 'This was a most impressive parade. The work was thoroughly well organized and carried out with great keenness. The weapon training seen was highly efficient...' Sometimes he was not at all satisfied: 'The office and store were most untidy.... This year's annual weapon training instructions could not be found amongst the many papers littering the Sergeant Instructor's tables'; 'The turn-out was very poor – dirty ammunition, two ill-fitting uniforms, two brown boots'; 'The light in the hall came from two Tilley lamps … it was totally inadequate'. There is little doubt, despite the resentment of the County Commandants, that Brigadier Knox's visits kept the units up to the mark and were very necessary after a long period of inactivity.

In 1950 the Inspector General had his attention called to the fact that County Commandants were not as young as they used to be. Their ages were as follows:

S. W. Kennedy, Esq	(Derry City)	77
Col Charley	(Belfast City)	75½
Lt-Col Blakiston Houston	(Down)	73
Captain Ensor	(Armagh)	72
Colonel Gregg	(Tyrone)	64
Captain Hanson	(Antrim)	58
Lt-Col Liddle	(Fermanagh)	51
Capt Lenox-Conyngham	(Londonderry)	47

All these officers had given splendid service to the Ulster Special Constabulary, Captain Ensor had been County Commandant of Co Armagh since the formation of the force, and Colonel Charley had joined the C 1 Specials in 1922. Colonel Liddle was the defender of Lisbellaw in the summer of 1920 with the early unofficial Specials, and Captain Hanson was an Area Commandant in the 'troubles' of 1922. Nevertheless it was decided that an age limit would have to be applied and Mr Kennedy, Colonel Charley, Lieutenant-Colonel Blakiston Houston and Captain Ensor were replaced by younger men during 1952. Captain Ensor had been awarded the OBE for his services as far back as 1924 and Lieutenant-Colonel Blakiston Houston in 1949. Lieutenant-Colonel Liddle had the same honour conferred on him in 1945, Captain Hanson in 1950 and Colonel Gregg in 1951. The men of the force were much younger. In January 1950 an analysis of ages in Co Londonderry was as follows:

Over 60	17
50–60	108
38–50	283
26–38	408
Under 26	286
	1,102

After a conference between the Ministry of Home Affairs and the Inspector General it was decided not to go ahead with the formation of a new Class A of the Ulster Special Constabulary as had been proposed a year before. Instead at the end of 1950 it was approved to form a Reserve force of three platoons composed of the regular RUC. Such a force could then be used for control of civil disturbances as well as active operations against the IRA. The place of the RUC constables used to form the Reserve force was taken by the mobilization of an equivalent number of B Specials. In 1950 there were five bomb explosions in Belfast, three of which were at RUC stations in the City. Some of the Belfast City Specials, although they were still in the Non-Patrol category, were used to make some patrols for which they were paid 5s. a night. Other B Specials were mobilized as barrack reinforcements through the Province as the RUC was under strength. The Reserve force was sent to the army camp at Ballykinlar for special training and arms and equipment for them were obtained from the War Office. The formation of the Reserve force was taken by the Press to be in answer to 'Captain Cowan's Army', an irregular body formed in Dublin to invade Ulster and end partition. On the occasion of the introduction of a supplementary estimate to cover the cost, the Opposition members at Stormont took the opportunity to attack the Special Constabulary again. The usual unfounded allegations were made. It was suggested, as usual, that they were a partisan force, they were compared to the Nazi Brown Shirts and were said to be a political police. The fact that the whole force had been in the Reserve category since the war and had not been used for any purpose was ignored. In reply the Prime Minister, Sir Basil Brooke, recalled that the Specials had been boycotted by the Nationalists from the beginning. The Minister for Home Affairs added that they had established an era of quiet and peace which members of the Opposition were anxious to disrupt. Unfortunately allegations against B Specials were occasionally true. In November 1950 a Special Constable at Rathfriland committed a robbery when off duty using his service rifle. He had a good record when he was enrolled into the Constabulary and there was no reason to suppose he could take to crime. When he did he was at once prosecuted in the civil courts, disarmed and dismissed from the force. On occasions even the best police forces have 'bent' members.

On 19 November 1950, the Co Armagh Ulster Special Constabulary held a church parade to commemorate the thirtieth anniversary of their formation. Nearly every Sub-District of the County was represented and the salute was taken by Sir Richard Pim, the Inspector General of the RUC. At another parade at Castlederg in Co. Tyrone, the Marquess of Hamilton said, 'I wish some of the people in England who talk about a "police-ridden State in Ulster" could be here and see your fine discipline and bearing, because they would very soon have different ideas'. He went on to say that the men on parade knew as well as he did that a peaceful, law-abiding citizen had nothing to fear from the Ulster Special Constabulary whatever his political opinions or religious persuasions. The members of the Special Constabulary by their self-sacrifice and service made it possible for every law-abiding citizen to go about without fear. Of a church parade in Belfast inspected by the Home Secretary (Mr W. B. Maginess, KC), one newspaper reported:

'Sunday's parade was in the main composed of young men – smart, alert ... (and) they made an impressive showing. Many of them were ex-Service men and the general bearing of the parade reflected credit not only on the officers, but also on the rank and file, who were prepared to sacrifice their spare time to do police duties.'

In 1951, new conditions of service were promulgated, the major change being that the bounty for the Patrol category was raised from £10 to £20 a year for which ten patrols had to be done each quarter. The Bounty for the Non-Patrol category remained at £6 a year. A recruiting poster giving these conditions ended: 'You will be expected to show a high standard of conduct befitting the traditions of the Force. You will be expected and required to carry out your duties towards all members of the community in an absolutely impartial manner.' At this time too the Minister of Home Affairs ruled that County Commandants were to be considered as part-time appointments. No part-time County Commandants had however been appointed by 1954 and with the increased preparedness required, this ruling seems to have died a natural death. The cost of the force in the 1951-2 estimates had risen to £270,277, £59,725 of which was to pay for the 171 Special Constables who were now mobilized for full-time duty with the RUC. Against this, the part-time members cost £75,500 and training £45,975.

In 1951 the IRA was still very short of arms and ammunition. In the summer the re-established Londonderry unit obtained the permission of the IRA headquarters in Dublin to carry out a raid on the Territorial Army's armoury inside the Joint RN RAF Anti-Submarine School which was situated in the old Ebrington Army Barracks. The raid was not an armed attack so much as a large scale burglary planned with the help of civilian employees in the barracks. The raid was carried out by the twenty-strong Derry unit on 3 June with complete success securing twelve modern service rifles, twenty sten guns and eight machine guns with ammunition to match. Not only were the raiders completely undetected, but the theft was not noticed for some time afterwards. RUC intelligence gave no warning and the B Specials were still in the Reserve category. The raid not only put a substantial quantity of modern arms in the hands of the IRA but greatly stimulated their morale and recruiting. At the same time, however, precautions against the IRA were improved and the security of armouries in Northern

Ireland was treated as a matter of urgency. During the next two years the IRA steadily increased in size and efficiency but at the same time it suffered a number of splits in which small groups left and followed their own devices. From the point of view of the RUC and the Specials, however, this was of academic importance as all types were dangerous and had to be countered. The B Specials' efficiency, under the watchful eye of Brigadier Knox, improved too and recruiting continued. The age limit was applied rigidly and at the end of 1953 the force was still 1,250 under its establishment of 11,250. During the year 1,417 men left the force and 1,399 were recruited.

On 25 July 1953, the IRA made another raid for arms, this time in England. Again it was really a burglary rather than an armed raid. It was carried out by members of the IRA from Ireland and the target was the armoury of the Officers Training Corps at Felstead School in Essex. At first all went well and over a hundred rifles and assorted weapons were stolen. Twice the quantity could have been taken if the IRA had provided better transport. The arms were recaptured by pure chance: unarmed police in two patrol cars thought the van was acting suspiciously and searched it. All the IRA involved received long sentences and some of the energy and money of the IRA was thereafter expended in trying to help them escape from prison.

It was nearly a year before the IRA struck again. In June 1954 they made a most successful raid on the armoury of the barracks of the Royal Irish Fusiliers at Armagh. The raid was planned after the IRA noticed that the sentries, although armed, had no ammunition.[1] The IRA first enlisted one of their men in the British Army and he was able to tell them all about the guards, sentries, the routine of the barracks and where the keys of the armoury were kept. The raid was executed on 12 June by nineteen men from a base near Dundalk. They crossed the border on a Saturday afternoon in a stolen lorry escorted by a car. They succeeded in securing the whole guard in broad daylight without firing a shot and drove back across the border eleven miles away with 254 rifles, thirty sten guns and nine Bren light machine guns. The first alarm was not given until a quarter of an hour after the lorry had left and the general alarm until an hour and a half after that. The B Specials were not therefore called out until the raiders were well over the border. The morale of the IRA soared and recruiting greatly increased. At the same time funds poured in from America where the keys of the barrack gates and the armoury at Armagh were auctioned! The Government of the Republic was embarrassed and slightly alarmed in case the arms were intended for use against it. The British Army looked very silly but the result was a great tightening of security all round. After this raid Stormont brought into force orders under the Special Powers Act giving the RUC the right to search for arms without a warrant and to stop and search vehicles or suspected persons.

On 14 July 1954, the Queen held a Royal Review in Hyde Park in London of the police forces of the United Kingdom. Northern Ireland was represented by a contingent of 200 under County Inspector R. T. Hamilton of the RUC. Most of the contingent was provided by the RUC, but the Ulster Special Constabulary was represented by a detachment of fifty-two under the command of Major N. F. Gordon, the District Commandant from Newcastle, Co Down. The men selected had to be smart and of good appearance and were chosen from those who had given good service to their County and the Province. Only thoroughly fit men were considered as the parade was expected to be a long one in hot weather. The number of men taken from each City and County was based on its establishment. Obviously there were a large number of suitable men available and the final selection was in most cases by ballot. Clearly it was a great honour to be chosen and the names of the contingent are given in Appendix II. They were mobilized for a week for the occasion and they assembled in Belfast on 12 July for a full scale rehearsal at which the salute was taken by Sir Richard Pim, the Inspector General of the RUC. They left for London that evening and were accommodated at the Guards Depot in Caterham. After the Review, Her Majesty sent a message of congratulation,

> 'I shall be glad if you will convey to ... all the men ... who took part in this afternoon's Review, my congratulations and those of my husband on the high standard of smartness and discipline shown by everyone on parade. ... I am glad to have this opportunity of expressing my warm appreciation of the loyalty, courage and efficiency with which they serve me and my people.'

Just before the Review, in May, in the debate on the estimates for the Ministry of Home Affairs, Mr Brian Faulkner called for an improvement in the type of uniform issued to the B Specials. He said they were old fashioned and not in keeping with the dignity of the duties they were expected to fulfil. The uniform was, indeed, somewhat out of date. They still wore tunics of the 1914–18 war-type with high turn-down collars. The RUC had already changed to jackets with an open neck worn with a collar and tie. The only change since the early days was that slacks had replaced puttees and boots. From the beginning the uniforms had been from ex-army stocks dyed green. On enquiry being made to find how many more of these garments were in stock it transpired that they had run out long before and the Ministry of Supply were actually making khaki tunics of the old pattern and dying them specially for the USC! There was also Parliamentary pressure for better conditions and pay for the Specials and some talk of Long Service medals. Dame Dehra Parker, replying for the Government said, 'What they receive is, in no sense, intended as remuneration. It is appreciation of magnificent services magnificently rendered.' Mr O. W. J. Henderson's statement that 'At the moment they carry on in a well-nigh voluntary capacity' was nearer the truth. Opposition suggestions on the other hand that their pay was a 'bribe for standing behind the Government' was as much nonsense as the trade union leader who said they were 'recruited on the basis of scab wages'.

The Armagh raid had produced plenty of weapons but not ammunition and the IRA began to plan another operation. Enheartened by their success at Armagh four months before, the IRA decided to repeat their exploit at the barracks of the Royal Inniskilling Fusiliers at Omagh. They again enlisted an IRA man in the army and the former agent who had been the inside man at Armagh paid a visit to Omagh as well. From their information an elaborate plan was worked out. Thirty-five men from the South crossed the border on 16 October, the intention being that sixteen of them should scale the back of the barrack wall and having silenced the sentry, take the guard-house from the rear. The main gates would then be opened and the rest of the party let in. Army lorries were to be used to transport the contents of the armoury to the border. From the beginning everything began to go wrong. IRA headquarters changed the leader of the raid at the last moment which was a great mistake. The sentry at the back of the barracks was not knifed silently as had been planned but succeeded in yelling so loudly that the whole barracks was awakened. The guard at the gate opened fire at the raiding party crossing the square and they had to run for it and scramble back across the wall as fast as they could.[2] Both cars and the lorry in which they had arrived then made at full speed for the border but in the confusion they left eight men behind including the leader of the raid. Omagh is farther from the border than Armagh, some twenty miles from Co Donegal and about the same from Co Monaghan and Co Cavan. The cars and the lorry crossed the border to Belturbet in Co Cavan successfully but the stragglers were captured in the very large security net which had been spread to catch them. The entire force of Tyrone Specials was mobilized for two days after this raid. At 0950 hours civilians reported to a B Special road block that they had seen a man with a blackened face hiding in a ditch. Special Constables of the Seskinore Sub-District went to the spot and arrested the man who, when searched, was found to be armed with a small pistol. A revolver was also found in the ditch and this man was subsequently identified as the leader of the raid. An hour later other civilians reported to Omagh RUC barracks that they had seen five raiders in the Loughmuck area and a party of Specials was at once sent to search. One of the IRA was captured by the Omagh Sub-District at 1415 hours and four others by a joint operation with Specials of the Edenderry Sub-District. After dark at 1915 hours a further report came in that two men dressed in overalls had been seen on the Omagh–Clogher road near Thompson's Cross. A combined party of RUC and Specials of the Clogher Sub-District at once left Clogher RUC barracks in two cars and arrested the two men. All this sounds very easy but of course arresting IRA fugitives could be a dangerous business. The operation involved placing a number of lookouts and spreading out a considerable number of men to comb the area. Great care had to be taken not to fall into an ambush. In this case most of the IRA had, in fact, thrown away their arms and this involved a large scale search for the weapons. When he heard no news of the raid, the 'Chief of Staff' of the IRA, waiting in Monaghan, hired a taxi and drove to Omagh. After picking up what news he could he returned the same way passing through a number of road blocks without being recognized. The B Specials were looking for wet and footsore raiders in boiler suits and gym shoes with black berets, so the 'Chief of Staff' to his amazement, got away with it. After this raid the IRA were determined not to upset the Government of the Republic in any way and issued strict instructions that the enemy was England and that the IRA in the South were not to use weapons even in self defence. On 7 December 1954 a van trying to smuggle arms across the border was stopped by HM Customs. The IRA occupants shot and wounded a customs officer and fled back across the border on foot.

An IRA plan to raid Omagh again came to nothing as they found great difficulty in getting anyone to undertake it. The IRA, however, had men enlisted in the British Army in both the barracks at Ballymena and at Armagh. Ballymena is far from the border and in a very 'Protestant' area, so it was decided to try again at Armagh on 6 March. A plan was made to use about a hundred men, including a number of the indigenous IRA from the six counties. This was a mistake as RUC intelligence got wind of the attack and a massive security operation was put into force all along the border. The lorries from the South were warned by the local IRA as they approached and the whole raid was called off. Two vehicles refused to stop at the border and fire had to be opened. The occupants of one of the vehicles in question near Keady were a youth aged eighteen who was killed and a sixteen-year-old girl who was injured by flying glass; another man was wounded in Co Fermanagh on the same night. These incidents were seized upon by the southern propagandists and the northern Nationalists. The usual allegations were made that the Specials were trigger happy and demands were made that they should be disbanded. Opposition members of Parliament also attacked the force for indiscriminate shooting and said they were irresponsible. In fact the first van had deliberately accelerated through the road block and only two shots were fired. The Minister of Home Affairs (Mr Hanna) pointed out that if it were not for the efforts of evilly disposed persons there would be no necessity for a Special Constabulary, which he affirmed were a well-disciplined force under proper control and well officered. The IRA, of course, would have very much liked to fight their approaching campaign with no B Specials to oppose them and would have been delighted if they could rush the road blocks without being fired upon. Fortunately Stormont stood firm and had the courage to support the police. It is of interest that in England shortly afterwards, the Press and general public were taking exactly the opposite line. They were furious when they found that the guard at Arborfield, when the IRA attacked, had been virtually unarmed. There was no such nonsense in the Special Constabulary and the prevention of this raid on Armagh barracks showed them to their very best advantage.

In August 1955, nearly a year after the failure at Omagh, the IRA decided to make another attempt in England. The raid was planned with the help of a traitor in the British Army of Irish extraction. Eleven of the IRA from Dublin crossed to England on 11 August and raided the REME depot at Arborfield in Berkshire. With the aid of the traitor they overcame the guard at the gate and took 60,000 rounds of assorted ammunition and another fifty Sten guns weighing five tons in all, which they loaded into two lorries. Again, with astonishing luck a police patrol car caught one of the lorries and from the information they obtained the police had little difficulty in finding the place where the rest of the ammunition had been dumped and recovered all of it. Nevertheless, the British Army looked silly again in spite of the fact that the IRA got no ammunition in the end. On 4 July 1955, a car within a quarter of a mile of the Parliament buildings at Stormont had been blown to pieces and an IRA man was killed. The man was in fact the leader of a splinter group from the IRA and was attempting to blow up the telephone exchange. In October 1955, B Specials stopped a car and the occupant subsequently alleged that he was ordered out of his van and struck with a rifle butt. The complaint was put in emotional language in a parliamentary question, 'What action the Minister proposed to take to prevent respectable citizens from being ruthlessly attacked by members of this force'. The 'respectable citizen' was subsequently charged with disorderly behaviour. Opportunities such as this were never missed to criticize the force especially when very occasional accidents occurred with weapons. Some of the allegations were ridiculous such as that members of the Special Constabulary were formerly confined in mental hospitals. Constant attempts were made to have the force disarmed or disbanded.

On 27 November 1955, the IRA placed a bomb alongside the RUC barracks at Rosslea in Co Fermanagh. The bomb blew in the side of the barracks but when the IRA tried to enter through the breach they were beaten off by the Sergeant in charge of the station with a Sten gun. A Constable was wounded but one of the IRA was shot dead. This attack was, in fact, made by a breakaway IRA group from Co Tyrone. During 1955 many of the Northern IRA journeyed to the

South to attend training camps which was a disturbing move.

The scheme for the resurrection of the A Specials was again considered and brought up to date at the end of 1955 and again submitted to the Minister of Home Affairs. It was decided, however, rather to increase the size of the regular RUC Reserve force. At the end of 1955 the conditions of service in the USC were again altered. The minimum age of enrolment was raised to eighteen from seventeen which it had been since 1947, and a one year probationary period was instituted after which a Certificate of Efficiency had to be obtained before confirmation. The Patrol and Non-Patrol categories were abolished and the bounty was fixed at £9 a year for which two drills a month had to be done. Patrols could be substituted for drills at any time, one patrol counting as two drills. Any additional patrols were paid at the rate of 15s a night. On this basis the cost of the force was estimated to be £300,000 a year. At about this time a change was made in the organization of the B Specials in Belfast who were put under the RUC Commissioner for the City. The City Commandant then became Deputy City Commandant and he no longer answered direct to the Inspector General as the other County Commandants. Early in January 1956, new scales of pay were introduced for all permanent and mobilized members of the USC and in June the pay of County Commandants was raised to £1,000 a year and Adjutants to £875. The estimates for 1956–7 for the force were £436,450. Finally in October 1956, no less than fifteen sizes of tunics and trousers were available for issue to the USC and most shapes and sizes could be catered for.

In 1956 the Ulster Special Constabulary Long Service Medal was instituted. It was a variety of the Special Constabulary Long Service Medal of 1919 for Special Constables in Great Britain. It was awarded for nine years' service in the Ulster Special Constabulary of at least fifty duties per year and had to be recommended by a Chief Officer of Police. A bar was awarded for each additional period of ten years. Service during the war counted treble. The medal was in bronze with the head of the Sovereign on one side and laurel leaves with the legend 'For Faithful Service in the Ulster Special Constabulary' on the other. Large numbers of men were eligible and the medals were awarded during the year. The ribbon has a red centre stripe one third of the whole bordered by white, black, white stripes on each side.

During 1956 the IRA wasted a great deal of effort and money trying to rescue Cathal Goulding, imprisoned in England since the Felstead raid in 1953. Nevertheless their plans went ahead for a regular campaign against the North and training began in earnest. During August they sent about twenty organizers into the Nationalist areas of the North and they set about training local units, making plans and gathering intelligence.

NOTES

1. The sentry at the gate was armed with a sten gun but with no magazine on it, so it was obviously not loaded.
2. In this battle, five soldiers were wounded.

CHAPTER EIGHT

The 1956–62 Campaign

The IRA Council voted to begin their campaign against Northern Ireland in November 1956 but for various reasons it had to be postponed for a month. On 11 November their plans were upset by the action of a splinter group, which made a number of attacks spread along the border including the blowing up of six Customs huts. They failed, however, to ambush any RUC or B Special patrols which they hoped would be drawn towards the trouble spots. Nevertheless the ambitious official IRA plans went ahead. They intended to use four columns of twenty-five men each based in the Irish Republic. The first column was to operate from the Dooish Mountains in Co Donegal between Letterkenny and Londonderry; the second from farther south in the same county near Lough Derg; the third from the Cuilcagh Mountains in Co Cavan south west of Enniskillen and the fourth from the Ballyconnel area opposite southern Fermanagh also in Co Cavan. In addition there was the indigenous IRA in the North working in the Nationalist areas which are situated in general in Fermanagh, Tyrone and the southern parts of Armagh and Down, the north-east of Antrim and parts of Co Londonderry. The IRA aim was 'to maintain and strengthen our resistance centres throughout the occupied areas (i.e.: Northern Ireland) and hold the enemy down to the larger towns by restricting his communications ... and to break down the enemy's administration in the occupied area until he is forced to withdraw his forces'. The method of achieving this aim was 'to use Guerilla Warfare, and propaganda directed at the inhabitants. In time as we build up our forces we hope to be in a position to liberate large areas – that is areas where the enemy's writ no longer runs'. The operations were to be carried out in three phases. In the first phase which was to last a month a number of targets thought to be of strategic importance were to be destroyed and the local IRA units were to do their best to cut all communications by attacking targets such as roads, bridges, telephones and petrol pumps. Phase Two would take three months in which forces would be built up and guerilla attacks continued and Phase Three was to be one in which the struggle would be continued 'into higher level'. As soon as the campaign began Sinn Fein announced that 'Irishmen have again risen in armed revolt against British aggression in Ireland. The Sinn Fein organizations say to the Irish people that they are proud of the risen nation and appeal to the people of Ireland to assist in every way they can the soldiers of the Irish Republican Army'. At first 'the enemy' were the British only and not the RUC and USC, who the IRA seemed to believe would not oppose them if they were asked nicely! They now maintained that no operations were to be carried out in Belfast because they feared this would lead to sectarian riots in which the Catholic population would probably suffer more than their opponents.

The IRA finally attacked on the night of 11–12 December 1956. They succeeded in destroying the BBC relay station at Rosemount near Londonderry; they blew up a new Territorial Army depot under construction at Enniskillen and set fire to the County Court House at Magherafelt. They failed to destroy three bridges over Lough Erne in Co Fermanagh, in two the mines cratered the roads and only rendered the bridges unfit for heavy traffic and in the third the mine failed to detonate altogether. An attempt to blow up the barracks at Armagh was a complete failure. The sentries were alert, the general alarm was sounded and the IRA put to flight. They got away across the border as the B Specials were not patrolling at the time and the RUC had moved north in response to intelligence which proved false. In all there were some twelve incidents, plenty in fact to show the authorities in the North that 'the balloon had gone up' and this was confirmed in the morning when the IRA proclamation was published.

The RUC, although they had been making preparations for an IRA attack for some time, received very little warning. The information they did obtain came in at the last moment and was somewhat garbled. It gave them enough to send a Reserve platoon from Belfast at full speed to North Antrim, where, in conjunction with the local RUC, they intercepted twelve men of the IRA on their way to blow up the RAF radar station at Torr Head. A gun battle followed and three of the IRA were captured. In Co Tyrone, patrols foiled IRA attempts on several targets, the most important of which was the Territorial Army Centre at Dungannon. An attack on a telephone exchange in Armagh was prevented by the RUC and a B Special patrol on the outskirts of Armagh City arrested two IRA men in a car.[1] A number of incidents failed through IRA inexperience, charges failing to go off or being badly placed and in some cases fires being extinguished before they could get a hold.

On 12 December, the strength of the RUC was 2,800 which was below establishment but 215 B Specials had been mobilized to make up their numbers. The Reserve Force still only had three platoons, all formed from the regular RUC and stationed in Belfast where it was normally employed on ordinary police duties. The total strength of the Reserve force was 113 all ranks, but it was fully mobile and self contained. It had its own vehicles, radio and cooking facilities. It was armed with Bren guns, grenades, 2-inch mortars and Piat antitank weapons as well as the usual pistols, rifles and Sten guns. The force was well trained and carried out periodic exercises with the USC in country areas. The B Specials were 11,600 strong and their patrol and road block plans were up to date and ready to put into effect at short notice. At the beginning of the campaign the County Commandants were:

Antrim	Captain R. S. Hanson, OBE, MC
Down	Lt-Col A. Turkington, OBE

Fermanagh	Lt-Col G. E. Liddle, OBE, DL, JP
Tyrone	Brigadier A. G. MacKenzie-Kennedy, CBE, DSO
Co Londonderry	Lt-Col R. W. E. Scott, OBE, JP
Armagh	Lt-Col R. E. Moody, MBE, JP
City of Londonderry	J. M. Harvey, Esq, OBE
City of Belfast	H. E. Geelan, Esq, OBE

There had been some patrolling during the summer and autumn mostly in response to the various IRA incidents, but few men were out on 12 December. When it was clear that the IRA had mounted a serious attack many units mobilized without more ado and patrolling began all over the Province.

On 13 December, the IRA attacked the RUC stations at Lisnaskea and Derrylin in Co Fermanagh. In both places the attacks were repulsed although the porch of the building at Lisnaskea was demolished. A diversionary attack was also made on Rosslea RUC Station in the same area. They also blew two more bridges, blocked some roads and cut telephone wires. The incidents continued throughout the Province but before many days all the IRA columns were back over the border in the Irish Republic. On 16 December the Irish Army and police raided the IRA General Headquarters which was in a farmhouse at Knockatallon in Co Monaghan. As they found no arms or incriminating documents, however, they had to release the men they had temporarily arrested. The raid was, needless to say, a shock to the IRA as they now had it brought home to them that there was to be no open sanctuary for them in the Republic. Mr Costello had already made his position clear on 30 November when he said, 'We are bound to ensure that unlawful activities of a military character shall cease, and we are resolved to use if necessary all the powers and forces at our disposal to bring such activities to an end. . . .' The IRA had also been condemned by the Hierarchy of the Roman Catholic Church in Ireland on 12 February 1956 when they declared that it was a mortal sin to be a member of an illegal organization and warned that no private citizen had the right to use force against another state. The Government of the Republic had already increased their border patrols. The

A and B Specials on parade at St Angelo near Enniskillen for inspection by the Secretary of State for War (Rt Hon the Earl of Derby), April 1923

The 1935 riots in Belfast

Small arms training on a rifle range

Revolver practice on the range

Fire with movement on the range

B Specials during a rifle competition

Lord Brookborough meeting B Specials

B Specials discover an IRA dugout during the 1956–62 campaign

Magherafelt Court House after fire, 1956

Captain Terence O'Neill, the former Prime Minister of Northern Ireland, presenting a shooting cup to Major Maclaren, County Commandant for Antrim

B Specials being inspected by H.E. the Governor of Northern Ireland, with Lord Brookborough in attendance, at Enniskillen. The men in the background are RUC

The Inspector General of the RUC inspecting B Specials of the
Maghera District in 1963

B Specials on parade at Enniskillen in the 1960s, wearing the
new uniform with stand-up collars

IRA hope that the campaign would 'snowball' and gain momentum on its own and set the North alight was very far from being realized. The damage they had done was small compared to their plans and they had expected to do much more. The 'Chief of Staff' of the IRA was so depressed that he considered calling the whole campaign off, but a meeting of the 'Army Council' decided to continue although all units would be recalled for Christmas to reorganize themselves.

Soon after the IRA campaign began, the British Ambassador in the Republic expressed concern over the incidents. On 15 December more regulations under the Special Powers Act were brought into force in the north of Ireland to allow for internment and curfew. A number of the IRA, especially in Belfast, were interned and this was the real reason why there were few incidents in the City. Thirty-five more B Specials had been mobilized by the end of the year and it was planned to take in another five hundred in the first quarter of 1957. On 19 December the British Prime Minister, Mr Anthony Eden, made it clear that Northern Ireland had the full support of the United Kingdom when he said in the House of Commons, 'The safety of Northern Ireland and of its inhabitants is ... a direct responsibility of Her Majesty's Government, which they will of course discharge'. Nevertheless the defence was left to the RUC and USC with occasional army support. The British Government's diplomatic pressure on the Irish Republic was, however, of great importance. Without it the repression of the IRA in the South might not have been as effective as it proved to be. On 22 December, the RUC and the Royal Engineers started to crater unapproved roads over the border. In a matter of weeks they had trenched or blown up 123 of them. On 30 December an unofficial IRA column was caught at Dunamore in Co Tyrone and three of them were captured. In the same area several IRA were wounded in an accident with a grenade and a sub-machine gun. Up to the end of the year, there had been twenty-five IRA incidents, that is over one a day, and they included the blowing up of more bridges and USC drill huts.

After Christmas, the IRA columns in the Republic crossed the border again. One of them made a second attack on the RUC barracks at Derrylin. This time they detonated a mine against the door and fired through a window mortally wounding an RUC Constable. Another Constable kept the IRA from entering with his Sten gun and, fearing the arrival of police reinforcements, they fled. The patrols and road blocks failed to catch them and they escaped across country and over the border. Two of them were subsequently arrested by the Garda. Another column spent its time trying to ambush B Special patrols but after four days had not succeeded in doing so. On New Year's Day they attacked the RUC barracks at Brookeborough. Twelve of them entered the village in a stolen lorry, stopped outside the barracks in the middle of the street and opened a heavy fire at the windows. Attempts to place two mines failed and neither detonated. The garrison of the barracks consisted of a single RUC Sergeant with a Sten gun and in two long bursts from an upper window he wounded six of the IRA, two of them mortally, as well as bursting two of the lorry's tyres and damaging the engine. To make matters worse for the raiders a hand grenade thrown at the first floor windows of the barracks bounced back and went off under the lorry. The IRA made their exit from the village in the lorry with its engine firing on only two cylinders, with two flat tyres. The tilting gear had been damaged also, the men in the back were in imminent danger of being tipped into the road. They drove five miles towards the border and then left the two men who were dying in a cowshed and took to the open country. After five hours' marching in constant danger from the many B Special patrols they crossed the border into the Republic. All were subsequently arrested by the Garda and the Irish Army. The RUC were in hot pursuit in land-rovers and soon found the two men dead in the cowshed. This raid was a disaster for the IRA by any standard. Practically everything went wrong; they outnumbered the opposition by twelve to one; they could only claim to have broken a few windows, and had suffered two killed, four wounded and the rest captured in the Republic. Yet the two men killed were made into martyrs, ballads were written and thousands attended their funerals.

In the following weeks the Southern Government acted under the Offences against the State Act and the Special Branch arrested large numbers of the IRA and interned them. The IRA insisted that they had no quarrel with the Government of the Republic and had orders not to resist its forces but next day most of the IRA leadership was caught in Dublin and arrested. Unfortunately these steps were weakened when a judge in the South let some of the interned men free and even ordered ammunition which had been taken from them to be returned.

During the first six months of 1957, IRA activity continued at a high level, there being 235 incidents in all. These included the blowing up of many road bridges, electricity transformers, USC and TA drill huts and other acts of arson and sabotage. Some of the incidents were major as when on 18 January, the local Tyrone IRA succeeded in blowing up the Territorial Army Centre at Dungannon. On 2 March the IRA from Londonderry stopped a goods train by using emergency detonators on the line north of Strabane and set it to run at full speed into the buffers of the station in Londonderry wrecking it and putting the station out of action. On 7 March, yet another attack was made on Derrylin RUC barracks and this time a Special Constable was wounded. Five days later an attempt to rescue a member of the IRA from the City Hospital in Belfast was frustrated by the RUC guard and two of the IRA involved were captured.

At 2330 hours on 12 April 1957 two automatic telephone exchanges were blown up by the IRA at Dunloy and Loughguile in the northern part of Co Antrim. A section consisting of a Sergeant and six Constables of the USC who were on patrol on the Clough–Cloughmills road, were ordered by the District Commandant to check another automatic exchange at Glarryford. When they arrived Special Sergeant Francis Wisener ordered Special Constable Andrew Russell to climb over the railings and inspect the exchange. He found a suitcase with a ticking noise coming from it concealed under some grass cuttings and returned and told the Sergeant. Sergeant Wisener then climbed in, picked up the suitcase and carried it as far as the railings. He then climbed out and went to report by telephone. While he was gone Special Constable Robert Patton, realizing that if the bomb went off it could seriously damage the exchange, told his son, Special Constable James Patton, to jump over the railings and hand the suitcase out to him. This he did and Constable Patton senior then carried it some thirty yards away and put it down. Later he thought that even this was not far enough and carried it a further seventy yards and put it in a ditch. When the army bomb disposal team arrived they found the suitcase contained thirteen and a half pounds of gelignite with a time fuse which had failed to function. The bomb was however in an extremely dangerous condition. Sergeant Wisener and Constables Patton, father and son, were subsequently awarded the British Empire Medal for Gallantry.[2]

In spite of the large number of incidents, the IRA campaign was not doing at all well. Their plan to hold and strengthen resistance centres throughout Northern Ireland had certainly failed. After four months there was no sign that their aim of 'breaking down the enemy's administration in the occupied area until he is forced to withdraw his forces' was more than a dream. In fact they had lost the initiative by the summer; their 'active service units' were on the run and had to spend their time evading the security forces rather than attacking. The RUC continued to make arrests; on 4 January, with army assistance, seven men were taken in the Mourne Mountains and on 15 January two more in the Glenshane Pass in Co Londonderry. By April the Londonderry IRA were practically all interned. IRA attempts to ambush the RUC, B Specials and British troops continued during the spring and early summer but were completely unsuccessful. Often IRA plans had to be abandoned: an attack on the RUC barracks at Carrickmore had to be called off as patrols were everywhere. An IRA column in Co Tyrone found it impossible to get supplies and had to retreat to Strabane. It was far from easy to cross the border. Only seventeen roads were left open and these were guarded day and night. In March most of the craters in unapproved roads were replaced by spikes set in concrete which could not be planked over or filled in so easily. There were now 122 roads that had been spiked and thirty-six which were cratered.

The IRA found that there was little sympathy for them among the Catholic population in the North. 'Safe' houses were very few and far between and lodging for the night could only be obtained by armed intimidation. The IRA could not use the roads and had to move across country. Many of their apparent successes such as the Derry train wreck were no more than small parts of larger plans which failed. It had been hoped to cause a number of train wrecks and to destroy the one break-down crane in the Province so as to bring rail transport to a halt. Even if they got back to the Republic, the Southern Government continued to harass them. This was however too much for the extreme Republicans in the Dail. At the end of the month the Coalition Government under Mr Costello fell apart when Clan na Poblachta moved a vote of no confidence. On 12 February the Dail was dissolved and on 5 March a general election returned De Valera and Fianna Fail to power. Sinn Fein won four seats polling 66,000 votes which showed considerable support for the IRA. What was worse was that the new Government began to release the internees in the South.

In January 1957, the Inspector General of the RUC set up a planning committee to co-ordinate all operations against the IRA. It was presided over by the Deputy Inspector General and consisted of the Army Chief of Staff of the Northern Ireland District, the Commander of 39 Infantry Brigade, the Staff Officer of the Ulster Special Constabulary and two County Inspectors of the RUC headquarters staff. Other officers were co-opted as necessary from time to time. By the end of April, 910 B Specials had been mobilized for full-time duty with the RUC. Two more platoons of the Reserve force were formed but this time half of the men were supplied by the USC. At the end of April they were stationed at Fivemiletown in Co Tyrone and Moneymore in Co Londonderry. The duty of taking the offensive against the IRA fell to the five platoons of the Reserve force. They were kept very busy making searches, setting up road blocks by day, planning ambushes and patrolling. They were equipped with armoured, long wheel-base Land-Rovers, larger armoured trucks and some scout cars. They took great care to avoid being ambushed and never followed the same routes at fixed times. They were very circumspect when approaching the scene of an explosion or any other incident. The B Specials made their patrols at the rate of one a week in most areas but rather less in the quiet areas. They were used as before to man road blocks, guard important people and places, including RUC Stations, and they made foot patrols on roads and on the border at night. They were always ready to turn out in force in emergency. The B Specials, as the Reserve force, followed tactics designed to prevent ambush. Their patrols were generally spread in pairs so that all would not be caught together and they set up their road blocks in different places and often changed them more than once during a night. The army and the Royal Air Force co-operated when asked, generally by making large scale sweeps by day in open country.

All these measures cost a lot of money. The estimate for 1956–7 for the Special Constabulary was £480,004 but for 1957–8 was £1,287,522. In February, tighter regulations were issued to control emergency mobilization of the USC as this was expensive. It was emphasized that Government authority was required for every mobilization and payment could not be made until reports had been received and approved. In ordinary circumstances, therefore, the approval of the Inspector General had to be obtained for any mobilization. In sudden emergency, however, the USC could be called out at once, but the County Commandant was required to obtain the concurrence of the County Inspector of the RUC, who had to report to headquarters without delay. If a unit was called out and the action was not subsequently approved, then the men got no pay. It was typical of the Specials, however, that they would rather this happened than that they should miss an opportunity of preventing some IRA outrage or capturing them afterwards.

By midsummer, the IRA was wholly on the defensive. It was at this time that they began to dig concealed dugouts in unfrequented places in which to live. The indifference of the Nationalist population and the grip which the RUC and the USC had on the Province had forced them to this extreme. One of their units in Co Tyrone ran out of supplies and four separate consignments sent from Dublin were intercepted. All movement had to be on foot by night, sleeping out in the open country. The situation was made worse by the short summer nights. After one unit had been on the run in Co Londonderry for two months they had to withdraw to the Republic, half starved and exhausted. The autumn was spent by the IRA setting up a new intelligence network and an organization for getting in messages and supplies. At the same time training camps were opened in the South. The general intention was to plan a new offensive for the next winter season when the nights would be long. It was decided to give up any idea of attacking police stations as these were now all heavily sandbagged with reinforced garrisons of Specials and they were in radio contact with each other. The hope was to ambush the RUC mobile patrols. This the IRA succeeded in doing very early in the morning of 4 July. An RUC Reserve force mobile patrol was caught close to the border near Forkhill in Co Armagh. Fire was opened from two places and one constable was killed and another wounded. The attack was clearly mounted from the Republic and the IRA retired across the border immediately afterwards. In the following days, the new Dublin Government, realizing that the campaign was not going to fade away of its own accord, made some sixty arrests under the Offences Against the State Act and opened the internment camp at the Curragh. From this time the IRA got very little support from the south of Ireland.

In spite of all their difficulties the IRA managed to keep the campaign going during the second half of 1957. There were twenty-two incidents in July, falling to seventeen and eighteen in August and September, rising to twenty-six in October and falling again to thirteen and ten in November and December. The total of 106 incidents was considerably less than half the number in the first six months of the year. The attempt to start a winter campaign in October was never allowed to develop by the security forces in the North. In fact counter measures led to the arrest of a number of the IRA and arms and explosives were captured. Nevertheless some of the IRA activities were disturbing. On 17 August an RUC Sergeant was killed and three constables and two soldiers were wounded at Coalisland in a deliberately planned booby trap into which they were lured by a telephone call. There were four attacks on RUC stations, mostly from long range and they were not pressed home. On 3 September shots were fired across the border wounding a Special Constable guarding a newly spiked road while the concrete set and on 8 October a bridge over the River Blackwater was demolished by an explosion. The IRA made many attempts to lure patrols into ambushes but no more succeeded. A Land-Rover was, however, blown up near the border in Co Fermanagh but no one was hurt. The majority of the remaining incidents were the blowing up or burning of customs huts, USC and TA drill huts, electricity transformers, telephone exchanges and kiosks and in one case a bus depot. Many of the incidents in August were in the Newry area and on 13 August a curfew was enforced there from 2300 hours to 0530 hours each night. The IRA urged people to defy it but they refused and after the situation had improved it was lifted on 9 September. On 11 November the IRA suffered a reverse when four of them were killed by the premature explosion of a bomb just south of the border at Edentubber, near Dundalk. On 9 August the IRA had issued a manifesto in which they threatened the RUC and the USC, 'The resistance can hardly be expected to differentiate between men, trained, organized and equipped along military lines (although clad in police uniforms) and British troops'. The Ulster Special Constabulary being British never wished for any such distinction. The IRA winter campaign of 1957–8 was therefore a complete failure. Much of what had been achieved was by local IRA units in the North. The morale of the rank and file was now low but they were still led by fanatics. There were reports that some members of the IRA preferred to emigrate rather than take part in raids on the North.

The security forces had had many successes. By October, fifty-one of the IRA had been convicted and had received prison sentences averaging five years. There were 136 of them interned in the North in October and by December this had risen to 167. A total of 133 weapons from machine guns to pistols had been recovered by the police as well as a large quantity of ammunition and explosives. On 27 July two more Reserve force platoons were formed and on 2 September four more making eleven in all. The proportion of Special Constables in these platoons was higher than before and the normal complement of a platoon was one RUC Head Constable, two RUC Sergeants, one Special Sergeant, eight RUC Constables and twenty-four Special Constables. In November a special training camp for the Reserve platoons was opened at Bally-kinlar. All mobilized B Specials of whom there were now some 1,300, received a course whether they were to join a Reserve platoon or not. Towards the end of the year, Brigadier Knox retired from the position of Staff Officer to the USC because of ill health and was replaced by Brigadier I. H. Good, DSO.

The year 1958 started with a considerable increase in IRA activity, there being twenty-five incidents during January. Three customs posts were destroyed, there were two attacks on police patrols and the usual attacks on electricity and telephone targets. Some bridges and roads were blown up in the hope of ambushing any security forces who closed on the spot. On the night of 14 January 1958, a patrol of a Special Sergeant and five Special Constables was sent from Upperlands in Co Londonderry to help guard the RUC Station at Swatragh. Swatragh is three miles from Upperlands and is in a Nation-

alist area. Some of the patrol were detailed to man the sandbagged emplacement in front of the station and others to set
up a road block on the Garvagh Road. At about 2200 hours,
distant explosions were heard and the road block men closed
on the RUC Station to report. As they arrived in the vicinity
of the station, a heavy fire was suddenly opened on them from
four places across the street. The patrol took what cover they
could and with two Special Constables in the sandbagged emplacement returned the fire. Almost immediately Special Constable James Murray was hit in the face and leg. Propped
against the wall of a house on one knee, he continued to fire
his sten gun[3] until it jammed and his head wound was bleed-
ing so badly that he could no longer see. He then told Special
Sergeant Thomas McCaughey of his plight. The Sergeant
took his sten gun and cleared it and decided to make a dash
for the station to summon medical assitance. This he did under
heavy fire covered by Constable McKeown of the RUC. When
an ambulance and doctor had been summoned, Sergeant
McCaughey returned to his patrol and together with members
of the RUC attempted to intercept the raiders, but they had
fled. Both Special Sergeant McCaughey and Special Constable Murray were subsequently awarded the British Empire
Medal for Gallantry.[4] B Specials from all over the district
heard the firing and at once threw on their uniforms, grabbed
their rifles and converged on the scene in their private cars. A
car with three Specials in it on a lonely road to the east of
Swatragh saw a car driving towards them at breakneck speed.
They recognized[5] it as the car of a well known IRA suspect,
stopped it and arrested the driver who had soaking wet feet
and had been slightly wounded in the chin. The attack on
Swatragh was made by IRA from the South with the assistance
of local men. Before the attack they had felled trees across
roads leading to the village. Next day a large combined search
by the police and army was made in the district and a dugout
was found. A second dugout was discovered the following day.
Aerial reconnaissance with helicopters was used on these
searches to photograph wild country and proved very helpful.

In February there was a substantial decrease in incidents and most of these took place in the border areas. The road blocks and patrols of the B Specials undoubtedly deterred the IRA from making deep thrusts into Northern Ireland. The most serious incident was a tip and run attack on Middletown RUC Station in Co Armagh. There were a few explosions in USC and Royal Observer Corps huts near the border, and some telephone and electricity targets were attacked as usual. The RUC found arms near Strabane and near Kilrea in Co Londonderry. There were now 178 men interned in the North and the approved roads across the border were reduced to fourteen. On 16 February, to try and obtain some heavier weapons to deal with the RUC armoured cars, the IRA raided the British Army establishment at Blandford in Dorset. They secured the guard at the gate but had to fire at one of the magazine sentries. Shortly afterwards the general alarm was sounded and the IRA had to run for it. They were empty-handed but managed to escape and get out of the country.

In March there were thirteen incidents but five of them were seizures of arms by the RUC and one the discovery of a tunnel out of Crumlin Road Gaol, which prevented an escape. The worst incident was the ambush of an RUC Land-Rover near Rosslea but although it was blown up and it was fired on by machine guns, there were no casualties. In April there were five explosions on Easter Monday but none of them was serious. The IRA made a propaganda demonstration in Clady, Co Tyrone, where they crossed the border, hoisted the tricolour, read the 1916 proclamation of the Republic and waited in ambush. The RUC were not going to be caught as easily as that, but reoccupied the village with armoured vehicles shortly afterwards. In this month the number of men interned in the North rose to 192 and in the South where there had been considerable activity against the IRA there were 131 interned in the Curragh. During May and June, IRA units in the North were almost completely disrupted. The RUC had by now succeeded in widening their intelligence net which made it very difficult for the IRA to operate at all. They succeeded in burning a bus or two, cutting down some telephone poles and blowing up the remains of two customs huts but there were prompt arrests after these incidents. The RUC also found another dugout and some arms near Newry. It seems probable that most of the IRA from the South had returned to the Republic.

In June 1958 the Nationalist Member for South Armagh produced a bus stop sign with bullet holes in it and alleged that Specials with nothing to do had indulged in indiscriminate target practice. This allegation was indignantly described by Mr Topping, the Minister for Home Affairs, as absurd and ridiculous. He said no facts or witnesses had been produced and his conduct in bringing the matter before the House could only be described as irresponsible! Nationalist animosity towards the Specials was always present. That all they could find to complain about was such a trivial matter is in itself significant.

In July the IRA returned to the attack and in the middle of the month caused some thirteen explosions damaging roads and customs houses on the border. They murdered an RUC Constable on his bicycle in Co Armagh and on 17 July attacked the RUC Station in Armagh City. The attack failed as the wires to the bomb broke: the miscreants were captured in Armagh Cathedral where they tried to hide. The security forces had considerable success during the month, they found another dugout in Co Armagh and interrupted the IRA trying to blow up the railway line near Newtownbutler. On 15 July the leader of the IRA in Co Fermanagh was killed in an accidental explosion in Co Cavan. On 24 August his successor led an attempt to blow up the customs post at Mullan in Co Fermanagh. His plan was to creep unarmed across the border with one companion to see if the coast was clear. Unfortunately for him the Special Constabulary was in ambush. The two men approached, walking on the grass verge and stopping now and again to listen. When they were close enough they were challenged, one man surrendered but the other tried to run back across the border. In the light of flares he was seen running across a field and as he ignored several orders to halt the Specials opened fire and he was shot dead. A van waiting on the Republic side of the border then drove rapidly away.[6]

During the rest of the year the number of incidents fell slightly from fourteen in August to eleven in December. Late in September the Special branch in the Republic arrested most of the IRA leadership and although two important men escaped from the Curragh at about the same time, control of IRA operations went to pieces. The northern IRA was left to its own devices and the campaign would have collapsed altogether but for the work of a few individuals. Nevertheless they were a considerable nuisance. Three RUC stations were fired at from long range and two B Specials' houses were raided for arms. There were nine explosions at USC and TA drill huts, customs posts and other places. The total number of incidents during the year was 126, forty-six of which were classed as minor, considerably less than half the number of the previous year. On the other hand the police found seven arms dumps and two dugouts. Their vigilance also prevented a number of IRA attacks along the border. By the end of the year the IRA were really losing heart and many wished to stop the campaign.

Two more Reserve platoons had been formed at the beginning of 1958 making thirteen in all. By now they were provided mostly by the USC with RUC leadership. They now consisted of a Head Constable, two RUC Sergeants, a Special Sergeant, four RUC Constables and twenty-eight Special Constables. The Reserve force had now reached its peak strength of 516 all ranks, 222 of whom were mobilized B Specials. The total number of B Specials mobilized for all purposes now reached 1,424. The rest of the B force were approximately 13,000 strong. In October 1958 there were waiting lists in all counties in Northern Ireland of men wishing to join the Ulster Special Constabulary. It was possible to pick and choose and many excellent men who had already had experience in the services were coming forward.

With experience, the methods of patrol became more efficient. In October 1958 in Co Armagh a scheme was introduced in which the patrols were designated Red, Blue and Green followed by a number. Red patrols were in the border areas and they operated on foot to check the movement of suspicious people moving other than on the approved roads. Blue patrols were used to set up check points on minor roads in a given area. Green patrols were for checking traffic on main roads and would remain on the same road although they would from time to time move along it to a different place. The number following the colour indicated the position or area of the patrol. Green 3 for example, was a road check on the Armagh–Caledon road while Red 10 was a border patrol centred on the townland of Carrickawilkin near Keady. Road blocks were set up by sections at least five strong. They were never put in exactly the same place and were moved during the night from time to time. The whole section was directed to conceal itself at the side of the road when there was no traffic. Two men would be detailed to use a red torch to order traffic to stop and would only step out into the road when necessary. The patrol commander with a white torch would examine the vehicle and the remainder of the patrol would remain in a concealed covering position. In this way attack from a vehicle or by the IRA creeping up on them would be made more difficult.[7] In Co Londonderry, a scheme had been in force for some time of transporting B Special patrols by RUC transport to set up their road blocks in Nationalist areas some distance from their homes. The IRA soon got to know the distinctive noise of these vehicles and could tell where the blocks had been positioned. A new scheme was therefore put forward for the B Specials to use their own cars. This was also cheaper and more patrols could be sent out in this way as there were never enough police vehicles. A parsimonious government agreed to pay a mileage allowance but refused to carry the insurance. All they would say was that they would consider any case of damage or loss of a car sympathetically. This added mobility spread the B patrols over a much greater area and contributed substantially to the problems of the IRA.

The USC always kept their eyes open when off duty and the

files are full of their contributions to RUC Intelligence. On 4 September 1958, the Sub-District Commandant of Tamlaght in Co Londonderry on his way to town saw a man acting suspiciously at a peat stack in Moyagney Bog. After returning home he went with another Special Constable and examined the spot finding two Thompson sub-machine gun magazines fully loaded. The Tamlaght Sub-District thereafter made ambush patrols nightly in the vicinity and two youths were later detained. On 28 July reports were made of a stranger who had a key to a disused house in the neighbourhood. On the same day it was also reported that an IRA suspect had been absent from home for four days during a particular IRA outrage. Such reports were endless – a report of hammering in the glen after dark – lights reported in a disused house – a strange formation of sticks discovered stuck in the ground, etc., etc. When analyzed by intelligence officers they were often of great value.

In spite of the lack of support amongst the Ulster minority for the IRA, Nationalist politicians never missed an opportunity to criticize the Specials. In October 1958 the *New Statesman* took up the Republican line of propaganda and suggested that B Specials were used to interfere with Nationalist voters going to the poll. Mr Brian Faulkner, the Government Chief Whip, refuted 'this utterly contemptible attack' maintaining that there was absolutely no truth in this allegation. The annual estimates were always an occcasion for the Opposition at Stormont to show their animosity towards the Specials. The estimate presented in February 1959 was £1,770,640, or four times what it had been before the emergency. Nearly a million of this was to pay the 1,600 mobilized B Specials, even so the cost of the part-time force was doubled to pay for the extra patrols. Predictably the member for Falls called this a scandalous waste of money. A Unionist member replied that no one more than he would like to see the day when it would be unnecessary for these young men, especially in the border areas, to leave their beds night after night for the paltry sum of 15s. to defend what was theirs by right. He emphasized that the RUC could not have contended with the emergency without the Special Constabulary. Sometimes of course the Specials were in the wrong. In 1959 two Special Constables were fined for practising shooting in their back yard with an air rifle for which they had no licence.

By the beginning of 1959 the IRA were, although neither side were yet sure of it, a spent force. The Government of the Republic had begun to release their internees at the end of 1958 and by February, a hundred of them were free and only forty remained. This was not so much due to their assessment of the situation as because there was a case before the European Court of Human Rights brought by one of the internees. During the first four months of 1959 there were as many captures of arms and explosives and arrests by the police as incidents caused by the IRA. Many of these incidents were also failures and the terrorists' only real success was the ambush of an RUC Land-Rover on 13 March near Clogher in which two policemen were wounded. Two days later the last internees in the South were out and the Curragh Camp closed. In the five months from May to September 1959, there were only two incidents but one of them was serious. On 26 August a Reserve force Land-Rover was blown up on the Crockada bridge near Rosslea and an RUC and a USC constable were both badly wounded. In spite of the ending of internment pressure continued on the IRA in the South. On 17 June, de Valera became President and Sean Lemass, the new Prime Minister, said about the IRA 'It is impossible to understand how any intelligent person can now believe that such activities can help any national interest. Far from contributing to the reunification of the country, it is obvious that they are having the very opposite effect and are indeed the main impediment to the development of a more constructive approach.' Throughout the summer the IRA spent the time arguing among themselves. Although it was obvious that the campaign had failed, the extremists swayed the annual convention and a motion to continue the campaign was accepted. This was not at all easy, many IRA members were emigrating and there was a lot of defeatism in their ranks. By October there had been a total of only twenty-one incidents since January and 166 men were still interned in the North. Nearly a hundred were in prison, many serving long sentences. In October, however, the hard core attacked two police stations on the border but only at very long range and they ran for it as soon as the fire was returned. An attempt to ambush police at Clady failed, not because the RUC didn't turn up but because when they did, the IRA thought discretion the better part of valour and withdrew. In November there were five incidents, all except one were minor and in border areas. On 20 November an RUC Land-Rover escorting a GPO van was ambushed and Special Constable F. W. Boyle was seriously wounded losing an eye.

At 1930 hours on 26 November 1959, a drill hall belonging to the Special Constabulary at Caledon in Co Tyrone was blown up by the IRA. The drill hall was about half a mile from the border and Special Constable Robert Allen who was off duty in his home about 400 yards from the border, heard the explosion. His brother, Special Constable Harry Allen, who lived elsewhere was also in the house. Robert Allen seized his service rifle and some ammunition and accompanied by his brother with a torch, ran as fast as he could to the bridge over the River Blackwater which at this point is the border. They took up positions in the ditch and waited. Very soon two men appeared running towards the bridge. When they were close, Harry Allen shone the torch on them and they were seen to be armed with sub-machine guns. Robert Allen ordered them to halt and when they brought their weapons to the ready, he fired over their heads. They then dropped their arms and were taken into custody, the two Allen brothers being assisted by other Specials who arrived on the scene. The brothers were awarded the British Empire Medal for Gallantry.[8] The police had other successes, as when they picked up an important IRA leader in Belfast on 4 November. On 10 November in the Ardboe area near Cookstown, a police patrol ordered three men to halt. Two obeyed and were found to be IRA men but the third tried to get away. After calling on him to stop the police opened fire and wounded him and he was subsequently captured. Two of these men were important IRA leaders.

Although IRA activity seemed to be declining drastically, it was judged prudent to continue the police counter measures. The number of mobilized B Specials reached its peak at the end of 1959 when it stood at 1,594, of whom 272 were with the Reserve force. The B Special patrols continued and the types of patrols were now laid down in the USC Patrol Orders. There were road patrols, road check points, road blocks, street patrols, tactical patrols, static guards and ambush patrols. The road patrol was the basic patrol of the USC generally made by a section of a Sergeant and six Special Constables. The object of the patrol was to ensure that the road was not used by the IRA and that bridges, culverts, telephone kiosks, electricity transformers and other targets were not interfered with. The patrol would move on foot along the side of the road facing oncoming traffic spaced out in pairs. The road check patrol was to provide a check on road users and to apprehend wanted persons. It would stop a proportion of vehicles or any acting suspiciously. The road block was to stop and examine every person and vehicle. Street patrols were normally carried out in towns with the RUC; sometimes the patrols were mixed but could be a pair of Special Constables 'on the beat'. Tactical patrols were used to search open country for the IRA and to pin them down and were normally made by full platoons. Static guards were posted at vulnerable points such as TV masts, electricity transformers, telephone exchanges, bridges and other places and could be open or concealed. Such a guard was never mounted by less than two Special Constables. An ambush patrol would conceal itself on the route to a likely target or on the border where it believed the IRA would probably pass and would wait keeping absolutely quiet. Anyone approaching would be allowed to pass the first members of the patrol and would then be challenged.

In the first three months of 1960, very little happened. There were only six incidents, none of them important and all near the border. On 2 February two members of the Lisnadill

Sub-District of the USC in Co Armagh when off duty found some arms in a disused house. Subsequently, they detained two youths acting suspiciously in the vicinity. The Northern Government then began to release the internees, the total falling from 152 in January to 126 in March. In April and May, the IRA tried a minor offensive and there were seventeen incidents. Some damage was done in a number of explosions against a GPO van, electricity transformers, customs posts, a bridge and USC drill huts. An RUC vehicle was ambushed near Belleek, but the landmine was fired too soon and the police opened fire and drove the IRA over the border. A grenade attack on an RUC Sergeant on a bicycle also misfired. In spite of a resolution at the IRA Convention in June to continue the campaign, there were only three incidents in the seven months to the end of 1960. There were two attacks on police stations and one ambush and all were complete failures. The internees continued to be released and by the end of the year there were only thirty-three left in custody.

The year 1961 began with the murder of an RUC Constable who had crossed the border to see his fiancée. In January and February there were only four other incidents but in March and April there were sixteen. These consisted of explosions against the usual targets which included five bridges all in the border area. The IRA plan seems to have been to try and isolate an enclave in South Fermanagh. On 26 April the main line railway bridge near Jonesborough in Co Armagh was damaged and traffic was stopped for some time. The IRA found it difficult to operate except in tip and run raids over the border and they could get no local support. Indeed the Nationalists in the North agreed with Sean Lemass and were actively hostile to the IRA. The Northern Government do not seem to have been unduly perturbed by the upsurge in activity in March and April and released all the internees by the end of the month.

On 29 January 1961, a USC road block near Draperstown in Co Londonderry had to open fire on a car which refused to stop and the driver was wounded. As the USC were always being unjustly criticized for being 'trigger happy' and loosing off at anything that moved, this incident is of interest and will be described in some detail. On the Sunday evening in question a section of the Tobermore Sub-District consisting of a Special Sergeant and seven Special Constables was driven in two police vehicles to a position four miles from Draperstown on the Omagh road. The road block was set up in accordance with the Standing Orders with the Sergeant and two Special Constables positioned at the chosen check point near a bridge over the River Moyola. A pair of Special Constables was stationed on either side along the road at a distance of seventy to a hundred yards. It was a dark night and had been raining heavily but the rain had just stopped. At 2250 hours a car approached from Draperstown at about forty miles an hour and one of the first two Special Constables signalled it to stop when it was a hundred yards away by waving a red torch. The car drove straight past them without slowing down, passing a large reflector 'Police Stop' board. The Sergeant also signalled the car to stop with his torch but he was nearly knocked down and so shouted to the last two men of the patrol to fire. One of the Special Constables fired a warning shot in the air as the car passed him and the other fired a single shot from the hip when the car still did not stop. The bullet went through the top of the rear offside mudguard but missed the tyre by a fraction of an inch only because the wheel at that moment was down on the springs. The bullet went on and hit the driver in the hip. The car then pulled up. The driver was aged sixty-seven, his eyesight was none too good and he had a charge of careless driving outstanding against him. He genuinely believed that the signals of the patrol were to indicate that the road was flooded, signs of which he had seen earlier in the evening. He was taken into a nearby house while a doctor and ambulance were summoned. The file on this incident consists of fifty closely typed pages of report, statements by everyone concerned and a meticulous investigation by the Royal Ulster Constabulary. A number of witnesses were traced who had stopped at the road block to enquire whether they could see the torches and signs clearly. The B Special patrol did everything in accordance with the rules and came out of this searching investigation with flying colours. The area was ardently Nationalist and had seen IRA activity and a number of subversive incidents so they had every reason to be suspicious. It was a remarkable shot which stopped the car and there was certainly no wild or indiscriminate firing. The driver was fortunately not badly wounded and recovered in hospital where he was visited on several occasions by both the County Inspector and the County Commandant. He was most reasonable in every way and made no complaint.

The IRA achieved little in May and June, when there were only five incidents but two of these were the destruction of bridges, the Moy Bridge over the River Blackwater being completely demolished. In July there were seven incidents which included explosions at no less than five bridges. On 19 July, a B Special off duty in his house at Lismore near Aughnacloy was held up by three IRA men and pushed into his kitchen. His sister shouted to another brother who was upstairs and who was also a B Special. He got his rifle and the IRA made off firing a burst from a sub-machine gun as they went. The brothers, both now with their rifles, pursued but the IRA escaped over the border. In August there were again seven incidents all in the border areas, four of which were attempts to 'unspike' spiked roads.

On 4 September 1961, the new Inspector General, Sir Albert Kennedy,[9] expressed his concern at the impunity with which the IRA were able to perpetrate outrages along the border despite the activity of police patrols. It seemed that the IRA often came into action just after a patrol had passed or withdrawn from the area. He advocated careful planning and more subtlety, such as pretending to withdraw and returning immediately afterwards. He also suggested that precautions in the safer areas could be relaxed so as to release men for the border. Even as he signed the memorandum, a patrol at Kinawley in Co Fermanagh surprised a party of the IRA and opened fire as they fled over the border. On 3 September, a train and bridge in Co Armagh were blown up and in the rest of the month there were five more minor explosions. In the last three months of 1961 there were twelve incidents, all carried out by a few hard-core IRA from the Republic. The worst of these was on 12 November near Jonesborough in Co Armagh where they crept up on a Reserve force road block and opened fire. An RUC Constable was killed and three wounded including Special Constable Gilmore. On 26 November an RUC Land-Rover was blown up by a land mine near Whitecross in Co Armagh and three were wounded including Special Constable Orr. The burning of a bus and two GPO vans during December were in fact the end of the campaign.

On 23 November the Government of the Republic set up a special military tribunal to deal with the IRA. By the end of the year they had handed out twenty-five heavy sentences. In January the IRA decided to call off the campaign. On 26 February they announced that they had 'ordered the termination of the Campaign of Resistance to British Occupation launched on 12 December 1956'. They went on to say, 'All arms and other material have been dumped and all full-time active service Volunteers have been withdrawn'. The statement ended as follows, 'The Irish Resistance Movement renews its pledge of eternal hostility to the British Forces of Occupation in Ireland. It calls on the Irish people for increased support and looks forward with confidence – in co-operation for the final and victorious phase of the struggle for the full freedom of Ireland.' This, of course, was not a 'termination' or 'withdrawal', it was defeat. The plain fact was that the morale of the rank and file of the IRA had collapsed and the fanatics who directed it simply could not get anyone to do their dirty work. The campaign had been futile from the start. The IRA manifestos showed that they lived in a dream world. Great Britain did not occupy Northern Ireland: Northern Ireland was part of the United Kingdom by the vote of the vast majority of its citizens. The idea that the IRA could fight the British whilst the RUC and the USC stood aside and watched was fantastic. The campaign in fact never even achieved the

IRA's first objectives. Operations in 1957, in which over half the incidents occurred, certainly did not 'break down the enemy's administration in the occupied area until he is forced to withdraw his forces'. The most that could be claimed was that the IRA did damage amounting to a million pounds and caused the Northern Ireland Government to spend some ten million pounds in increased security measures. Spread over five years this was no more than an irritation.

During the whole campaign there were 605 incidents, 271 of which were classed as minor. Of these incidents, 366 were in the the first thirteen months, in 1958 they fell to 126 and in the three years 1959–61 the total was 113. There were thirty-one attacks on RUC stations every one of which was beaten off. The IRA did not have any more success with their other plans. They hoped to destroy whole communication systems by their attacks on telephones, roads and bridges but they never caused much anxiety. They tried to disrupt the whole railway system in the Province by causing a number of accidents and then blowing up the only breakdown crane in Northern Ireland but this got no further than running a train into the buffers in Londonderry. They attacked a large number of electricity targets throughout the campaign but never caused more than local inconvenience. An interesting feature of the campaign was its very low casualty rate. The total on both sides was twelve killed and thirty-eight wounded. The RUC took the brunt with six killed and eighteen wounded. The USC had twelve wounded and the army two. IRA casualties were six killed and six wounded. The total seizure of arms and ammunition by the security forces amounted to 367 weapons, including Bren machine guns, sten and Thompson sub-machine guns, rifles, pistols, revolvers and a few shotguns. The haul of ammunition amounted to 13,756 rounds of various types and one and a half tons of gelignite.

Two large factors in the defeat of the campaign were the lack of support it received from the minority in Northern Ireland and the outright opposition of the Government of the Republic. The minority in the North were feeling the bene-

ficial results of the welfare state and a united Ireland did not
interest most of them at that time. The IRA therefore found it
very difficult to operate with a population two thirds of which
were hostile and one third indifferent. The opposition of the
Government in the South meant that there was no easy sanctuary and they still had to operate as an underground force.
Internment by the Dublin Government prevented any substantial expansion of the IRA and the setting up of the Special
tribunals was the last straw.

Of the security forces, the RUC must take most of the
credit for the defeat of the campaign. Its intelligence service
was excellent and its Reserve force provided first class well
trained mobile units to take the offensive against the IRA. The
Ulster Special Constabulary provided a police reserve which
raised the strength of the RUC from under 3,000 to 4,500.
They also provided half the Reserve force. It is difficult to
single out incidents in which they were involved because, unlike the troubles of the twenties, the RUC and USC worked
intimately together in 1956–62. The role of the part-time
USC was one of guarding and making movement by the IRA
very difficult. The result was that the IRA were frustrated in a
very large number of their plans without a gun battle actually
taking place. IRA attempts to ambush them or, for that matter, the Reserve force were very seldom successful and this was
not by chance but by carefully thought out tactics. At the same
time the USC provided a large reserve at very short notice
available for use in emergencies. It was their steady grip on
the Province which drove the IRA from vehicles on the roads
and 'safe houses' to the open country and dugouts where it was
possible to starve them of supplies. Finally, the unrelenting
pressure drove the southern IRA out of the Province and confined them to tip and run border raids for the last three years
of the campaign.[10] The campaign, in fact, took the form of an
attack on the Province from across the border. The defence of
the border was undoubtedly a United Kingdom responsibility
and the duty of the army, but, as in the twenties, it was done
by the police. No one seems to have questioned this policy and

it had the tacit agreement of the Governments at Westminster and Stormont. The army was kept busy guarding its own establishments and co-operating in large scale cross country drives when its help was requested by the RUC and such assistance was freely rendered. The defeat of the indigenous IRA was brought about by good intelligence, RUC and USC vigilance and by internment. The total number of men interned during 1956–62 was 335 and the maximum detained at one time was 187. All were released well before the end of the campaign, 179 on recognizances and the rest unconditionally. A total of 204 people were prosecuted and 113 of these were imprisoned for a total of 637½ years. Others entered into recognizances, were fined or put on probation.

NOTES

1. This was not strictly a patrol, it was a Sub-District Commandant and a Sergeant Instructor on their way to turn out Milford Sub-District.
2. Sergeant Wisener's employment was as a foreman of a Pig Farm and he was fifty-two years old. Constable Robert Patton was the same age and was a postman: he had served in the army during the war. His son was twenty-nine years old and a labourer.
3. Sten guns had recently been issued to the USC on the scale of one per section. They greatly increased the fire power of B Special patrols.
4. Sergeant McCaughey, a carpenter, was aged forty and had served in the USC for seventeen years, Constable Murray was forty-five and a textile worker who had two periods of service with the USC and had been in the army during the whole of the Second World War.
5. It was a Wolseley which had a small light in front of the radiator.

6. An attempt to make capital out of James Crossan's death was made in the South. He was described as a Sinn Fein organizer and an article in the *United Irishman* was entitled 'The Murder of James Crossan'. It was alleged that he had been with three friends in Northern Ireland and was walking back to the place where he had left his van across the border when he was shot dead. He was given an IRA funeral.

7. When a road block was ordered, all cars would be stopped but for a road check only a proportion would be examined.

8. Special Constable Robert Allen was a farmer aged thirty-five and his brother was a bus driver aged thirty.

9. On 15 January 1961, Sir Albert Kennedy, the Deputy Inspector General relieved Sir Richard Pim as Inspector General of the RUC and therefore as Inspector General of the USC as well. Sir Albert had started his career in the police as a B Special before joining the regular RUC.

10. The *Sunday Times* Insight team made the totally uninformed statement that the B Specials were unimportant in the 1956–62 campaign and quotes an anonymous soldier 'who has studied the records' as saying they were just a 'bloody nuisance'. A superficial perusal would indeed show that most of the incidents involved the Reserve force rather than the Specials, but this is only half the story. Certainly a study of IRA histories does not reflect such a shallow conclusion.

CHAPTER NINE

The Last Phase, 1962–9

After its decisive defeat, the IRA spent 1962 in recriminations and in arguments between factions. It was no real danger but its proclamation calling off the campaign issued in February had made it quite clear that it had no intention of giving up the struggle but was merely waiting for a more suitable opportunity. Patrols and road checks by the Ulster Special Constabulary did not cease immediately in case the IRA was bluffing and they continued with decreasing frequency for the best part of the rest of the year. The estimates for the USC for 1962–3, presented shortly after the IRA proclamation, were for £1,784,000, over a million of which was to pay the 1,141 B Specials who were still mobilized for full-time duty. During 1962 the number of mobilized men was gradually reduced and had fallen to 589 by the end of the year. Of these 148 were in the Reserve force, although three platoons were disbanded in July 1962.

In May 1962 the future of the Ulster Special Constabulary was considered by the Ministry of Home Affairs. It was agreed that the USC should remain in being for the foreseeable future but that its strength of 12,606 might be reduced to the pre-emergency figure of 11,008. Any reduction was to be made by limiting the number of men in each Sub-District rather than disbanding whole Sub-Districts. It was thought best not to revert to the old system of Active and Reserve categories but to keep all men fully trained in a single category. To the two principal roles of a reserve for the RUC and as a force in emergency to guard vulnerable points and provide a network of patrols a new function was considered. At the time in the United Kingdom a great deal of thought was being given to the problem of defence against nuclear weapons. It was considered that the USC might be required to be trained in the civil defence role as well.

In March 1963, there was a slight indication that the IRA was not entirely quiescent when two of its members blew themselves up in a premature explosion in Co Cork. Nevertheless patrols by the Ulster Special Constabulary had now ceased although it was decided to keep the strength at 12,500. The number of mobilized B Specials was reduced to approximately 300 who were required to keep the RUC up to strength. During the year the Reserve force was reduced to three platoons composed entirely of RUC personnel, based in Belfast. Some fifty-six B-men were still employed guarding important people. Lieutenant-Colonel S. Miskimmin had now relieved Brigadier Good as Staff Officer to the Inspector General for the Ulster Special Constabulary. Pay in the USC remained at the rate to which it had been raised on 1 April 1961 by which the annual bounty for a Special Constable was £12 and the sum of 20s. was paid for each extra patrol. At about this time the USC uniform was altered and a new type of tunic with a stand-up collar was issued. During 1964 the whole USC was rearmed with new 0.303-inch Mark IV rifles in place of the older types which had been in service for many years. In 1966 the sten guns were replaced by Sterling Machine Carbines to the scale of one for each section. It was planned to replace all the revolvers with a new type of automatic pistol but the force was disbanded before this could be done.

After 1964 the IRA began to recover from its defeat in 1962 and started to rebuild its strength. It seemed, however, to favour a political rather than a violent policy, mainly as a result of Dr Roy Johnston, a Marxist, joining the Army Council. Relations between the North and South of Ireland were, however, greatly improved when on 14 January 1965, the two

Prime Ministers met in Northern Ireland. Constitutional subjects were not discussed and the meeting was welcomed by all except the extremists on both sides. In 1964 the IRA had staged protests over the visit of HRH Princess Margaret to the Irish Republic and in 1965 they fired on HMS *Brave Borderer*, a British motor torpedo boat on a visit to Waterford. Then on 7 March they really showed their disapproval and blew up Nelson's Pillar in O'Connell Street in Dublin. Fears that the IRA were going to cause further trouble increased during the year and in November, fifty of the Ulster Special Constabulary were mobilized for full-time duty to provide guards for the members of the cabinet. Next month another 128 were mobilized for a minimum period of six months to guard various police headquarters, the RUC depot at Sprucefield and RUC stations in Nationalist areas.

By February 1966, with the approach of the fiftieth anniversary of the 1916 Rising greater precautions were considered necessary. At first these were confined to a warning to the RUC in their stations to be on guard against attack and when making road checks to be ready for trouble. In March, owing to the uncertain conditions prevailing, a few walking patrols a month were carried out by the USC to provide a steadying influence throughout the Province. At the same time it was decided to re-form three additional platoons of the Reserve force and station them at Londonderry, Clogher and Whitecross. Ninety Special Constables were mobilized for twelve months to relieve the RUC personnel required for this purpose. By April there were indications that the IRA were likely to resort to violence in Belfast to mark the Easter Rising and on 4 April it was decided to put the whole of the Ulster Special Constabulary in the Patrol category for the rest of the month and for each man to do one patrol a week. Next day the Counties were ordered to guard important electricity and telephone installations.

The actual Easter weekend passed over with only minor incidents but as the real danger point was believed to be 17 April, road blocks were put on all the approved roads across the border on 15 April and, to guard against those who crossed by unapproved roads, an inner line was manned to prevent intruders reaching Belfast. This line held the bridges across the River Bann north of Lough Neagh and the line of the old Newry canal south of Lough Neagh. In all, fourteen check points were required to hold these lines. For 17 April, over two hundred of the RUC from the counties were drafted into Belfast and their place was taken by 160 men of the USC. The result was that there was no trouble at all in the city. With the emotional atmosphere of the fiftieth anniversary celebrations of the 1916 Rising, however, both Sinn Fein and the IRA gained support. Sinn Fein attempted to organize itself in the North in the guise of Republican clubs until these were banned by Mr William Craig, the Minister for Home Affairs, in 1967.

The fact that the 1916 Rising Celebrations were allowed in Northern Ireland at all caused considerable tension in Protestant circles. About this time there was a sinister development when it became clear that there was a Protestant counterpart to the IRA operating. This body known as the Ulster Volunteer Force was fortunately very small and inefficient. Members of it attempted to murder some IRA men in Malvern Street in Belfast but instead shot the wrong men who were innocent Roman Catholics. They were speedily arrested, brought to trial and sentenced to long terms of imprisonment. The UVF was proscribed by Stormont in the same way as Sinn Fein and the IRA. The emergence of the Ulster Volunteer Force was worrying as it was feared in some quarters that the Special Constabulary would not be so effective against them as they had always proved to be against the IRA. There was an equally sinister development on the Republican side when in 1967 a splinter group of the IRA called the Saor Eire Action Group carried out a number of bank raids in the Republic.

On 7 May 1966, the police in the Republic found an IRA document parts of which were read to the Dail by the Minister of Justice. It was a plan for the future and included a great deal of social action. On 21 May the 'Belfast New Letter' published what purported to be the remainder of the document which related to Northern Ireland. It was a plan to take over the Catholic areas of Belfast and make an armed stand coupled with a worldwide appeal to the United Nations. The armed stand was to be similar to that made in the 1956 Hungarian Rising and, of course, the 1916 Rebellion in Dublin. The plan also envisaged the intervention of the Irish Republic in support of the northern Catholics. The document also contained plans for infiltrating labour, civil rights organizations, trades unions, the British Army and the RUC. The Republican publicity committee in Dublin said that the document only represented suggestions for future policy and it was obvious that the IRA was not strong enough to attempt anything so ambitious. Nevertheless it is of interest as it shows how the extreme members of the IRA were still thinking and that their real object was still the unification of Ireland by force. It also shows why the security authorities in Northern Ireland could not afford to ignore the IRA and why they took such elaborate precautions over the period of the 1916 Rising celebrations.

Throughout the period defence schemes were kept up to date in the USC. The scheme for Co Down, for example, was designed for rapid use if an IRA attack occurred without warning. Its principle aim was to seal the perimeter of the county by a ring of some fifty road blocks to prevent the IRA escaping. On the alarm being given the plan laid down exactly where the Sub-Districts were to set up their road blocks and these were arranged close to the homes of the B Specials so that the operation could be mounted extremely quickly. There were eight variations of the main plan which allowed for attacks in adjacent counties or on army barracks or other important places. The plan also provided for fifteen small mobile columns of up to a dozen men to be ready to proceed in private cars or taxis to the assistance of places under attack, to search particular areas or to set up special road blocks.

In May 1968 the establishment of the USC was still 12,542 and the estimates in 1967–8 to support this strength amounted to £744,100. Of this sum £27,000 was required to pay for the

Headquarters staff and £124,200 for the County Staffs,
£194,300 was needed for the mobilized members and
£194,000 for the part-time members. In June it was announced that as an economy measure the establishment was to
be cut to 8,285, a reduction of over 4,000 men. The reduction
was to be made partly by stopping recruiting and relying on
natural wastage and partly by rigidly applying the age limit of
sixty. This age limit had, in fact, applied to all new entries
since 1947 but members recruited before that date had been
exempt from this rule. The men who had to go included many
District and Sub-District Commandants but did not amount
to more than 5 per cent of the whole force. The reduction of
the force upset the men, especially those who had to go. The
Minister for Home Affairs, Mr William Craig, went to inspect
a church parade of the USC at Lisnaskea on 16 June 1968.
Only seventy men paraded out of some 400 in the District, a
poor performance which indicated the feelings in the ranks. As
a result the County Adjutant wrote to one of the Sub-District
Commandants who had not been present to ask for his reasons.
The reply came in the form of his resignation which, after
some weeks' delay, was accepted by headquarters. The officer
in question had some forty years' service in the USC and on
12 September his Sub-District failed to turn out for a road
block exercise. In the end ten Special Constables resigned in
sympathy with their Sub-District Commandant. Incidents
such as this have been cited to show that discipline in the
USC was poor. It must be remembered that these men were
civilians but if an emergency had arisen all of them would
have been at their posts. Nevertheless, tact and an understand-
ing of the Ulsterman were always required in the leadership of
the force. Any serious breach of discipline always led to the
dismissal of the member concerned. Such incidents were more
than balanced by others which showed the USC to advantage.
On 27 April 1968, nineteen teams from the regular army,
the Royal Air Force, the Territorial Army, the Royal Ulster
Constabulary and the Ulster Special Constabulary took part in
the Northern Ireland Command Rifle Meeting at Ballykinlar.

The Hamiltonsbawn Sub-District of the USC from Co Armagh came first winning the Queen Victoria Trophy. The runners up were Comber Sub-District from Co Down and Ballygowan Sub-District also from Co Down. This was the first time since 1897 when the competition began that the Trophy had been won by other than an army team. To take the first three prizes was a remarkable achievement for the Specials.

In midsummer 1969, the strength of the Ulster Special Constabulary had fallen to 8,579 and it is appropriate to review its organization. On 31 January 1969, Mr Anthony Peacocke, the Deputy Inspector General had relieved Sir Albert Kennedy as Inspector General and as the last head of the USC who was a policeman. At the Inspector General's headquarters in Belfast were the Staff Officer (Lieutenant-Colonel S. Miskimmin), an Assistant Staff Officer, a Paymaster, two Special Sergeants and ten Special Constables all on full-time duty. In the various City and County Headquarters were eight City and County Commandants, seven Adjutants, fifty-eight Sergeant Instructors, four armourers and eight Special Constables. The County and City Commandants were:

Belfast	(Deputy City Commandant) Colonel J. Brown
Londonderry	(City Commandant) Lt-Col K. B. L. Davidson, DL
Co Londonderry	Lieutenant-Colonel R. W. H. Scott, OBE, JP
Co Armagh	Captain F. M. A. Torrens-Spence, DSO, DSC, RN
Co Tyrone	Commander J. S. T. Reilly, RN
Co Down	Major A. D. Woods
Co Antrim	Major F. B. S. Maclaran
Co Fermanagh	Captain T. S. Anderson

The part-time members of the force numbered thirty-two District Commandants, 315 Sub-District Commandants and 8,134 Special Sergeants and Constables. The remuneration of the permanent staff had kept pace with police pay: the Staff Officer now received £2,925 rising to £3,140 per annum and County and City Commandants £2,190 per annum. The annual bounty for part-time members was £125 for District Commandants, £20 for Platoon Sergeants and £15 for Special Constables. For this bounty they had to do twenty-four training drills a year as well as an annual weapon training course. Patrols could be substituted for drills at the Inspector General's discretion, one patrol counting as two drills. For additional patrols Special Constables were paid 9s. an hour. The estimates for 1968–9 for the USC amounted to £669,900, £190,000 of which was to pay the mobilized men still serving as part of the RUC.

In 1968 the IRA had burned some buses in a labour dispute with an American firm at Shannon and they had also blown up a foreign fishing boat in the South. The next year they burned some German farms in the Republic. These acts did not, however, show their real policy at this time. The IRA had decided that their best course was to back a Civil Rights campaign in the North. In August 1967 there had been a meeting of people in Londonderry, including Cathal Goulding, the 'Chief of Staff' of the IRA, to form a Civil Rights Association. It was a year before they held their first demonstration which was a march from Coalisland to Dungannon on 24 August 1968. Its aim was to protest against housing policy in the area. It was re-routed by the police to avoid the square at Dungannon and the possibility of a counter demonstration. The marchers accepted the re-routing and there was consequently no trouble. Nevertheless it was seen by Unionists to be a Republican march masquerading under the Civil Rights banner. Seventy of the stewards were Republicans including ten members of the IRA.

The march from Coalisland to Dungannon encouraged the Civil Rights Association, which included left-wing and Republican elements in Londonderry, to organize a march in the city and to choose a route normally used by Loyalist and Protestant processions. On 3 October 1968 the Minister for Home Affairs, on the advice of the RUC, banned part of the proposed route to avoid a conflict with Loyalist factions. In spite of the ban, which it was certainly legal to impose, the organizers went ahead with the march over the original route. Inevitably this defiance of the law resulted in a clash with the RUC which was just what the extremists wanted. That night and the next there was serious rioting, damage to property and looting in the city. On 23 November and 4 December there were incidents in Dungannon in which there was a confrontation and some stone throwing between 'Loyalist' and Civil Rights supporters but which were on a small scale and were brought under control by the RUC. On 30 November in Armagh there was a more serious confrontation in which the Rev Ian Paisley and his supporters occupied the centre of the city and a Civil Rights march had to be diverted by the RUC.

On 1 January 1969, a march from Belfast to Londonderry was organized by the extreme left-wing People's Democracy. The objects of the march were not apparent but the result was to create trouble in a number of centres along the route. There were confrontations with Protestants at Antrim and Randalstown in which trouble was only averted by the re-routing of the march by the RUC. At Toome the march was joined by Republicans carrying a tricolour. When the march was diverted round Maghera there was a serious sectarian riot in the town. At Dungiven, the march had been swelled by 500 Republicans who refused to be re-routed by the police. That night in Londonderry, where tempers were rising, there was a serious riot outside the Guildhall where Dr Paisley was holding a meeting. Next day the leaders of the march decided to continue, realizing full well that there was a likelihood of further communal violence in Londonderry if they did. They were warned by the RUC that there was a hostile crowd ahead at Burntollet Bridge and a risk of stone throwing but they would not be diverted. As a result there was an affray at the bridge and at least thirteen people were injured, several of whom had to be taken to hospital. There was another ambush at Irish Street[1] as the march arrived in Londonderry in which at least thirteen more people were injured. That night there was more serious rioting in Londonderry. Of the march the Cameron report says 'We are driven to think that the leaders must have intended that their venture would weaken the moderate reforming forces in Northern Ireland. We think that their object was to increase tension so that in the process a more radical programme could be realized. They saw the march as a calculated martyrdom.' Captain O'Neill said 'The March was from the outset a foolhardy and irresponsible undertaking ... the RUC ... handled the situation as fairly and firmly as they could ... we are all sick of marchers and counter marchers. Unless these warring minorities rapidly return to their senses we will have to consider a further reinforcement of the regular police by greater use of the Special Constabulary for normal police duties.'

A week later, on 11 January, the People's Democracy group organized another march in Newry which was re-routed by the RUC to avoid a Unionist shopping area. The march led to a confrontation with the RUC followed by a serious riot in which several police vehicles were burnt and which lasted late into the night. There was no Protestant mob in this incident which took the form of an attack on the police. Its Republican character was obvious not only by the people who took part but by an attempt to occupy the post office.[2] There were serious outbreaks of rioting in Londonderry again on 19 and 20 April in which a large number of police were injured.

The Ulster Special Constabulary was not employed in any of these disturbances. The RUC Reserve force which was often used and which had become the 'Riot Squad' was now, unlike the 1956–62 period, composed entirely of regular police. Some 300 B Specials had, however, been mobilized since November 1968 to free regular members of the RUC for crowd and riot control. They were not used in the troubled areas but performed ordinary police duties in other districts. The RUC itself still contained 125 mobilized B Specials but these men had been in the force for ten years or more and were indistinguishable from the regular RUC.

In April 1969, there were explosions at an electricity transformer at Castlereagh, at the Silent Valley Reservoir and an electricity pylon at Loughgall. This was at first ascribed to the

IRA but later it transpired that it was almost certainly the work of its Protestant equivalent, the UVF Mobile patrols were at once instituted by the Ulster Special Constabulary using their own motor cars for which they received an allowance. These patrols consisted of four armed Special Constables in each car and they would visit all vulnerable places in their district, make spot checks on vehicles and investigate anything suspicious. One patrol was made each night in each district. In the border areas, forty-eight Special Constables were mobilized to protect twelve RUC stations and release RUC constables for mobile patrols by day. Patrols were, however, ordered not to fire on vehicles which refused to stop but to take their numbers and report by telephone as soon as possible to the nearest RUC station. The USC was also used to mount a large number of static guards at vulnerable places. In order to maintain these guards by day, the army was called in and an additional battalion was sent over to provide sufficient troops.

In July 1969, the house of a member of the USC was ransacked and his Sterling sub-machine gun and ammunition were stolen. The force was warned to conceal their arms in a safe place and to keep vital parts and ammunition separate. In another case some men called at a house when the Special Constable was away and tried to get his wife to hand over his rifle saying they had authority to collect it. Special Constables were reminded that they should hand in their arms to an RUC station for safe keeping when they were away from home.

During these disturbances in the spring the RUC was often seriously short of men. The total strength of the force, including policewomen was only 3,200. An expansion to 3,500 had been authorized but had not as yet been recruited. One third of the RUC was in Belfast and the Londonderry City strength was only 123. The Counties varied from 352 in Antrim to 110 in Fermanagh. The reserve force, eight platoons strong, with a total of 272 men was mobile and could be made available anywhere in the Province. The number of men that could be used for riot control was never, therefore, very large.[3] It may well be asked why the 8,000 men available in the Ulster Special Constabulary were never called upon. After the explosions which began on 20 April 1968, a great many B Specials were busy guarding water pipe lines, electricity supplies and other important places and people. The most important reason, however, was that the USC had never been given any training in crowd or riot control in urban areas. Basically it was an armed force and its members had all been taught to use revolvers as well as rifles during the sixties so that they could patrol 'on the beat' in the same way as the RUC. Without question there was a fear that if the USC was used in the disturbances they might be too tough and give Republican propagandists material with which to discredit the police. This fear was present in both political and RUC circles. There is no doubt that had they been employed they would have been subjected to intense provocation in the same way as the RUC.

Propaganda against and animosity towards the USC by the Republicans had never ceased. It had continued from the moment the force was formed and there was invariably, when the opposition members of Parliament were not abstaining, a row over the annual estimates for the force. There is no doubt that the extremists in the Civil Rights movement had as one of their aims the discrediting of the police. This they hoped to achieve by intense provocation leading to retaliation which could be presented on television and in the Press as police brutality. They were successful in discrediting the RUC in the riots in Londonderry in January and April, although the incidents were enormously exaggerated. Against the USC, as they were not used on the streets, they were unable to achieve any results at all. Nevertheless the Civil Rights Association demanded the disbanding of the USC soon after the first riot in October 1968 and the People's Democracy repeated the demand in their manifesto of February 1969. It was obvious nonsense to claim that guarding of vulnerable points against attack by terrorists could be claimed to be brutal or oppressive! The hostility of these groups must have stemmed from the Republican elements in their midst: they knew that it would be difficult to unify Ireland by force if the USC was in existence. The IRA, of course, fully realized that their defeat in 1956–62 was to a large extent due to the B Specials and that if they were to try again they must first get rid of them by political pressure.

As there was no way to discredit the USC if they were not used on the streets, some other way would have to be found. Allegations were therefore made that it was the B Specials who were behind the 'Loyalist' bodies which were involved in clashes and conflict with Civil Rights demonstrators. The Cameron Report states 'but there was nothing in the evidence to indicate that any deliberate or official use was made of members of the organization (USC) as such in support of those who made attacks on Civil Rights Demonstrations'. There were, however, a number of complaints that individual B Specials were present on such occasions. The Cameron Report suggests that this was so in Dungannon on 4 December and at Burntollet and Irish Street in Londonderry on 4 January. Of Dungannon the report says, 'There is also evidence which we accept – indeed it was not denied – that certain members of the USC, including at least one officer, not on duty, were present'. There is no indication of why they accepted the evidence or who they called who could have denied it. As the Minister for Home Affairs later said in Parliament, 'A person's presence at the scene, before, during or after the events is not in itself evidence that he was guilty of any offence'. When a member of the Special Constabulary off duty was watching a potential disturbance, it is quite wrong to assume that he was taking part. In any case where it was proved that a member of the Ulster Special Constabulary committed any offence of this type when off duty he was at once required to resign. Two Special Constables allowed themselves to become embroiled in the riot in Maghera on 2 January and were fined in the Magistrates Court. Both of these men were required to resign and it is interesting that Republican propaganda never referred to this fact at all. At Burntollet a determined effort was made to discredit the USC by this kind of allegation. Photographers accompanied the march and took a large number of photographs at Burntollet to try and establish the identity of the people there. Subsequently between 6 May and 8 July Mr Patrick Devlin, the Northern Ireland Labour MP for Falls, asked no less than 442 questions of the Minister for Home Affairs at Stormont. He produced, presumably from the photographs, some 180 names and asked the Minister if they were members of the Special Constabulary. Of these 117 had never been in the USC. Of the remaining names, forty-seven had been in the Special Constabulary at some time during their lives but were not serving members. There was, in any case, no RUC evidence that the majority of these men were even at Burntollet and if they were that they committed any offence. Twenty-five of the names were of serving members of the USC but of these there was only evidence that two were at Burntollet, one who lived nearby was watching from a point 250 yards from the bridge and the other was not known to have acted unlawfully in any way. The disappointment of Mr Devlin is obvious from the debate on the adjournment on 25 June in which he reiterated his charge that a hundred members of the USC were present.[4] He took the Minister to task for a genuine mistake in the answer to one of his many questions which had been put right with an apology. Subsequently, in an account of the incident called 'Burntollet' all the allegations were repeated and it was alleged that the Government of Northern Ireland did not even know the identity of the Special Constabulary. The suggestion is intended to convey the impression that anyone who turns up will be given a rifle and uniform providing he is a supporter of the Unionist Government. The records of the USC were kept by the staff of the Inspector-General and by the Counties and not in the Ministry itself. Nevertheless they were kept meticulously, and monthly returns were made showing enrolments, deaths, leave of absence, promotions, resignations and transfers. These returns were sent to the Inspector-General and the County Inspector of the RUC as anyone with any knowledge of the administration of the USC will know. No member of the force was allowed on patrol until he was fully trained and had done a probationary period.

The propaganda value of this barrage of questions, which cost the Government £3,315 to answer, was not entirely lost. If a question is asked 'Was so-and-so a member of the Special Constabulary' and the answer is 'Yes', then it is at once assumed that he was at Burntollet and that he was engaged in violence. When it is said 'of 320 people (approx) who took part in the attacks they identified 257, 100 of whom had records of service with the B Specials', the suggestion is that the Special Constabulary were present in force and took part in the ambush. In fact from the parliamentary questions, only forty-seven of the names put forward had records of service in the USC and of these there was very little proof that more than a handful were at Burntollet and if they were that they threw any stones! Some of those who had served at some time in the Special Constabulary had been out of the force for years. Their conduct, if they were at Burntollet and if they broke the law cannot be used to discredit the USC any more than Major Bunting's conduct can be used to discredit the army in which he once served. There is no proof that all the photographs were taken during or even at the disturbance at Burntollet. Mr Robin Chichester-Clark, the Westminster MP for the area, was in Londonderry on the day of the ambush. He motored to Burntollet but arrived after it was all over finding stones and rusted bedsteads all over the road. He stopped to clear some of them out of the way and was immediately photographed. On 17 June, Mr Devlin asked in the Stormont House of Commons, 'On what date and in which area Robin Chichester-Clark of Kells attested as a constable and what rank he holds' and 'whether police inquiries have established that Robin Chichester-Clark was present at Burntollet on 4 January', to which the Minister replied 'Mr Robin Chichester-Clark, MP has never attested as a special constable' and 'No police enquiries were necessary to establish whether or not Mr Robin Chichester-Clark, MP was present at Burntollet on 4

January 1969. It was known that he visited Burntollet on that date after the disturbances . . .' It is interesting that none of the parliamentary questions ask whether any of the people concerned were known to be Orangemen or members of the Ulster Protestant Volunteers or the Ulster Volunteer Force: it was the Ulster Special Constabulary they were trying to discredit.

Propaganda of this type often gains its effect by repeating something that is untrue over and over again until people really begin to believe it. Repetition here of the real situation will help to set the record straight. The Ulster Special Constabulary was not used for crowd or riot control in Northern Ireland before July 1969. The suggestion that the USC was used officially or deliberately to support attacks on Civil Rights demonstrations is utterly false and has been refuted by the Cameron Committee. At Burntollet it was not established by the RUC or anyone else that there were more than two serving members of the USC present and that they were other than innocent bystanders who had every right to be there. If a case was brought against any serving member of the USC leading to a conviction for riot or any such offence he would at once be required to resign. The Burntollet affair was, however, only the beginning of a mendacious campaign against the USC which unfortunately due to the skill of Republican propaganda was believed throughout the Catholic population of the North, in the Republic of Ireland and also in Great Britain.

NOTES

1. The Cameron Report notes that Mr John Brown, a District Commandant of the Londonderry City Specials, was present. The implication that he had something to do with the riot is without any foundation. He had every right to watch a procession and indeed, as an officer of the Special Constabulary, to observe during a riot.

2. A symbolic gesture in imitation of the seizure of the GPO in Dublin in the 1916 Easter Rising.

3. In the Grosvenor Square Riots in London in 1968, some nine thousand police were available. There were two thousand at the Springboks' Match at Manchester in 1970.

4. The *Sunday Times* Insight team repeat the untrue allegations that a hundred B Specials were identified as taking part in the ambush at Burntollet.

CHAPTER TEN

The Hunt Report and Disbandment

The Ulster Special Constabulary was put on stand-by duty on occasions during the summer of 1969 to assist the RUC in crowd control. It was not used until July when, in spite of the long list of reforms that had been promised by the Government of Northern Ireland, the situation began to deteriorate. With the summer 'marching season' for the Orange and other loyalist institutions, tension increased and the confrontation became openly sectarian. On 13 July 1969, serious trouble began in Dungiven in Co Londonderry when a Republican mob attacked two tenders with some twenty RUC which had been sent to protect the Orange Hall. The police were nearly overwhelmed and took refuge in the Orange Hall itself. Later they fought their way out and made their way to the RUC Station in which they were besieged by the mob, who then attempted to burn down the Orange Hall. The County Inspector was obliged to call out the Limavady District B Specials and fifty of them assembled fully armed at the farm of the District Commandant near by. Here on RUC instructions they left their firearms under guard and were issued with batons. They then entered Dungiven to relieve the RUC Station which was at the other end of the town. In the street they were assailed by the mob with taunts and then stones during which some shots were fired at them from a 0.22-inch rifle. Finding his men in a very difficult and dangerous situation the District Commandant sent for revolvers for the officers and sergeants. Subsequently some fifteen rounds had to be fired over the heads of the mob to disperse them.[1] By 0300 hours in the morning the detachment reached the police station and together with the RUC cleared the streets and order was restored. The steadiness and discipline of the USC during this night of violence was beyond reproach and contributed much to the restoration of law and order. They were warmly congratulated by the County Inspector and set a high standard of conduct for future operations. The County Commandant in his report to the Inspector General pointed out that the rioters were consumed with hatred and would not have hesitated to use weapons if they had them: they would undoubtedly have taken advantage of any show of weakness. He considered that batons were insufficient protection and that at the very least the officers and sergeants should carry revolvers in the same way as the RUC. If this could not be approved then he considered that it was unfair for the USC to be used in riot control.

In Belfast there was trouble with a Junior Orangeman's parade at the foot of the Shankhill Road near the Unity Walk Flats which were occupied partly by Protestants and partly by Catholics. The Protestants listened to rumours that some of their number had been attacked and became incensed. This led to riots which lasted from 2 to 5 August and fighting with the RUC who tried to prevent them attacking the Catholics. Inevitably relations between the RUC and the Protestants suffered and the Belfast B Specials, being more acceptable, were called out on 4 August to patrol the area and prevent looting and the gathering of crowds. In accordance with the orders in force they were armed only with batons.

After the riots early in August it was clear that the RUC might well need assistance to cope with the disturbances. The Government of Northern Ireland first asked the British Government for supplies of tear gas. The British Government agreed but stipulated that it was only to be used on the specific authority of the Minister for Home Affairs and when the situation was so grave that the only alternative would be to open fire. If tear gas failed then the Government of Northern Ireland had to decide whether to use the Ulster Special Constabulary in force or to call in the army in aid of the civil power. They were very reluctant to use the B Specials for riots mainly because they had had no training for this type of work. They were already using them fully for guarding key installations and relieving the RUC of duties in quiet areas. The USC were only trained to use firearms in which they were expert but to use them for crowd control would inevitably lead to shooting sooner or later. It was essential that it should not be the police who started a shooting war in Northern Ireland and the possibility that the army would have to be used in the end was freely discussed in the Press. Early in August the view was expressed that if this became necessary Stormont would be suspended and Westminster would take over direct rule. An enquiry by the Prime Minister of Northern Ireland (Major Chichester-Clark) of Mr Callaghan showed that this was indeed in the British Government's mind. Mr Callaghan emphasized that if the British Army had to be used on a continuing basis to keep the peace in Ulster, British public and parliamentary opinion would demand that the British Government should have an effective voice in the circumstances in which they were employed. He saw no other way than to take over the whole government of the Province. Major Chichester-Clark then demanded an interview with Mr Callaghan and went to London on 8 August. He made it clear that to replace a representative Government, freely and democratically elected, would be wholly unacceptable to the great majority of the people of Ulster and also pointed out that there were grave constitutional questions under the Government of Ireland Act of 1949. Mr Callaghan did not give way at this meeting and repeated that the United Kingdom Government must have proper control over a situation in which British troops were being used but clearly the arguments made an impression on him. Why the British Government took this line is debatable. Westminster certainly did not want to commit the army or take over direct rule.[2] British troops had been used in Ulster before, both in the riots in Belfast in 1935 and in the 1956–62 campaign, without any such consequence.

On 12 August the annual parade of the Apprentice Boys took place in Londonderry. This parade was to celebrate the relief of the City after its historic siege in 1689 and had been held annually for very many years without trouble. It followed a route which did not enter the Catholic areas of the city and before it began Dr Abernethy, the Governor of the Order, said: 'We are celebrating an event which secured civil and religious liberty for all and our celebration is an expression of determination to uphold and maintain this principle and practice for every section of the community.' Nevertheless, it was obviously going to be used by Republican elements to stir up sectarian feeling. The members of the march felt that as provocative Civil Rights marches had been permitted and those who had interfered with them prosecuted then anyone who interfered with their traditional march should also be prosecuted. The march itself was orderly and passed through the City without trouble except that a few stones were thrown at the very tail end of it as it passed Waterloo Place. No sooner were the Apprentice Boys in their buses on the way home than serious rioting broke out. It did not take the form of Catholics versus Protestants but of Catholics versus the RUC, the police trying to prevent the mob breaking out into the main shopping area. The rioting lasted most of the night, the mob using stones and petrol bombs and the RUC using water cannon and later tear gas. There were serious fires in the city and by morning there were ninety-four police injured as well as twenty-two civilians. A BBC newsman reported 'The RUC have been magnificent. It is difficult to explain how they have managed to keep their tempers.' Rioting was not confined to Londonderry and there were outbreaks in Newry, Strabane and Coalisland.

Next day, 13 August, the rioting continued in Londonderry and a small detachment of the USC was held in reserve in the city. The rioting now spread to Belfast where few USC were in the riot area but a considerable number were used to guard

Catholic public houses in Protestant areas. The USC were
however involved in riots on this day in Coalisland and Dungannon. There had been a disturbance in Coalisland on 12
August but it had been dealt with successfully by the RUC
who were on this occasion seventy strong. On 13 August after
dark a mob of 200 attacked the police station and its married
quarters: a constable was seriously burnt by a petrol bomb
and reinforcements were summoned. Among the reinforcements was a party of the Tyrone Specials who were armed and
were used to guard the police station. A subsequent attack was
led by a large mechanical shovel (similar to a bulldozer) with a
crowd throwing petrol bombs on each side of it and also lob-
bing them over the top. The District Inspector hoped to
counter this vicious attack with baton charges but as the mob
neared the station the USC fired a volley of 12 shots mainly
over the heads of the crowd but some shots were aimed at the
mechanical shovel causing some injury and damage.[3] The District Inspector at once ordered firing to cease and the police
advanced, captured the shovel and the mob retreated and finally dispersed. At the Scarman Tribunal the District Inspector
said that he had not intended to use firearms and considered
the shooting had been unjustified. In this he was supported by
the findings of the Tribunal who, however, said 'It is understandable that in what must have appeared to be a very ugly
emergency they (the USC) had resort to the only weapon with
which they were equipped...' There is no doubt, however,
that the volley was very effective and the attack might well
have succeeded if it had not been fired. Subsequently the
Army policy in Ulster was to shoot to kill petrol bombers and
this policy was put into practice. The batons with which the
USC were supposed to be armed seemed a peculiarly ineffec-
tive weapon with which to stop a mechanical shovel and petrol
bombers. In Dungannon, the RUC was reduced to seventeen
Constables because of the trouble in Coalisland. The County
Inspector was unable, because of the riots in Londonderry, to
obtain any reinforcements from elsewhere. He was left with no
alternative but to call up the local USC, forty of whom re-

ported for duty. The USC were very unhappy about being rearmed with batons and the County Inspector allowed them to carry their firearms as well. Throughout the evening there were both Catholic and Protestant hostile crowds on the streets and at about midnight the Catholics set fire to a bus and some buildings. The County Inspector with a party of thirty-five to forty mixed RUC and USC took steps to disperse them. In the course of the operation a party of USC were isolated and attacked by youths throwing stones and bottles. The USC charged and dispersed them but subsequently three civilians were found to have bullet wounds. The USC denied firing but the evidence before the Scarman Tribunal that four men of the Kilnaslee platoon did in fact use their weapons was overwhelming. The Tribunal, besides criticizing the County Inspector for allowing the USC to go on the streets armed, found that, even though the Specials were being pelted and taunted by the mob, that the shooting was unjustified.

At 2100 hours that evening Mr Lynch, the Prime Minister of the Republic, inflamed the situation by moving Irish Army troops to the border and making a broadcast in which he said 'the reunification of the national territory can provide the only permanent solution to the problem'. On this day too the Limavady USC were again called to assist in Dungiven after an attack on the RUC station. They provided a reinforcement for the Reserve force platoon which was in the town but arrived too late to help to escort the fire brigade in the riot area.

On 14 August, the rioting in Londonderry had been in progress without pause for nearly two days. The RUC all over the Province were stretched to the limit. Some of them had been on duty for forty-eight hours and there were no reliefs available. By midday the situation was so grave that it was obvious that the assistance of the troops would have to be asked for. It was by no means certain how long the British Government would take to comply with the request. Earlier in the day the Inspector General had given authority to the Police Commissioner in Belfast and the County Inspectors to call out members of the USC in their areas where necessary.[4] They were to carry their normal arms for the protection of RUC Stations and when patrolling in areas where they were unlikely to be involved in riots. They were only to be used as reinforcements for street disturbances in exceptional circumstances and they were still, if possible, to be rearmed with batons. Before this order was received in most places the situation deteriorated to such an extent that a general mobilization of the whole USC was broadcast and they were ordered to report fully armed and equipped at their nearest RUC Station. Where rioting was actually in progress, District Inspectors were given permission in new instructions to use the USC in their districts. Where possible, however, the USC should take over the guard of RUC Stations to release regular men for riot control. Any USC remaining were to be held in reserve and used as necessary.

In Londonderry the USC were assembled in Waterloo Place and sent to guard Castle Gate and Butchers Gate and to restrain the Protestant crowd in Fountain Street. They were, however, unable to stop a sectarian riot in Bishops Street. There was some stone throwing by the Specials but as Insight says 'The reason was simple: the B Specials were having stones flung at them, and they had neither helmets nor shields to protect themselves. Retaliation was their only defence'. The Scarman Tribunal summed up by saying 'There is nothing to justify any general criticism of the USC in the few hours that it performed riot duty in Londonderry.'

The request of the Government of Northern Ireland for the use of troops in aid of the civil power in Londonderry was at once approved by Westminster who were expecting it. The garrison of Northern Ireland consisted at the time of a single brigade of three battalions, one of which was busy guarding vulnerable points. One battalion at once relieved the RUC in the Bogside taking over before dark. The rioters, also exhausted, then stopped rioting and order was restored.[5] In Belfast it was a very different matter. As night fell shooting broke out, a machine gun being used against the RUC in the Divis Street area. The mobs on both sides broke loose, there was shooting, burning and throwing of petrol bombs. Five people were killed and over a hundred injured, twenty-nine by gunshot wounds. At dawn the city was at last quiet but smoke rose from many fires.

In the appalling riots in West Belfast, the Specials were employed to try and control the Protestant crowds in Dover and Percy Streets and they made a baton charge when a Catholic mob attacked them with stones and petrol bombs from behind mobile barricades. Subsequently when the Protestant mob counter attacked there were too few of them to keep the factions apart. In the shooting that later broke out from the Catholic side, only one of the USC returned the fire with his revolver. In the burning of Conway Street by Protestant civilians there were no USC involved at all. In the Crumlin Road area, the USC were used to try and restrain an angry Protestant crowd in Disraeli Street after the Catholics from Hooker Street attacked the RUC. Later they did the same in Bray Street and Palmer Street successfully. They were too few, however, to prevent a Protestant mob erupting out of other streets and following the RUC into Hooker Street.

In the evening of 14 August, too, the situation had become serious in Armagh. The RUC were by now very extended and there were only fifty police in the city. Some sixty USC answered the mobilization call and arrived at the RUC station in Armagh during the evening. At 2200 hours there was a serious sectarian confrontation in English Street and the RUC were used to deal with the Catholic mob and the USC to hold back the Protestants. At 2230 hours it was clear that more men were needed and the Tynan Sub-District of the USC were called into the city. This unit consisted of a Sub-District Commandant, three sergeants and thirteen Special Constables. They arrived at the RUC Station in four private cars at about 2300 hours. As they arrived, information came in by radio which showed that the situation was getting worse and there was a need to get behind the troublesome Catholic mob in Cathedral Road. The County Inspector came out of the barracks and ordered the Tynan USC to follow him. He then set off in his car followed by the USC in their four cars. Unfortunately, the USC lost touch with the County Inspector and arrived in Cathedral Road with no instructions to find a riotous crowd throwing stones and petrol bombs. To make matters worse shots were heard as they got out of their cars and there was a vehicle on fire in the middle of the road which might well have belonged to the County Inspector. Their cars were pelted with missiles and they were subjected to violent abuse by the hostile mob. In this dangerous situation in which they believed they had been deliberately ambushed thirteen of the B Specials fired over the heads of the crowd. Unfortunately not all members of the USC fired in the air and a man was found dead shortly afterwards from a bullet wound and two other people were wounded. As the Insight team said 'The Tynan platoon were appalled by what had happened and later made a clumsy effort to cover up their part in the shooting'. The Scarman Tribunal found 'After making all allowances for the strange, difficult and frightening situation in which they found themselves, there was no justification for firing into the crowd – as the USC themselves impliedly admitted by their strenuous denials that they had done any such thing' they also found that 'a measure of responsibility rests with the County Inspector, who put an untrained but armed party of USC drawn from a country area into an alarming town riot without briefing or leadership'. The Scarman Tribunal does not say that firing over the heads of the mob was unjustified and this is what most of the platoon did. There was clear evidence of the bullets whistling through the leaves of the trees overhead. The volley was certainly effective and the mob dispersed at once. If the Specials had been armed solely with batons, the fight would undoubtedly have continued; the Specials would probably have got the worst of it and their cars would have been burnt. At the same time in Newry the USC were well led and proved of great value. The USC answered the general call up on 14 August and were instructed to leave their rifles in the police station and re-arm themselves with batons, helmets and shields. They were used to restrain an angry Protestant crowd during a Catholic attack on the RUC which they did success-fully. Afterwards they assisted the RUC to dismantle barri-cades and compete with Catholic rioters while sporadic petrol bombing and stone throwing continued until 4 AM. The USC were a substantial reinforcement to the RUC and it was num-bers more than anything else which was successful in control-ling the trouble. There is no evidence that B Specials used in this predominantly Catholic town exacerbated the situation.

At the same time as the disturbances in Belfast and Lon-donderry were being brought under control by the troops, Re-publican propaganda launched a vicious campaign against the Ulster Special Constabulary. The allegation was that they had been responsible for all the Catholic casualties from gunshot wounds in Belfast and that they were responsible for the arson and looting which had been done by the Protestant mobs. In fact the number of B Specials in this area of Belfast was small and they were armed with batons and pistols. On the night of 15–16 August the USC were withdrawn from most areas to guard police stations and to form a reserve. The Republicans were given full scope for their allegations by television which broadcast heavily biased statements about the Specials without an opportunity for them to be contradicted. The following quotation from Miss Bernadette Devlin's book illustrates the theme, 'In Belfast the B Specials, alongside the police, fought the demonstrators. They did more. With small arms, machine guns, and armoured cars, they launched a vicious, well-planned attack on Catholic areas. They burned down row upon row of houses. Only the arrival of the British Army brought their destructive progress to a halt, and I have no doubt myself that the army came, not because Major Chichester-Clark asked for help, but because Harold Wilson wasn't prepared to tolerate the Unionist Party's private army of reserve police'. The Scarman Tribunal shows that there is scarcely a word of truth in this extract but this kind of propaganda seems to have been believed by Mr Wilson and Mr Callaghan. The propaganda was also directed at the force itself and this second extract from the same source shows the form, 'There are no regulations tests to get into the B Specials. You don't have to have a minimum or maximum height; there are no weight restrictions and no intelligence qualifications. All you've got to be is a supporter of the Government, but once you're in you are entitled to service pay, to a gun, to all the ammunition you want, and to a uniform which is usually either two sizes too big or three sizes too small.'[6] The first two sentences of course also apply to Members of Parliament! The description of the meagre emoluments as service pay would make many Specials smile. Even the ill-fitting uniforms had gone by the early sixties. One person interviewed on television even said that the Government were guilty of negligence as they kept no check on the arms issued to Specials. Mr Wilson and Mr Callaghan cannot really have believed this sort of propaganda but, as it was not contradicted, many of the British public did.

When on 19 August, the Northern Ireland cabinet went to 10 Downing Street to meet Mr Wilson and his senior colleagues, they found to their astonishment that the first item on the agenda was the disbandment of the Ulster Special Constabulary. The Northern Ireland ministers were horrified and made it clear that it would be irresponsible to do any such thing. They were, however, bargaining from a position of great weakness, it being quite possible that Stormont was about to be suspended. Fortunately they had two important concessions which they were ready to make. After the serious riots in the middle of August, the Northern Ireland Government wished to appoint a committee to investigate the Royal Ulster Constabulary's part in them. That the military had had to be called in at all showed that something was wrong. They were particularly critical of what could be called the logistic side of the operation. That is the system for relief of the men who had been facing rioters in Derry for periods of days and the arrangements for feeding them. The RUC in Londonderry had in fact to be supplied by civilians. The purpose of the enquiry was therefore to advise how to cope more satisfactorily with riots in the future. In this matter they themselves were not blameless. Sir Albert Kennedy, the Inspector General, had proposed an increase in the force in 1967 but it had been turned down on financial grounds.[7] Major Chichester-Clark outlined his proposals for a committee to advise on the RUC which were welcomed by Mr Wilson and agreed that it should also report on the Ulster Special Constabulary. Just before leaving for London, the Army Chief of Staff of the Northern Ireland District had suggested that it would be better if all the security forces in the Province were put under a single command as had been found essential in Malaya, Kenya, Aden and other similar situations. The Northern Ireland ministers had discussed this in the plane on the way to London. Major Chichester-Clark therefore proposed this to Mr Wilson and, after a pause to summon the Chief of the General Staff from the Ministry of Defence, it was agreed upon. The Northern Ireland ministers believed they had saved the Specials by these concessions and that it was no longer being suggested that they should be disbanded. In the middle of the meeting, however, both Mr Wilson and Major Chichester-Clark appeared on television where Mr Wilson said that the use of Specials for crowd control had caused very great concern. 'What we now want to see is that the Specials are phased out of this situation. They are already out of the areas where the British troops are, and progressively they will be phased out of the areas where, up until now, they have been exercising riot control duties and so on. Because that is not where they ought to be.' Major Chichester-Clark was at the other end of the studio at this time and did not realize what had been said until he returned to Northern Ireland. The Joint Declaration made by the two Governments after the meeting of 19 August, however, made no reference to the Ulster Special Constabulary. Nevertheless Mr Wilson's statement caused considerable misgivings in the Province.

On 20 August Lieutenant General Sir Ian Freeland the GOC Northern Ireland District took over responsibility for security as opposed to police work in the Province and the Ulster Special Constabulary were transferred to his command. On 22 August the GOC told the Inspector General that for reasons of security the Regular and Territorial Army in Northern Ireland kept their arms and ammunition in armouries and not in their homes. So far as possible he wished the USC to do likewise. He directed that arms should be called in as soon as possible in Belfast and Londonderry and, although he realized that it might be difficult in country areas he asked for a study to be made to see what could be done. He then said that weapons and ammunition would be issued to the USC on his authority whenever their duties required it. On 23 August, General Freeland directed that the USC might be employed to guard vulnerable points, RUC barracks and VIP houses and for road checks in country districts where this could not be done by the army or the RUC. When employed on road checks the USC were to be accompanied by at least one RUC policeman or a mobilized member of the USC. The General also said that the USC were not to be employed on any other tasks without his permission. The use of firearms by both the RUC and USC was to be brought into line with army orders for the use of weapons in security operations. The orders, issued by the Inspector General that fire was not to be opened on cars which failed to stop, was confirmed.

The County Commandant of Co Londonderry replied it would be wrong to conceal the fact that the order for the centralization of arms had caused dismay among the rank and file of the USC. He pointed out that they had kept their arms and some ammunition in their homes for the past fifty years. This was partly because the Specials needed protection while travelling to their place of duty in uniform. The imputation that arms had been used indiscriminately by the USC was certainly not justified in his County. During the whole of the 1956–61 IRA campaign only one man had been wounded and that was unintentionally due to a ricochet. Nor could they be accused of losing their arms. In the last fifteen years which included the 1956–61 campaign only one weapon had been lost in the whole county. In the same period the army, with its arms centralized in armouries, had had several of them raided. He might have added that they had lost nearly 300 weapons in the raid on Armagh alone. He pointed out that if the arms were now centralized in the four continuously manned RUC stations in the county, the men would have to travel so far to fetch and return them that they would not have time to carry out any normal duty. Finally, he said it had been frequently and incorrectly forecast in the past that the IRA were a spent force but there was evidence to show that they were still active and he said it would be taking an unnecessary risk to hamstring the USC in such a way especially by making it impossible for it to get into action after a surprise attack. The County Commandant in Fermanagh reported that there were only five full-time RUC stations in the county and all of these were close to the border. They were therefore unsuitable places in which to store arms and ammunition as the married constables lived out and often only the sergeant was there at night. A strong and permanent guard would obviously be necessary, which would mean the mobilization of a considerable number of Special Constables. In any case from some districts a round journey of twenty-five to thirty miles would have to be made to collect arms for a patrol and the same distance afterwards to return them. He pointed out that the personal security of the Specials and their families would be in jeopardy near the border owing to the existence of extreme Republican elements. The force would, in any case, be quite unable to fulfil any emergency task or mobilization effectively. The Londonderry City Commandant saw no difficulty in centralizing the arms of the City district in an armoury at Whitehall but in the Border district it was a very different matter. The USC in this district was the only protection for four customs posts and Loyalist farms in the area. With the organization at present, with arms kept in their homes, the USC could close the border within half an hour of the order. There was no RUC Station in this area and if the USC had to travel six to eight miles to Whitehall to collect their arms they would become virtually useless in emergency. The order that road checks were always to be accompanied by a regular member of the RUC often meant that the patrols could not go out at all because there was not one available. At the end of the month the Inspector General said that the number of USC kept standing by in RUC barracks was to be substantially reduced as the GOC had ruled that they were never to be used for the control of riots. In practice from this time on the USC was seldom used for any purpose other than the static guarding of vulnerable places.

In fact most of these restrictions were found to be impracticable. In the end only the arms of B Specials actually living near armouries of RUC Stations in towns were centralized and as this had always been so in Belfast, it did not make very much difference. These moves did not really affect the security situation. The problem at the time was one of preventing communal rioting rather than countering IRA outrages. Nevertheless they were bitterly resented by the USC. The order to centralize arms was given as one to ensure that they were not lost. This fooled no one. No arms had been lost by the USC and over the years they had kept them safely in their homes while the army had lost them from their armouries in hundreds. They saw it as an attempt by Westminster to disarm them at the request of the Republican elements in the Province. In their eyes it was a political act of appeasement and a sell-out to the IRA. They found the orders restricting their employment and insisting that they be accompanied by the Army or the RUC when on patrol, humiliating. They had carried out their duties over the years with great restraint. It was obvious to them that Westminster had swallowed the Republican propaganda whole and seemed to believe every lie and allegation made against them. What was worse was the obvious joy of the Republicans. It had always been the aim of the IRA to get rid of the B Specials and now, through the gullibility of British politicians, they seemed well on the way to success.

It was obvious that something would have to be done to try and placate the B Specials. The Deputy Prime Minister of Northern Ireland (The Rt Hon J. L. O. Andrews, DL) made a tour round the Province to meet and talk to members of both the RUC and USC but it did little to reassure them. On 25 August, Major Chichester-Clark met twenty-six District Commandants representing the part-time members of the force. He was emphatic that the force would not be disbanded. The committee met again on 30 August and, appalled by the adverse propaganda to which the force had been subjected, decided to raise a fund with which to promote publicity and refute the aspersions cast on the USC. On 26 August, General Freeland sent the following message to all members of the Ulster Special Constabulary,

'Message from the Director of Operations Northern Ireland to all members of the Ulster Special Constabulary. This message is to be pinned on notice boards and read out to all ranks at the earliest opportunity:

1. As you know I have now assumed full command and control of the Ulster Special Constabulary and I want you to know what the present position is.

2. Firstly there is no question of my disbanding the Ulster Special Constabulary.

3. Secondly, there is no question of the Ulster Constabulary being disarmed. I have issued orders for the storage of arms in central armouries in the two main cities of Belfast and Londonderry for security reasons, this will bring the Special Constabulary into line with the regular Army and TAVR Arms will be issued when required for specific duties.

4. Thirdly, I am grateful for all the hard work that the Ulster Special Constabulary has been doing recently, particularly in guarding vulnerable points and other installations. I realize that some of you have been on duty night after night and have found this a great strain. I am doing my best to ensure that some of your duties are reduced so that you are not over-strained and that your civilian work will not suffer.

5. Finally, whilst I am your commander and until the Hunt Committee has reported on any changes that might be

necessary, I ask you all to give me your support and carry
out your duties as loyally as you have done in the past.'

These measures reassured the USC to a certain extent and
they continued loyally with their duties which says a great deal
for their discipline.

The Advisory Committee on Police in Northern Ireland
was appointed by Mr R. W. Porter, the Minister for Home
Affairs, on 26 August, 1969. Major Chichester-Clark had
asked Mr Callaghan who he thought should serve on it. Lord
Hunt[8] and Mr Robert Mark were suggested by London and
Sir James Robertson was chosen by Stormont. The Committee
were to 'examine the recruitment, organization, structure and
composition of the Royal Ulster Constabulary and the Ulster
Special Constabulary and their respective functions and to recommend as necessary what changes are required to provide
for the efficient enforcement of law and order in Northern
Ireland'.

On 24 August, the security of the Province was decentralized by the GOC on to the Commander of 24th Infantry Brigade for Cos Londonderry, Tyrone, Fermanagh and Armagh
and of the 39th Infantry Brigade for Belfast and Cos Antrim
and Down. All security operations by the army, the RUC and
the USC were co-ordinated at county level between the Senior
Army Officer and the County Inspector who was responsible
for both the RUC and USC. In September the road checks
were made more effective by the use of dannert wire drawn
across the road which could force vehicles to stop without
opening fire. In October the rule that USC patrols had to be
accompanied by a member of the RUC was allowed to be
waived at the discretion of the County Security Committees.

The Hunt Committee Report was published on 3 October
1969, just five and a half weeks after its appointment. Lord
Hunt, in his covering letter says, 'We have completed our mis-
sion in the shortest possible time compatible with giving ade-
quate consideration to the principal problems, being conscious
of the urgency of clarifying the future patterns for the enforce-

ment of law and order and the responsibility for the protection of the Province, which we regard as an essential step towards resolving the present situation.

'Within the limited time available it has not been possible to make as detailed an examination as we would have wished. Indeed, in less serious circumstances we would have preferred to have several months at our disposal.'

The Hunt Report dealt mostly with the proposed changes in the Royal Ulster Constabulary but one chapter traced the history of the Ulster Special Constabulary and three short appendices gave its strength and conditions of service. Another chapter was entitled ironically 'The Future of the Ulster Special Constabulary'. It drew attention to the fact that earlier in the report it had been proposed that the Royal Ulster Constabulary should be relieved of its para-military duties and assume the character of an unarmed civil police force. It had also recommended that the RUC should have an unarmed unpaid reserve of Special Constables as in the rest of the United Kingdom. The Report went on to say:

'... we believe that it will be necessary for some time to come to protect key installations and to undertake such other tasks as may be necessary to guard against the threat of armed guerrilla-type attacks. We consider that all threats to the security of Northern Ireland from armed incursions and attacks, from whatever quarter and whatever form they may take, are a proper military responsibility and should rest with the Government at Westminster. It is, however, self-evident that the Government of Northern Ireland has a vital interest in the defence of the Province which must continue to be recognized, and appropriate arrangements should be made to that end. Furthermore, we see great merit in the continuing presence of a local force, with local knowledge, capable of being at instant readiness to deal with such threats in the first instance.'

It continued, 'We consider however that the protection of the border and the State against armed attacks is not a role which should have to be undertaken by the police, whether they be regular or special'.

The Hunt Committee then recommended that a new part-time force 4,000 strong under the command of the GOC Northern Ireland, should be raised. This new force and the police reserve should then replace the Ulster Special Constabulary. Throughout the report there is scarcely a word of criticism of the USC. They remark in one place, however, that 'Whilst there is no law or official rule that precludes any person, whatever his religion, from joining the USC, the fact remains that for a variety of reasons no Roman Catholic is a member'. In another place they are very complimentary, 'We know that to a man, members of the USC are devoted to the cause of Ulster and that they and their forebears have done gallant service and we recognize the value of the anti-guerrilla patrols and armed guard duties they have carried out, particularly in times of emergency'. The words 'disarm' and 'disband' do not appear in the report at all.

The Hunt report was available to the Northern Ireland Government about a week before it was published. The Cabinet decided to accept nearly every recommendation but not the replacement of the Ulster Special Constabulary. Several cabinet meetings confirmed this decision and, as Mr Callaghan was due in Ulster on the proposed day of its publication, Major Chichester-Clark thought it proper to inform him of the cabinet decision by telephone. Mr Callaghan made it perfectly clear that if the Northern Ireland Government was not prepared to disband the B Specials then the Government of Westminster would do so by legislating over their heads. Constitutionally, Westminster had the right to do this and as it was the British Government which had formed the Specials in the first place it seemed logical too. On the other hand the Westminster Government had never legislated over the head of Stormont before and the constitutional implications were serious. Furthermore Major Chichester-Clark received the distinct impression from Mr Callaghan that if Westminster had to disband the B Specials then they would not raise a force to replace them as recommended by the Hunt Committee. Major Chichester-Clark subsequently said that this decision did him more harm politically than any other in his term of office.

The Hunt Committee had tried to soften the blow in their report but they had no control over the Press and television. The early morning radio and newspaper accounts of the Report were reasonably accurate but by the evening television was saying with obvious relish that the 'Controversial' or 'Hated' B Specials were to be 'disarmed and disbanded'. This revelation, after the assurances given, especially by the Prime Minister of Northern Ireland and the GOC, was received first with incredulity among the Protestant population and then, as the day wore on and they were able to read the report for themselves, with slight relief that at least there was to be a force to replace the USC. Among the more extreme Protestant elements incredulity turned to anger and a sense of betrayal and on the Saturday evening there were very serious Protestant riots in which the army in the Shankhill Road area were involved and in which shots were fired by both sides. It was madness to have published the report in such a hurry at a weekend to suit Mr Callaghan, when the discontent was likely to be inflamed by alcohol. The Press and television's biased handling of the question must also bear a heavy responsibility for these disturbances. The B Specials themselves received the blow with a dignified silence while the Republican element exulted and asserted that every lie and allegation they had ever made against the USC had been proved to be true by the Hunt Committee. This was, of course, nonsense, as the Committee had no power or time to investigate allegations.

It was widely believed in Northern Ireland that the Hunt Committee were simply carrying out the Westminster Government's instructions in recommending the disbandment of the Special Constabulary. It would, however, be most unjust to assume any such thing. Lord Hunt would never have accepted the chairmanship under such conditions. Nevertheless, in spite of the fact that this was a Stormont Committee, the Westminster Government were clearly involved with it. In the letter of appointment the Minister for Home Affairs for Northern Ireland makes no mention of a need for haste and it is clear that this pressure, although agreed to by Major Chichester-Clark, came from the Government at Westminster. Mr Callaghan after his visit to the Province at the end of August announced his intention of returning in early October. There is no doubt that he wanted the answer by then. All the Officers of the USC who gave evidence to the Committee came away with the feeling that the tribunal had already made up its mind about the future of the USC and were not interested.

The statement on the role of the army and the police is open to some criticism. There can be little argument that the defence of the border against external attack had always been a Westminster responsibility and so the duty of the army. The reasons that had led to it being carried out by the RUC and USC from 1921–69 have been discussed in an earlier chapter. Why this change was thought by the Hunt Committee to improve the enforcement of law and order in Northern Ireland in 1969 is not apparent. There had been no threat on the border since 1962, and in the IRA campaign of 1956–62 the RUC and USC had discharged this duty with conspicuous success. That defence against internal attack should be the army's business was a completely new concept. In Great Britain this had certainly never been their responsibility. In the IRA bombing campaign of 1939 in England, all the counter measures were taken by the police and there had been no question of it being anything to do with the army. Admittedly the problem of the IRA in England was a very different one from that in Ireland. The Hunt Committee produced no arguments to support their suggestion that the IRA within Northern Ireland could be controlled by an unarmed police force or the Army. Over the years it had been found that the best solution had always been a 'para-military' force such as the armed RUC or the USC. People in Northern Ireland are therefore to be forgiven if they believe that there were other reasons for this new division of responsibility. Nevertheless the Hunt Committee did see the need for some kind of force and it seems probable that it was General Freeland's evidence which convinced them.

In seeking for the real reasons it must always be remembered that the British police have always been prejudiced against Special Constabularies, para-military forces and armed police. The two senior police officers sent over to Northern Ireland in the late summer by Mr Callaghan as 'advisers' certainly held these views. It is therefore understandable that the Hunt Committee felt the same way. Nevertheless there is little doubt that they accepted, as had Mr Wilson and Mr Callaghan, all the arguments put forward by the Republicans that the USC was a Protestant armed militia, many of them members of the Orange Order, and a force controlled by the permanent Unionist Government of Northern Ireland. They believed the force had wide powers as policemen which they shared with the RUC without corresponding training as police, as distinct from training for para-military duties and they were not accountable to the public for their actions. They believed that no change short of complete replacement would remove the grievances of the Catholic minority. It was therefore an act of appeasement in the hope that if the B Specials were disbanded and all the other changes made in the RUC, the minority would stop their riots and disturbances.

The first serious criticism of the B Specials had come from the Cameron Report which was available to the Hunt Committee. It alleged that members of the Special Constabulary were present in Protestant crowds but certainly did not prove this fact. They simply accepted evidence which, if the allegations made about Burntollet are any guide, was very suspect. They also say 'We have good ground for inferring that in the ranks of the Ulster Protestant Volunteer Force are numbered members of the USC.' Here again there is no proof but simply the acceptance of statements made by people whose names are not revealed. The Commission do not seem to have interested themselves with what would happen to a member of the USC if he was involved in riots or found to be a member of an undesirable organization. They do not seem to have tried to find out why the Republican section of the community really objected to the existence of the USC. The force had only been used occasionally since 1962 and then mainly for guarding vulnerable points against IRA or UVF attack. These water pipe lines, electricity and telephone installations and other public utilities were needed as much by the Catholics as the Protestants. It seems odd that this sort of work should irritate the Catholic community. The IRA, on the other hand, had every reason to want to get rid of the Special Constabulary and no doubt were active in spreading propaganda against them.

There is no question that the Hunt Committee were sincere and really believed that their proposals for both the RUC and USC would go a long way to solve the problems of the Province. As events in the last two years have shown that the very reverse has happened it is reasonable to dwell a bit longer on the charges accepted by the Cameron and Hunt Committees against the USC. The reasons why the USC were all Protestants have been followed in this book in some detail. Basically it was because the Roman Catholics would not join. Undoubtedly many Specials would rather not have had Roman Catholics for security reasons. In the troubles of the twenties in the South, the IRA bragged that it had infiltrated practically every organ of Government. Michael Collins, at the time of the truce, claimed that he had his agents serving in the RIC in every police station. The British Army since the second World War had been infiltrated many times. The raids on the barracks at Armagh and Omagh were both planned with the aid of traitors in the British Army as was the raid on the Arborfield Depot in Berkshire. In their whole fifty years of service the B Specials were never infiltrated by the IRA. Nevertheless, Roman Catholics were never barred officially, a very few did join but undoubtedly more loyal Roman Catholics would have liked to apply but fear of a rebuff or intimidation by their own people discouraged them. These loyal Roman Catholics had a genuine grievance but the majority of Republicans simply wished to make a propaganda point.[9]

A considerable number of the USC did belong to the Orange Order, but this organization had absolutely no say in the organization or recruitment of the force.[10] The fact that Orange halls were used as drill halls had no significance except that it was an economy. As the Hunt Committee says, 'Whilst we are prepared to accept that it should be possible to be a member, both of such an organization and a police force, and to act at all times with complete impartiality, ... the task of demonstrating complete impartiality at all times is difficult enough without complicating it further'. The crux of the matter is therefore whether being members of the Orange Order any members of the USC on duty failed to act impartially. There is no evidence of this whatever in the Cameron Report. The assumption that if they were members then obviously they were not impartial is quite unjust.

The charge that the USC was controlled by the permanent Unionist Government of Northern Ireland is an allegation which was made throughout the force's history. The so-called permanent Unionist Government is re-elected on the same basis as in the United Kingdom and by the same franchise and it still has a greater majority than most Governments in Europe. It is therefore wholly democratic. The police in Ulster are no more 'controlled' by it than the police in Great Britain are controlled by Westminster Governments. The wide powers as policemen which they were said to have had are illusory. For most of the time they had no powers at all and were not used for any purpose. When called out to man road blocks or guard vulnerable points their powers cannot be said to have been wide, and were never more than the army in Ulster have had for the last two years. Training as police was undoubtedly not enough but was more than the army in Ulster. In any case this could have been put right without disbanding the force.

Mr Wilson in his book, says that the Hunt Committee 're-flected' his views. Presumably he means to disarm the RUC and disband the USC. Mr Wilson and Mr Callaghan had wanted to disband the B Specials on 19 August before they had seen the Cameron Report and it is not believed that at that time they had any idea of replacing them with a locally raised military force. Certainly Mr Callaghan gave the impression

during his visit to Northern Ireland from 27–29 August that
he did not think the IRA were any danger at all. Mr Wilson
refers in his book to 'the controversial and indeed hated B
Specials'. He seems to have assumed that the hatred was
merited and that if the USC were disbanded it would dis-
appear. Hatred is in itself evil whether merited or not. It is
unfortunately an Irish characteristic. Since the B Specials
have gone the hatred has not disappeared it has simply been
transferred to the British Army. There is now an Act of Parliament to prevent incitement to hatred in Northern Ireland
but unfortunately it is very difficult to apply. Those who
stirred up hatred against the RUC and USC were certainly
culpable. It is difficult to avoid the conclusion that perhaps the
British Government had another reason for disbanding the
Specials which never came to light. This was the spectre of the
old Ulster Volunteer Force of 1914 which successfully defied
the British Government's attempt to force them into a united
Ireland. It seems quite likely that Mr Wilson wished to remove any form of armed force from the Northern Ireland
Government in case Mr Craig, with his alleged UDI thoughts,
gained power.

The Northern Ireland Government having been forced to
abandon the Ulster Special Constabulary, at once accepted the
Hunt Committee's suggestion of a locally recruited part-time
force under the command of the GOC Northern Ireland. On
13 October the British Government stated its intention to introduce legislation to create such a force. In November a white
paper was presented to Parliament. The new force was to
be called The Ulster Defence Regiment and would be part
of Her Majesty's military forces. Its task would be to support the regular forces in Northern Ireland in protecting
the border and the State against armed attack and sabotage. It
would undertake guard duties at key points and installations,
carry out patrols and establish check points and road blocks. It
was visualized that it would be used mainly in rural areas and
it would not be used for crowd control or in riots. The size of
the force was not to exceed 6,000 officers and men and would

be organized in battalions whose areas would be approximately the county boundaries. The regiment would be commanded by a regular army brigadier and the battalions by local officers with a regular army major responsible for training. Any part of the force could be called out by a regular officer not below the rank of major. The force was to be recruited from all male citizens of good character of the United Kingdom and Colonies normally resident in Northern Ireland whatever their denomination. Applicants would be subject to strict security vetting and would have to take the normal army oath of allegiance to Her Majesty the Queen. Training was to consist of twelve days a year including one consecutive period of a week and twelve two-hour periods. Pay was to be the same as the army when on duty (at least £2.58 a day) and a bounty of £25–£35 would be payable according to service. The Ulster Defence Regiment was therefore a very similar force to the Ulster Special Constabulary and was to carry out very similar duties. The difference was that they were soldiers instead of policemen. Recruiting was opened on 1 January 1970 with the aim of being operationally effective by 1 April 1970.

The B Specials continued with their duties for the last six months of the life of the force with attention and good discipline if not with enthusiasm. Their duties were directed by the County Security Committees and consisted mainly of guarding RUC stations, armouries, VIPs and other vulnerable places such as radio stations, dams, reservoirs, power stations, transformers and bridges. According to the importance of the place guards were provided for the full twenty-four hours, for night hours only or were confined to visits by patrols. There were in all fifty-eight of these vulnerable places in the Province, seventeen of which were guarded by the army and the rest by the USC. The 'enemy' was the IRA either from across the border or from the indigenous units. The IRA was still assessed as being weak but the Provisionals had already emerged as the more militant and they believed the official IRA had let them down. Attacks by the UVF were still considered possible. On 28 September, a force of unarmed B

Specials were used to patrol the Shankhill Road where they were received with cheers by the Protestant population. They were used partly because they were more acceptable in this area than the RUC and partly because the security forces were very stretched. At the end of February a Sterling machine carbine was stolen from the house of a member of the USC when he was out for two hours and a rifle and a revolver were stolen from a car. County Commandants were urged to warn members to be particularly careful as there might well be an IRA plot to steal their arms before disbandment. If they were going to be away the Specials were told to hand in their arms early. The last night that the USC were on duty was 31 March/1 April 1970, and the month of April was regarded as a run-down period. During April all arms were handed in to the army who sent parties with transport to collect them from the various drill halls.

The Hunt report visualized members of the USC joining the new regiment and in November Colonel Miskimmin sent out a form to enquire whether the B Specials wished to transfer. This caused a minor political storm and the form had to be modified. The Opposition professed annoyance that the form had been issued six weeks before recruiting was to begin but it was obvious that they were really continuing their vendetta against the B Specials and trying to hinder them joining the UDR. In the first month only 700 of the USC applied to join out of a total of 1,625 applications. The lower age limit, of course, prevented some from being eligible as well as the stiffer medical requirements. At the same time there was apprehension from farmers that the new force would not be sufficiently flexible. It was accepted in the USC that if when a man's duty came round he had a cow calving then he simply got a substitute. At the same time a summer camp of a week would be unlikely to fit in with the harvest. Some felt that there would be a lot of unnecessary battle school type training. The army did their best to reassure them and meet these difficulties, nevertheless many were put off. Probably the reason which deterred a great many was their feeling of humiliation over the disbandment of the USC with what they saw as the appeasement of the Republicans at their expense. There were many complaints that applications were turned down without explanation with the stigma that they had extremist affiliations which in their view were simply Loyalist. Many others on hearing of such rejections refused to apply to join. There was a definite feeling, although this is hotly denied by the army, that the approval of the applications of Protestants were being kept low in order to keep the percentage of Roman Catholics as high as possible.

At first most Roman Catholic organizations recommended their people to join. It was soon clear, however, that the extremists were against the formation of the regiment. This opposition increased as soon as they realized that an oath of allegiance would be necessary. Nevertheless the early figures showed that a number of Roman Catholics were joining. The regiment took over from the USC on 1 April as planned and by then seven battalions had been formed but total strength was only 1,236. In the summer of 1971, strength had reached 4,100, 17 per cent being Roman Catholics. In August 1971 the establishment was raised to 10,000 and three more battalions were formed. By May 1972 strength was 8,500 of whom 2,487 were ex-B Specials, 1,842 ex-servicemen and 426 Roman Catholics. After the introduction of internment in August, 1971, the hostility of the Republicans increased and there was a great deal of intimidation of Roman Catholic members of the Regiment. The number of resignations increased until the percentage was under 6 per cent.[11] Three Roman Catholic members of the regiment have been murdered in cold blood and the IRA are doing their best to try and make others resign. That more have not done so shows considerable courage and loyalty. Total casualties in the UDR have been fourteen killed and twenty-five wounded, only two of those killed being on duty, the rest being by accident or murdered when off duty.

The original intention was that arms should be kept centrally in armouries although it was always accepted that in certain circumstances some members would keep them at home. In fact most members now, as the B Specials, keep their arms at home and only those in towns keep them in armouries. The regiment now have modern SLR rifles and SMG carbines and some armoured cars. They also have radio communication and sufficient vehicles for the men on duty each night. Without question the Ulster Defence Regiment are better equipped, younger and better soldiers than the B Specials. Their transport, their training, their modern weapons and their radio communications make them a more powerful mobile force able to operate anywhere in the Province. They would be able to fight in platoons, companies or even battalions. There are plans to enable whole battalions to move in private cars. It is indeed a worthy successor for the defence of the Province. The UDR, however, costs very much more than the USC. In some ways, too, the B Specials were superior for the work they had to do. Their close association with the RUC, their knowledge of their area and the people in it and the speed with which they could man their road blocks were all great advantages. The Ulster Defence Regiment, is however, doing its best to embody all its predecessors' advantages and intends to reach the point where regular troops coming to the Province will ask their advice.

The RUC Reserve was originally to be unarmed and 1,500 strong. At the end of 1971 its establishment was raised to 2,500 and its members were permitted to be armed if necessary. A high proportion of this force was composed of ex-B Specials.

On Sunday 22 March 1970 a commemoration service for the Ulster Special Constabulary was held in the Kings Hall in Belfast. The service was conducted by the Moderator of the Presbyterian Church in Ireland, the Lord Bishop of Connor and the Chairman of the Belfast District of the Methodist Church in Ireland. The Prime Minister of Northern Ireland (Major J. D. Chichester-Clark, DL, MP) gave the address. In it he said:

'For you, with this magnificent record, and for me – conscious as I am of all that your service has meant to Ulster –

today's occasion inevitably has elements of sadness. . . .

'You have done magnificently, and will continue to do it, I know, up to the moment the force stands down. You have acted always, and will act to the last, as a loyal and disciplined force of patriotic Ulstermen. . . .

'All down the years you have had much to endure – not only the physical attacks of enemies of this State, which you have so valiantly and resolutely beaten off time and again, but the insidious tactics of slur and innuendo. I have read with indignation and anger some of the distorted accounts of your force which have appeared in Britain and elsewhere. . . . Ulster owes you an immense debt – for the years of training; for the lonely hours on watch in desolate places at dead of night; for the courage and sense of duty which you have displayed; for the way you have kept alive the ideals of service and of loyalty to Queen and Country.' He might have added that they were victims of the least endearing characteristic of British governments in recent times that they have a tendency to sell their friends to appease their enemies.

The B Specials handed in every weapon with which they had been issued and obeyed orders to the last. Only one platoon resigned and handed in its arms and equipment early. This in itself gives the lie to its detractors who forecast that it would have to be disarmed by the army. So went a force of dedicated patriotic men whose only real crime was that they were all Protestants. They were prepared to take on a dangerous and arduous job for very little reward. The force was killed by a vicious and mendacious propaganda campaign which was widely believed in Great Britain. This disbandment solved nothing, the 'troubles' in Ulster escalated and their old enemy the IRA flourished and was greatly encouraged by their departure. There is no doubt that the IRA believed that with the USC out of the way, they had a good chance to unite Ireland by force. It was as the B-men were being disbanded that they redoubled their efforts and the gun-running scandals in the Republic came to light involving the dismissal of two government ministers. In the months following, the split widened between the two factions of the IRA and both began to expand and arm themselves in the north.

There is little reason to suppose that had the B Specials had their full quota of a third of their total of loyal Roman Catholics they would have been any more acceptable to the extremists. The old RIC who were 82 per cent Roman Catholic were denounced as traitors and agents of the British; they were murdered, discriminated against and boycotted. The British Army which has fallen over backwards to be impartial is now hated in the same way. If there had never been an Irish Republican Army, an Ulster Special Constabulary would never have been necessary. Far from being a political police force to oppress the minority the USC protected Northern Ireland for fifty years from many attempts to seize power by force against the wishes of the vast majority of the population.

NOTES

1. Most of the crowd of over a thousand strong were dispersing from a dance at the Castle Ballroom. The Scarman Tribunal found that this firing was unjustified. Nevertheless no one was injured and it proved effective in dispersing a dangerous mob. A month later the RUC fired over the heads of the crowd in Dungiven in a similar situation and, in this case the Tribunal found that they were justified in doing so.

2. Direct rule would mean twenty-five instead of twelve MPs at Westminster to represent Northern Ireland and two thirds of these would be Unionists.

3. One shot wounded the driver of the mechanical shovel and two others extinguished its headlights. Another shot wounded a man in a car well beyond the riot.

4. Surprisingly the Scarman Tribunal confirms that the NI Government were well aware that they must call out the USC before seeking the aid of the army.

5. Nevertheless the troops did not attempt to enter the Bogside.

6. The Insight team repeat this sort of propaganda which can now be seen to be what they describe as 'Catholic mythology'.

7. It is also very odd that steps had not been taken to equip and train the USC in riot control. This was especially so as the Northern Ireland Government knew they had to commit them before they could call in the army. There is no doubt that Ministers and the RUC always believed that the USC would exacerbate riots in which Catholics were involved. In the event the Scarman report shows that although the sight of them may have angered Catholics, it never made the riot worse. Indeed the intervention of the USC often stopped the riot. This was sometimes by the use of firearms but also because 'Catholic mythology' had for fifty years made them out to be monsters and the principal emotion among them when the Specials appeared was fear.

8. Lord Hunt had seen much service in India in communal riots and had for a time been seconded to the Indian Police.

9. It could surely be held that hatred of a police force because it is composed of Protestants is itself religious discrimination!

10. The Insight team tries, without producing any evidence whatever, to support the contention that the Orange Order controlled the B Specials. Republican propaganda shows through when, referring to the RUC and USC, it says 'Both forces carried arms and had very little compunction about using them. . . . Nearly 300 people died violently in the first two years of the new state's existence'. The inference the reader is supposed to draw is that those 300 were killed by the police. In fact the majority were murdered by the IRA including 49 of the USC. To descend to this level of journalism for a moment, it should be noticed that 300 people have now been killed in Ulster since the disbandment of the B Specials and the disarming of the RUC. In fact the Army killed more

people in Londonderry recently in an afternoon than the USC in over forty years.

11. This is not as bad as it seems. Some Roman Catholics are still joining but the total fell from some 700 to 426 at which point it stabilized.

APPENDIX I

Ulster Special Constabulary Roll of Honour

1921

Robert W. Compston
William Gordon
James Hall
Thomas Sturdy
John Cummings
John Fluke

Robert Coulter
Hugh Gabbie
Samuel Nixon
George Graham
George Lyness
William Lyttle

1922

Charles McFadden
James Lewis
Robert W. McMahon
Alexander Kirkpatrick
James Harper
Joseph Plumb
Thomas J. Hunter
William T. McKnight
James Murphy
John Megarrity
James Murray
William Mitchell
Samuel D. Holmes
Joseph Abraham
James R. McCullogh
James McInnes
William Chermside
David Allen
Alexander Compton, MC

Edward Hegarty
Samuel J. Milligan
Herbert Martin
Andrew Roulston
Thomas Sheridan
Samuel Young
William Dougherty
William J. McFarland
Charles V. Vokes
Thomas Cunningham
Thomas Hall
Nathaniel McCoo
Robert J. Cardwell
George E. Connor
Albert T. Rickerby
Thomas W. Dobson
Thomas Russell
Samuel Hayes

1941

James Thompson   William M. Howe   John McCombe

1942

James Lyons   Samuel Hamilton

APPENDIX II

Contingent of the Ulster Special Constabulary which attended the Royal Review of the United Kingdom held in Hyde Park on 14 July 1954

Major N. F. Gordon	District Commandant (Newcastle, Co Down)
Mr C. F. Palmer	Adjutant (Co Fermanagh)
Mr W. H. Patterson	Sub-District Commandant (Co Tyrone)
Mr J. C. Nesbitt	Sub-District Commandant (Co Armagh)
W. Burrows	Sergeant Instructor (Co Londonderry)
J. H. Johnston	Sergeant Instructor (Co Antrim)
R. W. Paul	Platoon Sergeant (Co Londonderry)
V. Kerr	Platoon Sergeant (Co Fermanagh)
F. E. Strickland	Platoon Sergeant (City of Londonderry)
G. E. McClintock	Platoon Sergeant (Co Antrim)
T. N. Hadden	Platoon Sergeant (Co Tyrone)
J. K. Leggett	Special Sergeant (Belfast)
J. Cush	Special Sergeant (Co Armagh)
W. Bickerstaff	Special Sergeant (Co Down)
T. Atkinson	Special Constable (Co Londonderry)
M. J. Dillon	Special Constable (Co Londonderry)
K. Kempster	Special Constable (Co Londonderry)
J. Allen	Special Constable (Co Fermanagh)
F. Johnston	Special Constable (Co Fermanagh)
M. Hassard	Special Constable (Co Fermanagh)
J. F. Clanaghan	Special Constable (Co Fermanagh)
R. Finlay	Special Constable (City of Londonderry)
A. G. S. Marskell	Special Constable (City of Londonderry)
R. J. Burns	Special Constable (City of Londonderry)

G. L. Alexander	Special Constable (Belfast)
W. Cousins	Special Constable (Belfast)
S. Logan	Special Constable (Belfast)
W. E. McCord	Special Constable (Belfast)
S. Downes	Special Constable (Belfast)
N. McNaught	Special Constable (Belfast)
M. Hughes	Special Constable (Co Antrim)
J. B. Hillock	Special Constable (Co Antrim)
M. McAlreavy	Special Constable (Co Antrim)
A. Simpson	Special Constable (Co Antrim)
J. Rankin	Special Constable (Co Antrim)
N. A. Dougan	Special Constable (Co Armagh)
F. Cunningham	Special Constable (Co Armagh)
P. Taylor	Special Constable (Co Armagh)
I. Fergus	Special Constable (Co Armagh)
C. Turner	Special Constable (Co Armagh)
R. Hewitt	Special Constable (Co Down)
J. Bradford	Special Constable (Co Down)
D. G. R. Green	Special Constable (Co Down)
W. Dickson	Special Constable (Co Down)
R. McKelvey	Special Constable (Co Down)
W. Arthurs	Special Constable (Co Tyrone)
C. McKinley	Special Constable (Co Tyrone)
W. Watson	Special Constable (Co Tyrone)
R. Millar	Special Constable (Co Tyrone)
J. Wilkinson	Special Constable (Co Tyrone)
W. Whiteford	Special Constable (Co Tyrone)
W. A. Bonis	Special Constable (Co Tyrone)

APPENDIX III

A Typical Sub-District of the Ulster Special Constabulary, 1960

Aghadowey Sub-District

Rank	Name	Age	Marital Status	Civilian Occupation	Years service in the USC
Sub-District Commandant	A. Shirley	46	S	Linesman	23
Platoon Sergeant	W. Anderson	32	S	Farmer	12
Special Sergeant	R. Harte	32	M	Labourer	12
	D. K. Martin	49	S	—	17
	T. McNeill	35	S	Farmer	12
	S. Shirley	48	M	Labourer	14
	A. Smyth	43	M	Farmer and Traveller	5
Special Constable	J. Anderson	47	M	Clerk of Works	3
	H. Allen	25	S	Farmer	3
	J. Blair	36	M	Lorry Driver	4
	J. Conley	29	S	Lorry Driver	5
	J. Cunningham	28	S	Farmer	3
	R. Campbell	23	M	Wholesale Grocer	3
	D. Campbell	20	S	Electrician	—
	J. Devennie	62	M	Labourer	21
Special Constable	W. R. Dickie	50	W	Farm Labourer	12

Rank	Name	Age	Marital Status	Civilian Occupation	Years service in the USC
	R. J. Dickie	49	M	Farm Labourer	9
	S. E. Dickie	36	S	Farm Worker	3
	B. Downs	38	S	Inspector Electrician	6
	W. Doey	38	M	Bus Driver	6
	W. Doherty	50	M	Labourer	3
	W. McF. Graham	51	M	Flax Scutcher	16
	I. Graham	37	S	Farm Labourer	20
	D. F. Hull	25	S	Farmer	3
	R. A. Holmes	27	S	Carpenter	8
	T. W. Jamieson	45	M	Bus Driver	3
	S. P. Lynd	49	S	Farmer	23
	H. McFadden	52	M	Flax Mill Worker	17
	R. McMaster	49	M	Labourer	12
	G. Miller	63	S	Farmer	40
	M. S. McKinney	32	M	Electrician	3
	R. McFadden	25	S	Farm Worker	3
	J. A. Mitchell	33	M	Creamery Worker	3
	J. Macauley	57	M	Carpenter	3
	J. Pollock	26	S	Farmer	4
	R. A. Reid	34	S	Farmer	5
	A. Shiels	73	S	Retired Engine Driver	39
	J. Simpson	41	S	Labourer	3
	J. F. Wilson	21	S	Farmer	3

NOTES ON SOURCES

I had hoped to publish a list of the large number of people who have given me interviews and verbal accounts of the Specials. As time went on some people began to ask that I refrain from mentioning their names. In the end I decided not to publish any of them. If any genuine historians wish to write to me, I may be able to put them on to some of my sources, providing of course that the 'source' agrees. (Members of Sinn Fein or either wing of the IRA need not apply!)

The rest of the material comes under three main headings. The first is a mass of administrative papers of the Ulster Special Constabulary which were collected on disbandment with a view to a history. These vary from interminable lists of B-men and rifle numbers or administrative correspondence on pay, allowances, uniform, etc. to occasional policy statements. There is very little on operations and nothing on intelligence. These papers will in due course be deposited in the Public Record Office. The second heading comprises some interesting papers in the Public Record Office in London. These are to be found in the Cabinet Papers for the period and in the Dublin Castle records which are filed under the Colonial Office. There is nothing of interest in the Public Record Office in Belfast as yet. The third heading comprises the published works, the most important of which are listed in the bibliography. I have also consulted newspaper cuttings and files.

For information on the IRA activities I have relied mainly on J. Bowyer Bell's *The Secret Army*, Tim Pat Coogan's *The IRA* and Calton Younger's *Ireland's Civil War*.

BIBLIOGRAPHY

ASH, BERNARD *The Lost Dictator* – Cassell, London 1968.

BEASLAI, PIARAS *Michael Collins and the Making of a New Ireland* Vol II – George G. Harrap & Co Ltd, London 1926.

BOWYER BELL, J. *The Secret Army* – Anthony Blond Ltd, London 1970.

CALLWELL, MAJOR-GENERAL SIR C. E. *Field Marshal Sir Henry Wilson* Vols I and II – Cassell, London 1927.

CAMERON REPORT *Disturbances in Northern Ireland* – HM Stationery Office, Belfast 1969.

CHURCHILL, WINSTON *The Great War* Vol III – George Newnes Ltd, London *c* 1933.

CHURCHILL, WINSTON *The Second World War* Vol II – Cassell & Co Ltd, London 1949.

COLVIN, IAN *The Life of Lord Carson* – Victor Gollancz Ltd, London 1934.

COOGAN, TIM PAT *The IRA* – Fontana/Collins, London 1971.

DANE, MERVYN *The Fermanagh 'B' Specials* – William Timble Ltd, Enniskillen 1970.

DEVLIN, BERNADETTE *The Price of my Soul* – Pan Books Ltd, London 1969.

ERVINE, ST JOHN *Craigavon* – Allen and Unwin, London 1949.

HANSARD *Parliamentary Debates* Vol 73, Nos 1, 2, 5, 8, 15, 21, 24, 25, 27 and 30 – HM Stationery Office, Belfast 1969.

HOOD, DISTRICT INSPECTOR W. J., AND SHEPHERD, HEAD CONSTABLE J. E. Article on 'Police in Ireland' – in *Ulsterview* Vol 4 No 5, February 1969.

HUNT REPORT *Report of The Advisory Committee on Police in Northern Ireland* – HM Stationery Office, Belfast 1969.

'I.O.' *The Administration of Ireland 1920* – Philip Allen & Co, London 1921.

JONES, THOMAS *Lloyd George* – Oxford University Press, London 1951.

MACREADY, GENERAL SIR NEVIL *Annals of an Active Life* – Hutchinson & Co, London, *c* 1925.

O'CALLAGHAN, SEAN *The Easter Lily* – Four Square Books, London 1967.

SCARMAN REPORT *Violence and Civil Disturbances in Northern Ireland in 1969: Report of Tribunal of Inquiry* – HM Stationery Office, Belfast 1972, 2 vols.

STREET, C. J. C. *Ireland in 1921* – Philip Allan & Co, London 1922.

SUNDAY TIMES, THE (Insight team) *Ulster* – Penguin Books Ltd, London 1972.

WHITE PAPER 4188 *Formation of the Ulster Defence Regiment* – HM Stationery Office, London 1969.

WILSON, HAROLD *The Labour Government 1964–70* – Weidenfeld and Nicolson and Michael Joseph, 1971.

YOUNGER, CALTON *Ireland's Civil War* – Fontana/Collins, London 1970.

INDEX

INDEX

Abercorn, Duke of 101–2
Abernethy, Dr 221
Abraham, Sp Const Joseph 62
ABWEHR 8, 139
Air Raid Precautions Head-
    quarters 147
Allen, Sp Const David 70
Allen, Sp Const Harry 191, 200n
Allen, Sp Const Robert 191, 200n
American troops 145
Anderson, Sir John, 15, 25
Anderson, Sgt William 150, 152n
Andrews, J. L. O. 232
Anti-Submarine School, joint
    RN RAF 161
Apprentice Boys
    parade 221
Assizes 5
Auxiliaries 8

Barton, Col 80
Barry, Thomas 94
Battle of the Boyne 49
Belfast News Letter 204–5
Better Government of Ireland
    Bill 4, 15
'Black and Tans' 7, 8, 16, 17,
    24, 25, 36, 58
Boundary Agreement 116
Boyle, Sp Const F. W. 191
Brave Borderer, HMS 203
British Broadcasting Corpora-
    tion (BBC) 172, 221
Brook, Captain Sir Basil 11, 29,
    41, 79, 80, 108, 125, 159–60
Brown, John 216n
Bunting, Major 215
Byrnes, General Sir Joseph 3, 6,
    26n

Callaghan, James 227, 228, 234,
    236, 238, 239, 241–2
Cameron, General A. R. 58, 66,
    114
Cameron Report, The 213, 216n,
    239, 241
    committee 240
Cardwell, Sp Const Robert 76
Carson, Sir Edward 8, 10
Carter-Campbell Col 50
Charley, Col 158
Chermside, William 69
Chichester-Clark, Robin 215–16,
    220, 227, 229, 233, 234, 236,
    238, 246
Chittik, George 68
Churchill, Winston 1, 15, 57, 67,
    69, 81, 84, 96, 113, 119, 141,
    151n
Civil Rights Association 208–9,
    212
    banner 208
    campaign 208
    demonstrators 213, 215–16
    march 209, 221
    movement 213
Clark, Sir Ernest 22, 25
Clones Massacre 63, 64
Collins, Michael 50, 55, 60, 71,
    74–5, 96–7, 240
Compston, Sp Const Robert
    32
Connor, George 78
Constabulary Bill (Northern Ire-
    land) 79
Coogan, Tim Pat 119–20
Cosgrave, William T. 97, 111
Costello, John A. 174, 179
    Costello's Government 154

Craig, Sir James 14, 15, 19, 23, 42, 48, 51, 55, 60, 63, 64, 67, 71, 85, 92n, 94, 97–8, 100–1, 105, 106, 108, 111, 114, 115–17

Craig, William 204, 206, 242

Cranagh Hall 57

Crawford, Lt-Colonel F. H. 53, 54

Crossan, James 200n

Cunning, Sp Const John 33

Cunningham, Sp Const Thomas 69

Davies, Moorhouse 6

Defence of the Realm Act 8, 16

De Valera, Eamon 47, 48, 109, 112, 128, 133, 136, 154, 179, 190

De Valera's Government 130

Devlin, Bernadette 227

Devlin, Patrick 214, 215

Dobson, Sp Const Thomas 82

Donegal Pass Police Station 148

Donnelly, Francis 70

Dougherty, Sgt William 62

Dublin Metropolitan Police 3, 4, 6

Dublin Resident Magistrate 5

Easter Rising, 1, 2, 10, 203, 217n celebrations 204, 205

Eden, Robert Anthony, 1st Earl of Avon 175

Elizabeth II, Queen, 163, 164, 243

Elizabeth, Queen Mother 134

Emergency Powers Act 139

Ensor, Capt 158

European Court of Human Rights 190

Fail, Fianna 154, 179 party 128

Faulkner, Brian 164, 189

Fitzalan, Lord 42, 99

Fluke, John 40

Foreman, Hugh 143

Freeland, Lt-General Sir Ian 229–30, 233, 238

Free State Bill 73

French, Viceroy Field Marshal John D. P., 1st Earl of Ypres 4, 8

Gabbie, Sp Const Hugh 45

Gelston (Belfast City Commissioner) 71

General Officer Commanding (GOC) 6, 66, 114, 137n, 141, 144, 148, 229, 232, 234, 236, 237, 242

General Post Office (GPO) 15, 26, 57, 191, 193, 196, 217n

George V, King 43

George VI, King 134

George, Douglas 44

Gilmore, Sp Const 196

Good, Brigadier I. H. 183, 202

Goodwin, Lt-Col W. R. 82

Gordon, Major N. F. 163

Gordon, Sp Const, William 38

Goulding, Cathal 208

Government of Ireland Act (1920) 66

Government of Ireland Act (1949) 220

Greenwood, Sir Hamar 6, 57

Gregg, Col 158

Griffith, Arthur 96

Halifax, E. F. Lindley Wood, 1st Earl of 135

Hall, James 41

Hamilton, R. T. 163

Hamilton, Sp Const Samuel 148

Hanna (Minister of Home Affairs) 167

Hanson, Captain 158

Harper, Sp Const James 70

Hayes affair 144

Henderson, O. W. J. 164

HM Customs 166

Home Rule Bill 1

Hopper, Albert 40

Houston, Lt-Col Blakiston 158

Howe, William 144

Hungarian Rising (1956) 205

Hunt, Lord 234, 237, 249n committee 233, 236, 237–41, 242

report 234, 235, 236, 244

Irish Administration 14
Irish Republican Army (IRA) 2,
    3, 4–5, 8, 10, 12, 16–18, 21,
    23–4, 25, 26, 29, 32–4, 36–8,
    39–45, 46, 47–9, 50, 52n,
    53, 57–9, 60–4, 67, 68, 69,
    70, 72–3, 74–7, 78, 79–81,
    82, 83, 84–7, 89, 90, 91n,
    92n, 93n, 94–6, 98–9, 101,
    107, 109, 112, 114, 115,
    116, 119–20, 120n, 121–2,
    124, 128, 132–3, 135, 136–7,
    138–44, 147–8, 150–1, 153–
    5, 159, 161–3, 164–70, 171–
    83, 184–93, 195–9, 200n,
    201, 202–5, 208, 211, 213,
    230–1, 232, 238, 240, 243–4,
    245, 247–8, 249n

Johnston, Dr Roy 202

Kennedy, Sir Albert 158, 195,
    200n, 207, 228–9
Kilpatrick, Sp Const Alexander
    68
Knox, Brigadier F. Y. C. 156,
    157, 158, 162, 183

Laird, Sp Const Samuel 68
Law, Bonar 8, 18–19, 20, 100
Lemass, Sean 190, 193
Lendrum, Captain 20
Lester, Sp Const 34
Lewis, James 62
Liddle, George E. 11, 158
Lisbellaw Parish Church 12
Lloyd-George of Dwyfor, (David
    Lloyd George) 14, 17, 26n,
    51, 55, 82, 100
Local Defence Volunteers (LDV)
    140–1, 141–2
Logue, Cardinal 86, 92n, 98
London Metropolitan Police
    120n
Lunny, Sgt Henry 150
Lynch, John 223
Lyness, Sp Const George 44
Lyons, Sp Const James 148
Lyttle, Sp Const William 56

McAteer, Hugh, 121, 150
McCallum, Major J. 28

McCappin, Adam 143
McCaughey, Sgt Thomas 184,
    199n
McClintock, Col 57, 58, 93n, 108,
    134
McCombe, John 144
McCoo, Sp Const Nathaniel 73
McCullough, Sp Const 25
MacDonald, James Ramsay 111
McGrath, Joe 74
M'Garrity, Sp Const John 83
McInnes, Sp Const James 63
McKeown, Sp Const 184
McMahon, Robert 25, 62
    family 69
Macpherson, Ian 6
Macready, General Sir Nevil 6, 8,
    14, 20, 24, 34, 35, 39, 41–2,
    48, 50, 52n, 55, 58, 64, 67,
    81, 91, 97, 100, 101
McRory, Dr 71
Magilligan, Sp Const Samuel 76
Maginess, W. B. 160
Margaret, Princess HRH 203
Mark, Robert 234
Miskimmin, Lt-Col S. 202, 207,
    244
Mitchell, Sp Const William 83
Montgomery, John 41
Mountjoy prison 8, 94
Murphy, Sp Const James 78
Murray, Sp Const James 184,
    199n

New Statesman 189

OBE 156
Observer, The 92n
O'Callaghan, Sean 52n
O'Duffy, Eoin 49, 50, 73–4, 94,
    130
O'Neill, Lord 77
Orange Order 24, 26, 60, 239,
    240–1, 249n
    Parade 13
    Junior Orangeman's parade
    219
Orr, Sp Const 196

Paisley, Rev Ian 209
Parker, Dehra, Dame 164
Partition Bill (Home Rule Act) 4

Patton, Sp Const James 178, 199n

Patton, Sp Const Robert 178, 199n

Peacocke, Anthony, 207

Pim, District Inspector, R. P. 56–7, 91n, 151n, 160, 163, 200n

People's Democracy 209, 210, 212

Plumb, Sp Const Joseph 72

Porter, R. W. 234

Princess Royal 124

Protestant shipyard workers 14, 37

Public Safety Act 124

Queen Victoria Trophy 207

Rebellion in Dublin (1916) 205

Redmond (Assistant Commissioner) 4

REME 168

Republican Courts 10

Restoration of Order in Ireland Act (1920) 16, 32, 65–6

Ricardo, General 29, 85, 92–3n

Richardson, Lt-Col H. S. 125

Rickerby, Sp Const Albert 80

Robertson, Sir James 234

Roulston, Sp Const Andrew 83

Royal Air Force (RAF) 142, 173, 180, 206

Royal Irish Constabulary (RIC) 3, 6–7, 8, 10–12, 13, 14, 16, 17, 18, 19, 21, 22, 23, 26, 26n, 28–35, 36, 37, 39, 40, 41, 43–7, 49, 50, 51, 52n, 57, 58, 61, 62, 64–8, 69–70, 72, 75, 77–9, 80, 84, 91, 119, 240, 248

Royal Observer Corps 185

Royal Ulster Constabulary (RUC) 66, 79, 85, 88, 89, 91, 95, 102–4, 122, 124, 129–32, 134–5, 137n, 139–43, 147–8, 153–5, 159–63, 192–4, 196–9, 200n, 202–4, 205, 206, 208–12, 214, 216, 218–20, 221–4, 225–7, 228–9, 230–5, 238–9, 240, 241–2, 244, 246, 248n, 249n, 250n

Russell, Sp Const Andrew 177–8

Russell, Sp Const William 83

Saor Eire Action Group 204

Sargent, Lt-Col J. 102, 122, 156

Sinn Fein 2, 3, 5–6, 7, 8–10, 13–14, 15, 18, 23, 25, 26, 33, 34, 36, 37, 38, 39, 41, 42, 43, 47, 49, 50, 51, 53, 54, 56, 58, 60, 69, 73–4, 78, 84, 86, 87, 91, 92n, 114, 119, 155, 172, 179, 200n, 204

Smith, J. 6

Smith, Lt-Col M. F. Hammond 134, 149

Smyth, Col 13, 14

Solly-Flood, Major General A. 66, 71, 83, 87, 102

Sommerville, Admiral 133

Spain, Civil War 133

Special Power Act 65, 73, 175

Spender, Col Sir Wilfred 91n

Sperrin Mountain 57, 68

Stewart, Major 45

Stormont 228, 234, 236
  Committee 237

Sturdy, Sp Const Thomas 43

Sunday Times 200n, 217n

Swanzy, District Inspector 26

Tallents, Stephen 84–5, 87, 92n

Territorial Army (TA) 126, 172, 177, 182, 187, 206, 230
  TAVR Arms 233

Thompson, James 144

Thurles shooting 2

Todd, A. 45

Tone, Wolfe 128

Topping (NI Home Affairs Minister) 186

Treasonable Offences Act 114

Treaty, British–Free State 115, 120n

Tudor, Major General H. M. 6, 14, 15, 22, 23, 24, 33, 40, 43, 51, 54, 55

Twaddell, W. J. 78

Ulster Defence Regiment 242–3, 244–6

Ulster ex-Service Men's Association 13

Ulster Home Guard 142–3, 144–5, 148–9, 150, 151, 153
UHG order of battle 146
Ulster Labour Association 20
Ulster Special Constabulary (USC) 95–6, 121, 122–3, 125–7, 138, 140, 142, 144–5, 151, 154, 155–9, 163–4, 169–70, 172, 173–4, 175, 176–8, 179–81, 182–3, 185, 186, 187–90, 192–4, 196–9, 199n, 201–4, 205–7, 210–16, 219–20, 221–4, 225–34, 235–46, 246–7, 248, 248n, 249n
Ulster Protestant Volunteer Force 239
Ulster Unionist Council 19
Ulster Unionist Party 23–4
Ulster Volunteer Force (UVF) 20, 24, 53, 54, 56, 204, 211, 216, 242, 243
United Irishman 200n

Vernon, Lt-Col A. J. 91n
Vesey, General 87
Vokes, Sp Const Charles 64

Walsh, A. 6
Wickham, Lt-Col C. G. 22, 28, 32, 35, 51, 54, 55, 66, 71, 79, 99, 100
Wilson, (James) Harold 228, 229, 239, 241–2
Wilson, Sir Henry 20, 50, 51, 58, 64–6, 83–4, 91n
Wisener, Sgt Francis 177–8, 199n
Wylie 15, 25

Young, Samuel 83

DO YOU ALWAYS CHOOSE THE RIGHT GIFT?

You can be sure with Book Tokens! Why? Because when you give a Book Token you give the pleasure of choosing. A Book Token can be exchanged, without time limit, for any type of hardback or paperback book. Book Tokens can be bought at any one of over 2,000 Bookshops in the British Isles, and exchanged in any other — ideal for long-distance gift giving! From as little as 20p up to £5·00 or more, a Book Token is right for every age and occasion.